ANNUAL REPORT
of the
SECRETARY *of* STATE
to the
GOVERNOR *of* OHIO

—Appendix B—
RETURN OF THE NUMBER OF DEAF AND DUMB,
BLIND, INSANE AND IDIOTIC PERSONS

MAY ✣ 1856

HERITAGE BOOKS
2010

HERITAGE BOOKS
AN IMPRINT OF HERITAGE BOOKS, INC.

Books, CDs, and more—Worldwide

For our listing of thousands of titles see our website
at
www.HeritageBooks.com

A Facsimile Reprint
Published 2010 by
HERITAGE BOOKS, INC.
Publishing Division
100 Railroad Ave. #104
Westminster, Maryland 21157

Reprint of:
Appendix B of the 1856
*Annual Report of the Secretary of State
to the Governor of Ohio*

— Publisher's Notice —
In reprints such as this, it is often not possible to remove blemishes from the original. We feel the contents of this book warrant its reissue despite these blemishes and hope you will agree and read it with pleasure.

International Standard Book Numbers
Paperbound: 978-1-55613-089-2
Clothbound: 978-0-7884-8336-3

Introduction

This reprint of Appendix B of the 1856 *Annual Report of the Secretary of State to the Governor of Ohio*, relays the names of deaf and dumb, blind, insane, and idiotic persons in eighty-two counties of Ohio as of 1856. The information contained in this tabulation is extremely detailed considering the time period. The inclusion of age, birthplace, name of parents, and the birthplaces of the parents should prove very helpful to anyone finding a person of interest within. All the columns are clearly labeled and are self-explanatory.

As of 1856, Ohio had eighty-eight counties and eighty-two of those submitted names; the following counties did not comply: Athens, Belmont, Butler, Gallia, Hancock, and Henry.

An original copy (1857 printing) of this report may be found in the Documents Section of the State Library of Ohio at Columbus where it is bound in a volume entitled *Report of Secretary of State, Ohio Statistics, 1836-1860*. It may also be found, probably more frequently, in *Ohio Executive Documents*, 1856, part 2, pp.113-368; this volume is available at the State Library of Ohio, the Public Library of Cincinnati and Hamilton County, and may also be found in other major libraries.

Additional records for persons appearing in these lists may possibly be found at the county level in Probate Court records such as lunacy hearings, guardianships, etc. as recorded in the Journals, Complete Record and case files. Additional information for some individuals may be found in institutional records available at the Library/Archives Division of the Ohio Historical Society in Columbus. State institutions were operated for the deaf and dumb, blind, and insane.

I would like to acknowledge Susan Kober, First Assistant History Department, of the Public Library of Cincinnati and Hamilton County for her helpful assistance and guidance.

W. Louis Phillips, C.G.
P.O. Box 24111
Columbus, OH 43224

RETURN of the Number of Deaf and Dumb, Blind, Insane and Idiotic

Townships.	Names of Persons.	Nature of Affliction.	Duration of Affliction.	Cause where known.	Age.	Sex.	Color.
Oliver	Frances A. Atwell	Dumb	3 years	By a fall	4	Male	White.
"	Sarah Roads	Blind	8 "		55	Fem'le	do
"	Isabella Creswell	Insane	27 "	Obstruse study	61	do	do
"	Martha E. Wallace	Insane	9 "		9	do	do
"	Eliz A. McCleughen	Idiotic	9 "	Sickness	11	do	do
Monroe	George Rater	Idiot		Unknown	9	Male	do
"	Mary Ann Collings	Idiot		"	30	Fem'le	do
"	Nancy Collings	Idiot		"	18	do	do
"	Nancy Miller	Idiot		"	62	do	do
"	Jane Miller	Idiot		"	60	do	do
"	Isaac Foster	Insane	7 years	"	70	Male	do
Sprigg	Van Pence	Idiotic	During life			do	do
Scott	Jefferson L. Hagerty	Idiotic & dumb	From birth		12	do	do
"	Lesse Callader	Idiotic & dumb	34 years	Unknown	34	do	do
"	John McCormack	Idiotic	36 "	"	36	do	do
"	William S. McAllister	Idt'c d'b & bl'd	7 "		7	do	do
Green	Moses J. Baird	Blind		Cataract	26	do	do
"	Rodney Fields	Fits	8 "	Unknown	26	do	do
"	Nancy E. Terry	Palsy	8 "	"	10	Fem'le	do
"	Peter W. Hozellaker	Insane	24 years	Calomel	28	Male	do
Jefferson	Rosa Anderson	Deaf & dumb	49 "		49	Fem'le	do
"	Mitchel Young	Blind	4 "		27	Male	do
"	Benjamin Sutherfield	Insane	5 "				do
Wayne	Frances A. Plummer		4 "		4	Fem'le	do
"	Thomas Mahaffey	Deaf & dumb			7	Male	do
"	James H. Mahaffey	Deaf & dumb			4	do	do
"	T. W. Sutton	Deaf & dumb			4	Fem'le	do
"	Elizabeth McNeil	Blind	26 years		26	do	do
Tiffin	Samuel Rader	Idiotic	26 "		26	Male	do
"	Malcom McCollum	Insane	9 "		36	do	do
"	Richard Cadic	Insane	20 "		47	do	do
"	William Ames	Idiotic	12 "	Hereditary	12	do	do
"	Mary Garwood	Insane	9 "		38	Fem'le	do
"	Nancy Roe	Insane	20 "	Trouble	45	do	do
"	Elizabeth Pittenger	Insane	10 "	Love	50	do	do
"	Van Grooms	Blind	18 "	Hurt by a horse	26	Male	do
"	John Trotter	Idiotic	19 "	Unknown	19	do	do

Persons, in the county of Adams, State of Ohio, on the 2d Monday of May, 1856.

Occupation.	Birthplace.	Educated or not.	Names of Parents.	Occupation.	Birthplace.	No. of child'n	No. children thus afflicted	Relationship of parents before marriage.
....	Ohio	....	Frances & Susannah Atwell	Physician	Va. & Ohio	4	1	None.
....	Virginia.	Educated	Enoch & Ellen Grice	Farming..	Pen. & N.J.	7	1	do
....	Penn....	Educated	James Edgar	do	Pennsylv'a	6	1	
....	do	....	Mary Creswell	do	Maryland.	3	1	do
....	Illinois..	....	Elizabeth W. Brown	....	Pen'vania.	7	1	
....	Ohio.....	Not	J. and Minerva Rater	Farming.	Ohio	5	1	do
....	do	Not	Elijah & Hannah Collings..	do	Md. & Ky.	10	2	do
....	do	Not	same............	do	do	10	2	
....	Penn.....	Not	Jas. and Eliz. Miller......	....	Ireland ...	9	6	
....	do	Not	same....	....	do	9	6	
....	Virginia.	Educated	Nathaniel Foster.........	Farmer ..	New Jersey	..	..	Unkn'wn
....	Ohio.....	....	Elijah Pence	....	....	..	1	None.
....	do	Not.	W. and Eliz. Hagerty.....	Carpenter.	Penn.	8	1	Cousins.
....	do	Not'.	J. and Anna Cadwallader .	Farmer ..	Virginia ..	8	1	None.
....	do	Not.	Eppa McCormack.........	....	Penn	..	1	do
....	do	Not.	Elizabeth McAllister	....	Ireland ...	2	1	do
Sawyer	do	....	James Baird............	Sawyer ..	Unknown .	9	1	
....	do	....	Jacob & Elizabeth Fields..	Carpenter	Penn	8	1	do
None ..	do	....	Dan'l and Sarah Terry....	....	Ohio & Va.	3	1	do
do	do	....	J. and Mary Hozelbaker ..	....	Switzerl'nd	6	1	do
do	do	....	Jas. and Eunice Anderson.	....	....	..	..	
Farmer.	do	Not.	Wm. and Mahala Young.	....	Ohio	..	..	
None ..	Ohio.....	Not.	Wm. Plummer...........	....	Ohio	..	1	do
do	do	Not	Jas. & and Sus. Mahaffey .	....	....	..	2	
do	....	....	do do	....	....	..	2	
....	Ohio.....	....	Julia A. Sutton...........	....	....	..	1	
....	do	....	James McNeil	....	....	..	1	do
None ..	do	Not	Martin and Sarah Dillon..	Farmers.	Ohio	6	1	do
Farmer.	do	Educated	John McColum	do	....	..	..	
....	England.	Educated	Unknown.................	....	England ..	..	..	
None ..	Ohio.....	Not	T. and Matty Gilpin......	Laborer ..	Penn. & O.	5	1	do
do	Kentucky	Educated	....	....	Kentucky .	2	1	do
....	Ohio.....	Educated	Elrad ——....	Minister .	Ohio	4	1	Unk'wn.
None ..	do	Educated	Unknown	....	....	7	1	Cousins.
do	do	Not	Zachariah and Mary	....	....	..	..	
do	do	Not.	James T. and Rebecca....	Carpenter	....	8	1	

RETURN of the number of Deaf and Dumb, Blind, Insane and Idiotic pesons,

Townships.	Names of Persons.	Nature of Affliction	Duration of Affliction	Cause, where known	Age.	Sex.	Color.
Sugar cr'k.	Sarah Ridenour	Blind	12 years	Winter fever	13	Fem'le	White.
German	Ellen M. J. Leaser	Iditoic	2 "	Fits	4	do	do
"	Samuel Brown	Insane	From birth		40	Male	do
"	Elizabeth S. Hood	Insane	12 years	Fits	24	Fem'le	do
"	Gotleib Rummell	Idiotic	18 years	Sickness	22	Male	do
"	Zebedah Creman	Deaf and Dumb	34 "	Fever	35	do	do
"	Bartemus Terry	Blind	22 "	Not known	22	do	do
Marion	Nicholas Sherwick	Idiotic	From inf'cy	Fits	15	do	do
"	Mary E Schrader	Insane	5 weeks	Not known	45	Fem'le	do
"	Mary Weihart	Insane	5 years	do	26	do	do
"	Elizabeth Weihart	Insane	13 "	Sickness	34	do	do
"	John Lance	Insane		Fits	38	Male	do
"	Elizabeth T. Ludwig	Idiot and Dumb	From inf'cy	Fits	11	Fem'le	do
"	Samuel Lance	Idiotic	" "	Not known	33	Male	do
Spencer	Nicholas Firebaugh	Deaf and Dumb	3 weeks	Cold in Head	13	do	do
Shawnee	Edward	Idiotic			22	do	do
Auglaize	James W. Keith	Insane	13 years	Fits	14	do	do
"	Hannah Jane Keith	Insane		Wh'ping cough	22	Fem'le	do
"	Elizabeth C. Keith	Insane	19 years	Fits	20	do	do
Perry	John McElroy	Idiotic	13 "	Not known	13	Male	do
"	Mary Franklin	Insane	24 "	do	21	Fem'le	do
"	John McPheren	Deaf	21 "	Sickness	45	Male	do
Marion	Elizabeth Spikermyer	Idiotic	14 "	Fits	18	Fem'le	do
"	Henry Myer, jr	Idiotic	6 months	Fits	15	Male	do
Jackson	Sarah M. Barnes	Idiotic	6 years	Unknown	7	Fem'le	do
Amanda	Elisha Shock	Idiotic	15 "	Fits	15	Male	do
Monroe	Alfred Downing	Deaf and Dumb	19 "	From gathering	19	do	do
"	Leonard Fullerton	Deaf and Dumb	14 "	Sudden cold	19	do	do
"	Daniel Sheets	Blind	4 "	Sickness	19	do	do
"	Adam Rummel	Deaf and Dumb	36 "	do	38	do	do
"	Jacob Miller	Insane	11 "	Not known	33	do	do

in the County of Allen, State of Ohio, on the 2d Monday of May, 1856.

Occupation.	Birthplace.	Educated or not.	Names of parents.	Occupation.	Birthplace.	No. of child'n	No of child'n thus afflicted.	Relationship of parents before marriage.
....	Allen co..	Not.....	Geo. & Mary Ridenour	Farming .	Penn. & Md	8	1	None
....	do	....	Joseph Leasers.......	do	Penn......	6	1	do
....	Penn.....	Not.....	Saml. Brown........	Shoemk'r	Penn......	7	1	do
....	Ohio	Not.....	Geo. W. Hood	Farmer...	Ohio	8	1	do
Farmer	Europe...	Not.. ...	Unknown............	....	Europe ...	8	1	Unknown
Shoem'r	Ohio	Educated	Wm. Creman........	Shoemk'r	Maryland .	9	1	None
....	do	Not.....	Enos Terry.........	Farming .	Ohio......	3	1	do
Farm'g	Perry co..	Not.....	Sml. & Barb. Sherwick	do	Fairfield co	7	1	do
Servant	Germany.	Educated	A.Meiker & M'ry Grove	do	Germany..	5	1	do
None ..	do	Educated	H. and Mary Wiehart.	do	do	5	2	do
do	do	Educated	do do do	do	do	....	....	....
Various	Penn.....	Not.....	G. & Kathrrine Lauce.	Laborer ..	Penn......	12	2	None
None ..	Picka'y co	Not.....	G. W. & Ele'or Ludwig	House w'k	Pickw'y co	6	1	do
do	Penn.....	Not.....	G. & Katherine Lance.	Laborer ..	Penn......	12	2	do
....	Seneca co	Not.....	C. & Eliz. Firebaugh..	Farming .	Germany..	6	1	do
....	Fr'klin co.	Not.....	Not known..........	....	....	....	....	....
None ..	Allen co..	Not.....	J. H. & Mary Keith...	None	....	....	3	None
do	do	Not.....	do do	None	....	....	....	....
do	do	Not.....	do do	None	....	....	....	....
....	do	Not.....	Miles & Mary McElroy	Farmer ..	New York .	4	1	None
....	Miami co.	Not.....	C. Franklin, f. not k'n	....	Not known	1	1	Unknown
Farmer.	T· nnessee	Educated	Wm. & Jane McPheren	Farmer...	Tennessee.	14	1	None
None ..	Germany.	Educated	Henry Spikermyer ...	....	Germany..	5	1	do
do	....	Educated	Henry Meyer........	Carpenter.	do	3	1	do
....	Knox...	Not.....	L. & Sally Barnes....	Farming .	Harrison co	....	1	do
None...	Holmes co	Not.....	S. G. & Sarah Shock .	Mason...	Penn......	13	1	....
....	Allen co..	Educated	A. & Sarah Downing..	Farming .	Va & Penn.	9	1	None
None...	do	Educated	A. & Cath'ne Fullerton	do	Highl'd co	5	1	do
do	do	Educated	Jos. & Nancy Sheets .	do	Pa. & Md..	6	1	do
Shoem'g	Germany.	Not.....	G. & Cath'ine Rummel	Shoemk'r	Germany..	8	1	do
Farm'g	Penn	Educated	H. & Elizabeth Miller.	None.....	Penn. & Va	1	1	do

RETURN of the number of Deaf and Dumb, Blind, Insane and Idiotic persons in

Townships.	Names of Persons.	Nature of Affliction.	Duration of Affliction.	Cause where known.	Age.	Sex.	Color.
Lake	Newton Weioff	Idiotic	8 years		8	Male	White
"	Sidney C. Akins	Idiotic	From birth		19	do	do
"	Jasper N. Chandler	Dumb	"	Fall of mother	13	do	do
"	Mary Metcalf	Insane	3 years		22	Fem'le	do
Ruggles	Charles Malcolm	Insane	5 "	Not known	29	Male	do
"	Hugh McKee	Blind	12 "	Whip lash	45	do	do
"	Bramen Johnson	Blind	12 "	Ox horn	62	do	do
"	Geo. Taylor	Insane	15 "	Unknown	38	do	do
Troy	M. A. Smith	Insane	4 "		32	Fem'le	do
"	Mary Lowry	Deaf & dumb	11 "		11	do	do
"	Henry Haun	Insane	1 "	Domes'c trouble	25	Male	do
Milton	John Cordell	Insane	5 "	Not known	26	do	do
Hanover	Henry McEwen	Idiotic	From birth	Fits	28	do	do
"	Ma y Carnagey	Blind	4 years	Old age	92	Fem'le	do
"	Eliza Carnagey	Bl'd, d'b & Id'c	42 "	Skull cracked	44	do	do
"	Eleanor Parrat	Blind	35 "	Measles	71	do	do
Mifflin	Mary Sunday	Deaf and dumb	22 "	Sickness	32	do	do
"	Samuel Lewis	Deaf and dumb	From birth	Unknown	30	Male	do
"	Simon Lewis	Blind	30 years	Measles	35	do	do
Jackson	Jacob Biers	Blind	23 "	Salt rheum	61	do	do
"	Mary A Ott	Idiotic	10 "	Unknown	10	Fem'le	do
Vermillion	Albert McIntire	Insane	30 "	Sickness	31	Male	do
"	Samuel Ludwig	Idiotic	From birth		27	do	do
"	Oliver Sloan	Deaf and dumb	"		36	do	do
Perry	Ester Helman	Deaf and dumb	1 year	Measles	15	Fem'le	do
"	Wm. Marks	Idiotic	From birth	Fits	33	Male	do
"	James Allison	Idiotic	"		16	do	do
Orange	Frederick Switzer	Blind	45 years	Cataract	65	do	do
"	William Webster	Blind	17 "	Fever	45	do	do
"	Barbara Cassell	Deaf and dumb	14 "		14	Fem'le	do
"	Catharine Hartman	Deaf and dumb	40 "		40	do	do
Greene	Ahirah Hill	Blind	20 "	Hard labor	65	Male	do
"	Evens Burgan	Deaf and dumb	11 "	Sickness	20	do	do
"	James Cook	Idiotic	From inf'cy	Not known	27	do	do
Sullivan	Geo Manor, jr	Insane	2 years	" "	16	do	do
"	Hiram B. Ross	Idiotic	From birth		18	do	do
Montgom'y	Benjamin Crone	Blind	1 year	Sickness	36	do	do
"	Lewis Deal	Idiotic	From birth		41	do	do
"	Sally Deal	Idiotic	"		35	Fem'le	do
"	Henry Deal	Idiotic	"		30	Male	do
"	Harriet Deal	Idiotic	"		24	Fem'le	do
"	Lewis Zimmerman	Idiotic	"		26	Male	do
"	Margaret Figley	Idiotic	"		34	Fem'le	do
"	John Smith	Blind	20 years	Cut with knife	30	Male	do

the County of Ashland, State of Ohio, on the second Monday of May, 1856.

Occupation.	Birth place.	Educated, or not.	Names of Parents.	Occupation.	Birth-place.	No. Children	No. Children thus afflicted	Relationship of Parents before marriage.
None....	Ohio....	Not.....	Wm. & Sabina Weioff...	Farmer.	Pa. & Ohio	5	1	None
"	do	do	Joel Akins & wife.......	do	Pa	2	1	Cousins
"	do	do	Rob. & Hannah Chandler	do	Md......	14	1	None
Housek'r.	do	do	Wm. & Casander Goudy.	do	Pa.......	11	1	do
Farming .	Scotland	Educated	Alex. & Barbara Malcolm	do	Scotland ..	10	1	do
"	Ireland ..	do	John & Jane McKee....	do	Ireland ...	2	1	do
Miller	Vermont.	do	....	....	....	16	1	do
Farming .	Conn	do	Enoch & Cynthia Taylor.	Shoemak'r	Conn	4	1	do
Housek r .	Vermont.	do	Wm. & Lydia Smith	Farmer ..	....	11	2	do
....	Ohio	Not.....	Walter & Mary Lowry....	....	Ireland ...	7	1	do
Farmer...	do	Educated	John & Olive Haun	Farmer ..	Virginia ..	6	1	do
Farming .	Not kno'n	do	Sam'l & Catharine Cordell	do	Not kno'n.	10	1	do
None	Penn	Not.....	Henry & Sarah McEwen .	do	Pa..... ..	7	1	do
Farming .	N. Jersey	Educated	....	....	....		1	do
None	Penn	Not.....	Wm. & Mary Carnagey ..	Farming .	N. Jersey .	13	1	do
Housek'r .	N. Jersey	Educated	Jacob & Eliz. Vanwenkel.	do	do	5	1	do
"	Ashl'd co.	do	John Sunday Leak......	do	Pa.......	5	1	do
Shoemak'r	do	do	Charles Lewis Hand	do	Ohio......	9	1	do
....	do	Not.....	Nathan Lewis	do	....		1	do
Pedler ...	Penn	Educated	Fred. & Catharine Biers..	do	Pa.......	12	1	Cousins
None	Ohio	Not.....	Jacob & Sarah Ott	Butcher .	Pa.......	2	1	None
"	N. York..	do	D. & Isabella McIntire...	None	N. York ..	14	1	do
"	Ohio	do	Philip & Barbara Ludwig	do	Pa.......	7	1	do
" ...	do	do	Oliver & Parsalla Sloan..	Farming .	Pa.......	7	1	do
....	Ashl'd co.	do	David & Eliz. Helman...	....	Pa.......	8	1	do
None	Penn	do	Elizabeth Marks	....	Pa.......		1	do
"	Ohio	do	Alex. & Elce Allison	Farming .	Pa.......		1	do
"	Penn	Educated	Peter & Margaret Switzer.	do	Europe		1	do
"	N Jersey	do	Thos. & Catha'e Webster.	Clothier .	Pa..... ..	6	1	do
"	Ohio	....	John & Margaret Cassell.	Farmer ..	Pa......	5	1	do
"	do	....	David & Mary Hartman..	Tailor ...	Md.......	13	1	do
Pedler ...	Vermont .	Educated	Calvin & Mary Hill......	Farmer ..	N. & Mass.	11	1	do
....	Ashl'd co.	Not.....	James & Nancy Burgan..	Blacksm'h	Pa.......	5	1	do
None	do	do	J. E. & Mary Cook......	Merchant	Md.......	8	1	do
Farming .	do	Educated	Geo. & Arenath Manor...	Farming .	Vermont ..	10	1	do
"	do	Not.....	Samuel & Sarah Ross....	do	Vt. & Mass.	6	1	do
Chairma'r	Penn	do	Henry & Mary Crone....	Wagonm'r	Va	9	1	do
None	do	do	Fred. & Catharine Deal..	Farmer ..	Md.......	10	4	do
"	do	do	" " " ..	Housew'k	Pa.......	..	....	do
"	do	do	" " " ..	do	Pa.......	..	....	do
"	Ohio	do	" " " ..	do	Pa.......	..	....	do
"	Penn	do	Jos. & Eliz. Zimmerman.	Farming .	Pa..... ..	11	1	do
"	Ohio	do	Jacob & Sarah Figley....	do	Pa.......	11	1	do
Farmer ..	Penn	do	John & Larra Smith.....	do	N. Y......	11	1	do

28

RETURN of the Number of Deaf and Dumb, Blind, Insane and Idiotic persons in

Townships	Names of Persons	Nature of Affliction	Duration of Affliction	Cause	Age	Sex	Color
Pierpont...	Speeda Wright......	Blind	2 years..	....	81	Fem'le	White.
"	Nancy Shellenbeger..	Blind	9 "	.. Scrofula.......	70	"	do
Denmark..	Sarah Jacobs........	Insane........	52 "	.. Fits	53	"	do
"	Sarah Ann Gilbert...	Deaf and dumb	From infcy	....	30	"	do
Rome.....	Lorenzo Tinker......	Insane........	12 years..	Intense study..	35	Male..	do
Harpersf'ld	Louisa Frink........	Blind	Infancy...	Born blind....	17	Fem'le	do
"	Daniel Prentice......	Blind	14 years..	Cataract......	83	Male..	do
"	Sarah Rogers........	Blind	7 "	.. "	59	Fem'le	do
Wayne ...	John Rice..........	Blind........	15 "	.. Sickness	66	Male...	do
"	Windfield S. Loomis.	Idiotic........	14 "	.. Natural.......	14	"	do
Plymouth.	Almon Dart........	Blind	23 "	.. Rash & ch'n pox	27	"	do
"	Ber j. Lagrange.....	Insane........	3 "	....	20	"	do
"	Orra Upson.........	Insane........	11 "	.. Injury	55	Fem'le	do
Austinburg	Eliza Smith.........	Idiotic........	From birth	Neural........	12	"	do
"	Edward Lewis.......	Insane & dumb	20 years..	Protr'ted meet'g	54	Male...	do
Conneaut..	Martha Smith.......	Idiotic........	13 "	.. Blow f'm father	19	Fem'le	do
"	Franklin Hunt......	Idiotic........	8 "	.. Bath. while wrm	20	Male..	do
"	Sarah Wright.......	Blind	30 "	.. Inflammation..	45	F ...	do
"	Mary Huston........	Deaf and dumb	5 "	.. Cancker rash..	19	"	do
"	Stephen Bemus......	" "	51 "	.. Measl's & mu'ps	54	tale.	do
"	W. E. Cleveland.....	" "	2 "	.. Measles.......	8	"	do
Richmond.	....	....	....	....	..	......	do
Windsor..	Ralph Barnard.......	Deaf and dumb	57 years..	Unknown......	63	Male...	do
"	John McIntosh......	Blind	7 "	.. Inflammation..	47	"	do
Ashtabula.	Eliza J. Fields......	"	33 "	.. Accident......	35	Fem'le	do
"	Thos. H. Hopkins....	"	14 "	.. "	23	Male...	do
Orwell	Nancy Herrick......	Insane........	7 "	.. Unknown......	67	Fem e	do
"	Gardner Stone.......	Blind	....	....	48	Male ..	do
"	Ruth Jordan........	Idiotic........	10 years..	Fits	18	Fem'le	do
"	Lucy Northway......	Idiotic........	10 "	.. "	16	"	do
"	Wm. Paterson......	Idiotic........	18 "	.. Unknown	21	Male...	do
Monroe....	Luther Everett......	Blind	20 "	.. Hard labor....	60	"	do
Sheffield...	Sarah Smith........	Insane........	16 "	.. Taking cold...	40	'em'l	do
"	Alvin W. Colgrove...	Deaf and dumb	7 "	.. Scarlatina.....	11	tale	do
"	Elizabeth Burk......	Idiotic........	34 "	.. Unknown......	35	Fem'le	do
"	Albert Gage.........	Insane........	12 "	.. Epileptic fits...	13	male...	do
Kingsville.	Calvin Bugbee	Insane........	8 "	.. Disease.......	32	"	do
"	Lucius Sanderson....	Idiotic........	10 "	.. Congenital	10	"	do
"	Henry Sanderson.....	Idiotic........	13 "	.. "	13	"	do
"	Helen Surline.......	Idiotic........	10 "	.. Epilepsy......	15	Fem'le	do
"	Cynthia Bancroft.....	Insane........	3 "	.. Intemperance..	79	"	do
Co. Infirm.	Wm. Whitney.......	Idiotic........	14 "	.. Congenital	14	Male...	do
"	Anthony Ellison	"	28 "	.. "	28	"	do
"	Adelaid Countryman..	"	13 "	.. Masturbation of parents....	13	Fem'le	do
"	Fanny Monger......	Insane........	20 "	.. Deran. menstr'n	44	"	do
"	Sally House.........	" ...l...	20 "	.. Unknown.....	60	"	do
"	Susan Bartholomew..	"	38 "	.. Cruel husband..	..	"	do
"	Hall Smith..........	"	30 "	.. Loss of property	71	Male...	do
"	Caroline Donnell.....	"	....	....	40	Fem'le	do
"	Celestia Smith.......	"	12 years..	Disappointment	24	"	do
"	Zedekiah Fisk	"	10 "	.. Intemperance. .	59	Male .	do
"	William Barton......	Blind	4 "	.. Injury	50	"	do
"	Charles Hall	Blind	1 "	.. Intemperance..	62	"	do
"	Lorette Plympton....	Insane........	20 "	.. Disappointment	53	Fem'le	do

the county of Ashtabula, State of Ohio, on the second Monday of May, 1856.

Occupaiton.	Birth-place.	Educated or Not.	Names of Parents.	Occupation.	Birth-place.	No. Children	No. children thus affected.	Relationship before Marriage.
....	Connec'ut	Educated	....	....	....	..	..	....
....	Penn	"	....	....	....	..	..	....
....	Vermont.	Not.....	Levi and Lydia Jacobs..	Farmers...	Mass......	10	1	None.
Laborer..	Conn	Educated	Lewis and Lydia Gilbert	"	..Conn.....	3	1	"
Farmer ..	Rome, O.	"	Lynes and Polly Tinker.	"	.. "	4	1	....
....	N. York..	Not.....	B. W. and Clarissa Frink	"	..New York.	8	1	None.
Farmer...	Conn	Educated	....	....	....	..	..	....
Dairy ...	Mass.....	"	....	....	....	..	..	....
Farmer...	Mass.....	"	Amos and Sybil Rice....	Farmers ..	Conn.....	7	2	None.
....	Ohio.....	Not.....	M. and Sopha Loomis...	"	..Mass.....	6	1	"
....	Vermont.	Educated	S. and Hannah Dart....	"	.. "	9	1	"
....	N. York..	Educated	And.&Angelica Lagrange	"	..New York.	7	1	2d cous.
....	Conn	Educated	Bela and Olive Blakeslee	Tanner ..	Conn.....	7	2	None.
....	Austinb'g	Not.....	A. A. and Eliza Smith..	Teaching,	Mass. & Ct.	4	1	"
Farmer...	Conn	Common	Martin Lewis............	Tanner...	Conn......	2	1	"
None	N. York..	Not.....	....	....	....	..	..	....
"	Ohio.....	Was.....	....	....	....	..	..	....
"	"	Educated	....	....	....	..	..	....
"	....	At asyl'm	....	....	....	..	..	....
"	Conn	....	....	....	....	..	..	....
"	Conneaut.	....	....	....	....	..	..	....
Farmer...	Conn	None....	Moses and Reliance B...	Farmer...	Tolland,Ct	11	2	....
Merchant	Vermont.	Educated	Milt. and Lydia McJ....	Tanner...	Connectic't	3	1	....
....	Ohio	"	Aaron L and Diana F...	Farmers..	Vermont..	4	1	None.
Music t'ch	England..	"	Wm. and Emelia H.....	Laborer,	England ..	9	1	"
....	N.York..	Not.....	Stutely Stone.........	Farmer ..	New York.	5	1	....
None	Orwell, O.	"	Ralph and Abby Jordan,	"	"	11	1	....
"	" "	....	Geo. and M. Northway..	"	.. "	4	1	....
"	Penn	Not.....	John Paterson..........	"	....	..	..	....
Farmer...	....	Educated	....	....	....	..	..	....
....	Vermont..	Educated	....	....	....	..	..	None.
....	King-ville	Not.....	L. and Mary Colgrove..	....	....	..	..	"
....	N. York..	"	A. and Margaret Burk ..	....	....	..	..	"
....	Sh. ffield.	"	Josh. and Anna Gage...	....	....	..	..	"
....	Kings'ille	Educated	Z. and Polly Bugbee....	Farmer ..	Mass......	6	1	....
....	"	Not.....	....	"	.. ..	4	2	Cousins
....	"	"	....	"	....	..	..	....
....	"	"	John and Harriet Surline	Cab't mak	Unknown,	4	1	None.
....	Mass.....	Educated	Silas and Lois Tinker....	Farmers ..	Conn.....	10	1	"
....	Shef'ld, O	....	....	....	....	..	..	....
....	Jeff'son, O	....	....	....	....	..	..	....
....	Ashtabula	....	....	Laborer .	....	..	..	....
Housewfe	Unknown	Educated	....	....	....	5	1	None.
"	"	"	....	....	....	..	..	"
"	England ..	"	Thomas Atkin...........	Farmer...	England ..	22	1	None.
Merchant	Mass.....	"	....	....	....	..	..	....
Housewfe	....	"	....	....	....	..	..	....
Teacher .	Jefferson .	"	....	....	....	..	..	....
Butcher..	....	"	....	....	....	..	..	....
Laborer ..	Ireland ..	"	....	....	....	..	..	....
" ..	N.York..	"	....	....	....	..	..	....
Milliner..	N.York..	"	....	....	....	..	..	....

RETURN of the number of Deaf, Dumb, Blind, Insane and Idiotic persons

Names of Persons.	Nature of Affliction.	Duration of Affliction	Cause where known.	Age.	Sex.	Color.
Henry Goodwin	Idiotic	Birth	Unknown		Male	White.
Barbara A. Coil	Insane	29 years	Obstruc. menses	44	Fem'le	do
Reuben Wilkins	do	14 months	Spiritualism	48	Male	do
Mary Sturgeon	do	2 years	Do		Fem'le	do
Wm. Hollingsworth	Blind	4½ do	Inflamation	44	Male	do
Mary A. Hein	Idiotic	32 do		32	Fem'le	do
Peter Miller	Blind	2 do		60	Male	do
Albert Clawson	Deaf and dumb	7 do		7	Male	do
Ann Sibert	do	43 do	Fever	46	Fem'le	do
John Harshberger	do	53 do	Unknown	53	Male	do
E. C. Branen	Blind	2 do	Erysipelas	55	Male	do
James H. Mitchell	Idiotic	18 do		18	Male	do
Mary Jane Fitzpatrick	Deaf and dumb	21 do	Whoop. cough.	22	Fem'le	do
John W. Williams	Blind	4 do	Accidental	46	Male	do
Eve Brockert	do	1 do	Fever	67	Fem'le	do
Susan Barr	Deaf and dumb	14 do	Sickness	15	Fem'le	do
Mary M. Zangline	Insane	12 do	Jealousy	38	Fem'le	do
Christopher Harvey	do	14 do		38	Male	do
John Haroff	do	11 do	Cholera	60	Male	do
Franz Trentman	Blind	5 do		59	Male	de
Joseph Konig	Idiotic	12 do		46	Male	do
Francisco Hengster	Insane	12 do		47	Fem'le	do
Magdaline Stegle	do	7 do		60	Fem'le	do
Mary Henskey	do	10 do		28	Fem'le	do
John English	Blind	30 do	Measles	68	Male	do
John Miller	Insane	35 do	Unknown	60	Male	do
Abraham Wagner	Idiotic	25½ do	Fits	27	Male	do
Randall Wells	Deaf and dumb	47 do		47	Male	do
Sarah Pearce	Insane	30 do		30	Fem'le	do

31

in the County of Auglaize, State of Ohio, on the second Monday of May, 1856.

Occupation	Birth-place	Educated or not	Names of Parents	Occupation	Birth-place	No. children	No. afflicted	Relationship of parents before marriage
Farmer	New York	Not	Unknown		Unknown	2	1	
....	Ohio	do	Peter and Sarah	Laborer	do	7	1	
do	Maryland	do						
....	Ohio	Educated						
Carpen'r	Virginia	do	John and Jane					
....	Germany	Not	James and Mary	Farmer		4	1	
Shoe'ker	Do	Educated						
....	Ohio	Not	Isaiah and Lydia	do		3	1	None
Sewing	Virginia	do	Peter and Jane	do	Virginia	11	1	do
....	do	do	Henry and Elizabeth	do	do	12	1	Cousins.
....	N. H	Educated	John and Catharine	do	Connecticut	3	1	None.
Farmer	Ohio	Not	John F. and Sarah	do				
Dress'ker	New York	Educated	Edward and Clarissa	do	Ireland	9	1	do
Farmer	Ohio	do	John and Margaret	do	N. Y. &Va.	10	1	do
H's. wife	Germany	do	John and Catharine	do	Germany	1	1	do
....	Ohio	do	Christian and Martha	Attorney	Penna	2	1	do
....	do	do	H. Miller & Catharine	Farmer	do	6	1	do
Farmer	do	do	Christopher	do		8	1	
do	Penna	do						
do	Europe	do				6	1	
do	do	do						
....	Germany	Not						
....'..	do	Educated						
....	do	Not						
do	New Jersey	Educated	J. English & M Sutton	do		10	1	4th Cousins
do	Virginia	do	D. Miller & M Batey	do	Virginia	11	1	None.
do	Ohio	Not	John and Rachel	do	Va. & Ohio	13	1	do
Mech'nic	do	do	Joseph Wells	Dead	Rhode Is'd	3	1	2d Cousins.
....	Tennessee	do	William Pearch	Farmer	Tennessee	14	1	

RETURN of the number of Deaf and Dumb, Blind, Insane and Idiotic persons

Townships.	Names of persons.	Nature of Affliction	Duration of Affliction.	Cause where known	Age.	Sex.	Color.
Eagle.....	Nelson Surber.......	Deaf and dumb	25 years..	....	25	Male .	White.
"	Catharine Surber.....	do	5 "	....	5	Fem'le	do
Pleasant..	W A. Evans........	do	....	....	19	Male .	do
"	Peter Foerst.........	do	....	....	23	do	do
"	Charlotte Price.......	Deaf..........	6 years ..	Fever........	21	Fem'le	Mul'to
"	Robert Cahol........	Deaf and dumb	....	Unkuown	14	Male .	White.
"	Sanders J. Waterman.	do	....	"	9	do	do
Union	Daniel B. Fryer......	Idiotic........	13 years ..	"	13	do	do
"	Cena Pangburn......	Insane.......	40 "	A fall........	46	Fem'le	do
"	Ezekiel Rogers	do	26 "	Study	53	Male .	do
"	Fanny Chapman.....	Idiotic........	....	Unknown	40	Fem'le	do
Sterling...	Margaret Bengaman..	Blind..........	12 years ..	From hurt....	17	do	do
Byrd	Eugene Wyle........	do	....	....	5 m	do	do
"	Margaret M. Robe....	Deaf and dumb	3 years ..	Abscess......	16	do	do
"	Wash. Howlen) ..	do	30 "	Unknown	30	Male .	do
"	Clarinda, his wife) ..	do	12 "	Fever	24	Fem'le	do
"	John Maxwell	Idiotic........	20 "	....	20	Male .	do
Pike......	John Russel	Insane........	20 "	Sickness	54	Fem'le	¾ do
"	Sally Hughes........	do	15 "	"	53	do	do
"	Sanford Robbins.....	do	21 "	Unknown ..	21	Male .	do
"	A. J. Wilson........	do	17 "	Fits	20	do	do
Jackson...	Lovicy Moore.......	D'mb & part Ins	14 "	Worms.......	15	Fem'le	do
Green	Lonzo Fite	Idiotic........	9 "	....	9	Male .	do
"	Mary Donnily	Insane........	20 "	....	45	Fem'le	do
Franklin ..	Caleb Pifer.........	Idiotic........	....	Unknown ...	45	Male .	do
"	Jacob Roustberer.....	do	....	....	38	do	do
Jefferson..	Isaac N. Deming.....	Deaf and dumb	45 "	....	45	do	do
"	James Perry.........	Idiotic........	28 "	Fits	36	do	do
Clark.....	Hugh Kenedy	Insane........	16 "	"	30	do	do
"	Andrew J. Walker....	do	8 "	Study	34	do	do
"	Matilda Applegate...	Blind..........	21 "	Unknown ..	21	Fem'le	do
"	George L. Coffman ...	Idiotic........	2 "	Probably fits .	2	Male .	do
Huntington	James S. Jones.......	Idiotie & dumb	16 "	....	16	do	do
"	Daniel B. Jones......	do	11 "	....	11	do	do
"	Isaac Paul...........	do	30 "	....	20	do	do
"	Timothy Simmons....	Deaf and Dumb	25 "	Teething	26	do	do

in the county of Brown, State of Ohio, on the second Monday of May, 1856.

Occupation	Birthplace	Educated or not.	Names of Parents.	Occupation	Birthplace	No. children	No. children thus afflicted	Relationship of Parents before Marriage.
Farmer	Ohio	Not	L. and Margaret Surber...	Farmer ..	Ohio	14	7	None.
None ..	do	Not	do do	do	do	14	7	do
Clerk ..	do	Educated	Geo. D. and M. A. Evans..	Merchant	do	7	1	
Laborer	Germany	Educated	Adam and Eliza Foerst	Farmer ..	Germany	3	1	
Cook ...	S. Caroli'a	Not	Chas. and Eliza Price	....	S. Caroli'a	5	1	
Farmer	Ohio	....	Thos. and Rachel Cahol ..	Joiner ...	Ohio	6	1	
....	do	Not	N. A. & Barbara Waterman	Farmer ..	do	7	1	None.
None ..	do	Not	Alexander Fryer	Ch'rmak'r	do	8	1	do
do	do	Not	Sines & Rebecca Pangburn	Farmer ..	Penn	12	1	do
Teacher	Kentucky	Educated	Thos. and Nancy Rogers..	do	Virginia.	11	1	do
None ..	Ohio	Not	Henry and Fanny Chapman	do	do	11	1	do
do	do	Not	Solomon and Rebecca ....'.	do	Penn	6	1	do
do	do	....	T. B. and S. A. Wyler	Physician	do	4	1	do
....	do	Educated	Wm. and Johanna Robe ...	Farmer ..	Ohio	4	1	do
Farmer	do	Educated	Izatus and Sarah Howlen	do	Virginia.	6	1	do
....	do	Educated	Christian Hall	Unknown	Penn	8	1	do
....	do	Not	David Maxwell	Farmer ..	Mass	2	1	do
Farmer	do	Not	John and Nancy Russel ...	do	Va & Pa.	11	1	do
....	....	....	Robert and Phebe	Butcher.	Ireland...	7	1	do
....	Ohio	Not	Carl & Delilah Robbins ..	....	Ohio	5	1	do
....	....	....	Reuben and Lydia Wilson	....	New York	15	1	do
None ..	Ohio	Not	Robt. & Elizabeth Moore ..	Farmer ..	O. & Penn	7	1	do
do	do	Not	Reuben Fite	do	Ohio	3	1	Cousins
do	Kentucky	Educated	Unknown	do	do	1	1	Unknown
do	Germany.	Not	Unknown	....	....	..	..	Unknown
do	do	Can read	Unknown	....	....	..	..	Unknown
Bl'ksmth	Ohio	Not ...,	Job and Mary Deming	Farmer ..	Ohio	3	1	
....	....	....	John C. and Margaret	Bl'ksmith	....	5	1	
....	Ohio	Educated	John and Hannah Kenedy	Farmer ..	Penn	24	1	None
Doctor .	do	Educated	Nicholas & Phebe Walker.	....	Delaware	9	1	None
None ..	do	....	Benj. & Rebecca Applegate	....	....	16	1	Cousins.
....	do	....	....	....	....	5	2	
Farmer	do	Not	Ephraim & Sarah Jones...	Farmer ..	Ohio	4	2	2d cousins
do..	do	Not	do do	....	do	2	2	do
do..	....	....	James and Fanny Paul	....	....	2	1	Unknown
....	do	Educated	....	....	New York	2	1	Unknown

3—SEC. OF STATE.

RETURN of the number of Deaf and Dumb, Blind Insane and Idiotic persons

Townships	Names of Persons	Nature of affliction	Duration of Affliction.	Cause where known	Age.	Sex.	Color.
Monroe..	Harriet M. Miller...	Deaf and Dumb	10 years...	Unknown........	10	Fem'le	White
do	Abraham Pearch...	Blind.........	28 "	Blasting rocks...	50	Male..	do
Union.....	Daniel Wagoner....	Dumb.........	23 "	Disease of mother.	23	do	do
do	Elizabeth Smelts...	Insane........	3 months..	Unknown........	27	Fem'le	do
do	Robert Rutledge...	do	42 years...	do	42	Male..	do
Centre....	Virginia Stidger....	Idiotic........	generally .	Spasms when born	8	Fem'le	do
Brown....	Wm. Brown.......	Wht. swel.& b'd	36 years...	Unknown........	45	Male..	do
do	Milton Brothers....	Deaf and Dumb	4 "	do	4	do	do
do	Wm. Seaton.......	Insane........	8 "	Personal abuse...	57	do	do
Loudon...	Arthur Gruber.....	do	19 "	Fits.............	19	do	do
do	Lydia Rutledge....	Blind.........	2 "	By asthma......	75	Fem'le	do
do	James Clutz.......	Idiotic........	28 "	Unknown........	28	Male..	do
do	Julia Ann Scott....	do	28 "	do	28	Fem'le	do
Harrison..	Harriet E. Moore...	Insane........	6 "	Chronic Disease..	24	do	do
do	Thomas Bosler.....	Idiotic........	33 "	Fits.............	33	Male..	do
do	Hewit Henderson...	do	29 "	Unknown........	29	do	do
do	John Clice.........	do	22 "	Crossing the sea..	22	do	do
Perry.....	Ellen Post.........	Blind.........	2 "	Sickness	6	Fem'le	do
do	Francis Hess.......	Deaf and Dumb	23 "	....	23	do	do
do	Lydia Manchester..	D'f, d'b & ins...	25 "	Sickness	50	do	do
do	Francis Barnhouse..	Deaf..........	2 "	Unknown........	85	Male..	do

35

in the County of Carroll, State of Ohio, on the second Monday of May, 1856.

Occupation.	Birthplace.	Educated or not.	Names of Parents.	Occupation.	Birthplace.	No of child'n	No. of child'n thus afflicted.	Relationship of parents before marriage.
None..	Ohio....	Not.....	Solomon & Eleanor Miller.	Farmer.	Penn.....	3	1	None.
Farmer.	Penn.....	Educated	Conrad & Barbara Pearch..	do	do	7	1	do
do	Ohio....	Not.....	Henry and Susan Wagoner	do	Ohio.....	7	1	do
....	do	Educated	Lewis & Catherine Smelts.	do	Germany.	5	1	do
Farmer.	Ireland..	Not.....	....	....	Ireland...	7	1	do
....	Ohio....	do	Henry A. & Annie Stedger	Merchn't	Maryland	6	1	do
None...	Penn.....	Educated	George and Mary Brown..	Farmers.	Irel. & Pa	8	1	do
....	Ohio....	Not.....	A. & Marianna Brothers...	do	Penn. & O.	8	1	do
Farmer.	Ireland..	Educated	Ezekiel & Margaret Seaton.	do	Ireland...	10	1	do
None...	Ohio.....	Not.....	Saml. & Rachel Gruber....	Tanner..	Penn.....	10	1	do
Weaving	N. Je sey	Educated	Joseph and Hannah Beedle	Carpen'r	N. Jersey.	12	1	do
None...	Maryland	Not.....	Geo. and Catherine Clutz..	Sheom'r.	Penn.....	11	1	Cousins.
do	Penn.....	do	Robt. and Elizabeth Scott..	Farming	do	12	1	None.
....	Ohio.....	¯ducated	John and Sarah Moore....	Mech'nic	Ireland...	9	1	do
....	do	Not.....	Abraham & Sarah Bosler..	Laborer.	Penn.....	10	1	do
.....⌣.	do	do	Ed & Issabella Henderson.	Farmer..	Ireland...	9	1	do
....	U. S. A...	do	George and Mary Clice....	do	France...	11	1	do
....	Ohio.....	do	James and Rachel Post...	Laborer.	Ohio.....	1	1	do
Laborer.	do	do	Daniel and Elizabeth Hess.	Farmer..	Penn.....	1	1	Not kno'm.
....	New York	do	Not known...	....	New York	1	1	
Laborer.	Maryland	Educated	do	Not kn'n	Not kno'n	1	1	Not kno'm.

RETURN of the number of Deaf and Dumb, Blind, Insane and Idiotic persons in

Townships	Names of Persons	Nature of affliction	Duration of affliction	Cause where known	Age	Sex	Color
Salem	Susan Eichholtz	Dumb	20 years	Scarlet fever	21	Fem'le	White
Adams	Mary Martz	Insane	11 "	Not known	11	"	"
Jackson	James West	Blind	From birth	"	24	Male	"
"	William Johnson	Idiotic	"	"	24	"	"
Union	John G. Sullivan	Deaf and dumb	21 years	Scarlet fever	24	"	"
"	Nancy Sullivan	Insane	17 "	Relig's excitm't	45	Fem'le	"
"	F. A. Morrison, jr	Deaf and dumb	6 months	Mumps	19	Male	"
"	Sarah Ellen Kist	Idiotic	From birth	Fits	16	Fem'le	"
"	Eve Grove	Blind	20 years	Fever	59	"	"
Madison	Rachel Brian	Insane	15 "	Hereditary	71	"	"
"	Henry Clayton Idle	Deaf	4 "	Sickness	7	Male	"
"	Samuel Arrowsmith		14 "	"	15	"	"
"	Jane Jenkins	Insane	8 "		8	Fem'le	"
Goshen	Nicholas Wynant	Insane	20 "	Not known	46	Male	"
"	Lucinda Coffey	Idiotic	23 "	Fits	33	Fem'le	"
Wayne	Mary Johnson	Demented	22 "	Not known	25	"	"
"	Joseph J. Baker	Deaf and dumb	32 "	"	32	Male	"
Concord	Benjamin Long	Blind	2 "	"	76	"	"
Johnson	Samuel Brubaker	Deaf and dumb	From birth	"	20	"	"
"	Finly Davis	Deaf and dumb	"	"	5	"	"
"	George Davis	Deaf and dumb	"	"	3	"	"
"	John H. Evernham	Deaf and dumb	"	"	10	"	"
Urbana	Marshal Ward	Idiot	"		36	"	"
"	Patrick Comeford	Blind	4 years	[forehead] Stroke across the	38	"	"
"	Anna Blalock	Insane	15 "	Trouble	63	Fem'le	"
"	Margaret Mitchel	Idiotic	From birth		30	"	"
"	Lorenzo Mitchel	Idiotic	"		24	Male	"
"	Albion Taylor	Idiot	7 years	Sickness	18	"	"
"	John McCoy	Idiotic	From birth		9	"	"
"	Sidney W. Addison	Insane	18 years	Intemperance	58	"	"
"	Joana Donahoo	Insane	4 "	Trouble	30	Fem'le	"

the County of Champaign, State of Ohio, on the second Monday of May, 1856.

Occupation.	Birthplace.	Educated or not.	Names of Parents.	Occupation.	Birth-place.	No. Children	No. children thus afflicted.	Relationship of parents before marriage.
....	Lan. co. Pa	Not.....	John and Mary Eichholtz	Farmer ..	P-nn'a....	8	1	1st cous
....	Champ. co	"	B. Hand and F. Martz..	Farming .	Virginia ..	14	1	Cousins
Farming .	"	"	J. W. and Mary A. West	"	Ohio & Ky.	7	1	"
None	Clark co.O	"	Fred. and Eliza Johnson	"	Irel'd,N.Y.	6	1	None.
Plasterer.	Champ. co	Educated	Wm. and Nancy Sullivan	Potter....	Va. & Ohio	7	1	"
....	Ohio.....	Not	Wm. and Eliz'h McFarlin	Farming .	Virginia ..	11	1	"
Farming .	Champ. co	"	F. A. and Jane Morrison	"	Baltimore	5	2	"
"	"	"	John and Nancy P. Kist	"	Va. & Ohio	8	2	"
"	Virginia..	Educated	John and Eve Demeny ..	"	Virg nia ..	12	11	"
Housek'pr	"	"	Powell..................	....	....	..	..	....
....	Ohio ...	Not	Martin and Lavina Idle..	Farming .	Ohio	1	1	None.
....	"	"	W. R. and J. Arrowsmith	"	Va. & Ohio	4	1	"
....	"	"	David and Mary Jenkins	Shoemakr	Ohio	6	1	"
Cabin't mr	....	Educated	P. and Millie Wynant ..	Farming .	....	9	1	"
....	Ohio	Not	T. and R Coffey........	"	Ohio	9	1	"
None	Virginia..	"	Gould and Susan Johnson	Physician	Connectio't	8	1	"
"	N Jersey .	"	Joseph and Phebe	Farming .	N. Jersey.	7	1	Unkn'n
Carpenter	Penn.....	Educated	....	....	....	..	..	....
Farming .	Champ. co	"	Jacob and Sar. Brubaker	Farming .	....	2	1	None.
None	Hardin co.	Not	A. J. and A. E. Davis..	Carpenter	Mar'n co }	3	2	....
"	"	"	do do	"	" " }			
Farming .	Champ. co	"	Henry and E. Evernham	Farming .	Not known	..	1	None.
None	"	"	Wm. and Margaret Ward	"	Virginia...	4	1	"
Broom mr.	Ireland ..	Educated	Ed. and J. Comeford....	Laborer .	Ireland ...	8	1	....
....	Delaware.	Educated	Ed. and Sarah Covington	....	Maryland .	10	1	....
....	Ohio.....	Not	Samuel Mitchell........	Farming .	Not kn'n }	8	2	....
None	"	"	do	"	" }			
"	"	"	T. Taylor..............	"	Ohio	5	1	....
"	"	"	Not known.............	....	Va. & Ohio	..	1	....
"	England...	Educated	W. and Cathrine Addison	Mechanic.	England ..	6	1	....
"	Ir-land ..	Not	Not known.............	....	Ireland ...	..	1	....

RETURN of the Number of Deaf and Dumb, Blind, Insane and Idiotic Persons,

Names of Persons.	Nature of Affliction.	Duration of Affliction.	Cause where known.	Age.	Sex.	Color.
PIKE TOWNSHIP.						
Michael Hess...............	Insane......	Unknown.	Unknown	40	Male .	White.
John Brandenburg	do	Du ing life.	do	16	do	do
James P. Welch............	Blind	Born blind.	do	21	do	do
MAD RIVER TOWNSHIP.						
Mary A. Drake...............	Deaf........	12 years..	do	14	Fem'le	do
SPRINGFIELD—1ST WARD.						
Aaron Roll	Lunatic.....	10 or 11 y's.	Study at college....	30	Male .	do
William. H. Eaton.........	do	6 years ...	Unknown	35	do	do
Elizabeth Barr	do	Unknown .	do	50	Fem'le	do
Andrew Borer....	do	5 years...	Sickness	40	Male .	do
Hillic McGiffin........	Idiot	From birth.	Unknown	16	Fem'le	do
Sarah Williams	do	do	do	31	do	do
Martha Hughes...........	do	do	do	16	do	do
Sarah Green.............	Lunatic.....	Unknown .	do	45	do	do
William Swaney..........	do	5 years...	Onanism...........	26	Male .	do
Thomas Moore	Blind	3 years...	Intemperance.. ...	69	do	do
John Newton	Idiot	18 years..	Dropsy of the brain [1 year old]	20	do	do
SECOND WARD.						
David Henderson	Blind.......	10 years..	Strong medicine at }	10	do	do
David Anderson Moore	D'mb & ins'e.	23 years..	Born in that condit'n	23	do	Col'rd.
Lemuel Hoak	Idiotic......	10 years..	Unknown	15	do	White.
Mary Hoak	Blind.......	2 years..	Erysipelas	55	Fem'le	do
THIRD WARD.						
Tacey Bruce	Dumb.....	26 years..	Unknown	26	do	do
MADISON TOWNSHIP.						
Harvey W. Packer	Blind.......	8 years..	do	27	Male .	do
Eveline McCollum............	Idiotic......	From birth.	do	40	Fem'le	do
Caleb Meritte	Deaf........	33 years..	Sickness	35	Male .	do
PLEASANT TOWNSHIP.						
Amanda Shaul,)	Deaf & dumb.	From birth.	Unknown	25	Fem'le	do
Emma Shaul, } Same family .	do	do	do	23	do	do
Newton Shaul,)	do	do	do	20	do	do
Samuel Marsh	Idiotic......	do	Fits	50	Male .	do
Andrew Jackson Dixon.......	do	do	do	19	do	do
Mary Jones,)	do	do	Unknown.	20	Fem'le	do
William Jones, } Same family.	do	do	do	17	Male .	do
Jeremiah Jones,)	do	do	do	15	do	do

All in County Infirmary.

in the county of Clark, State of Ohio, on the second Monday of May, 1856.

Occupation.	Birthplace.	Educated or not.	Name of Parents.	Occupation.	Birthplace.	No. children.	No. children thus afflicted.	Relationship of parents before marriage.
Farmer	Germany	Educat'd	Unknown	Unkn'n	Unknown			Unk'wn.
None	Ohio	No	Saml. Brandenburg	Farmer	Virginia	20	1	None.
Tech'r music	"	Educat'd	Jas. Welsh	"	Unknown		1	None.
None	"	Educat'd	J. S. & Cath. Drake	"	"	1	1	None.
"	Clark co.	Educat'd	Unknown	Unk'wn	"			Unk'wn.
Farmer	Unk'wn	Educat'd	"	"	"			"
None	"	Educat'd	"	"	"			"
Laborer	Ireland	Not	"	"	"			"
None	Ohio	Not	"	"	"			"
"	Unk'wn	Not	"	"	"			"
"	Clark co.	Not	"	"	"			"
"	Unk'wn.	Not	"	"	"			"
Laborer	Ireland	Educat'd	"	"	"			"
Teamster	U..k'wn.	Educat'd	"	"	"			"
None	England	Not	Jos. & Eliz. Newson	Gardner	Englaud [Engl'd]	6	1	None.
None	Clark co.	Not	T. & Eliz. Henderson	Laborer	Ireland &	4	1	None.
"	Virginia	Not	J. & Hannah Moore	"	Virginia	12	1	"
"	Ohio	Not	John & Mary Hoak	"	"	12	1	"
Laborer	Virginia	Educat'd	J. & Chris. Huffman	"	"	2	1	"
None	Clark co.	Not	G. and Jane Bruce	Merch'nt	"	7	1	"
None	Ohio	Not	John and Ann Packer	Unk'wn	Penn	3	1	"
"	"	Not	J.& Elizabeth McCollom		Virginia	7	1	"
"	Pen	Educat'd	J. & Marg. Meritte		N. Jersey	3	1	"
House keeper	Ohio	Educat'd	M. and Sarah A. Shaul	Farmer	Virginia	19	3	"
"	"	Educat'd	" "	"	"			
"	"	Educat'd	" "	"	"			
"	"	Not			N. Jersey	1	1	Cousins.
None	"	Not	David Dixon	Farmer	Musk'm co.	1	1	None.
House keeper	"	Not	James and Mary Jones	"	Virginia	6	3	"
Farming	"	Not	" "	"	"			
Nothing	"	Not	" "	"	"			

40

RETURN of the number of Deaf, Dumb, Blind, Insane and Idiotic persons

Names of Persons.	Nature of Affliction.	Duration of Affliction.	Cause where known.	Age.	Sex.	Color.
BATIVIA TOWNSHIP.						
Jemima Ellen Black	Blind	From birth	Unknown	10	Fem'le	White.
Nancy Clark	Idiotic	Unknown	do	26	do	do
Eliza Gill	do	do	do	30	do	do
Joshua Stuart	do	do	Epilepsy	35	Male	do
Rhodes Noble	Insane			50	Fem'le	do
Mary Pool	do			49	do	do
WILLIAMSBURG TOWNSHIP.						
John Emerson	do	8 months	Not known	18	Male	do
Pauline Homan	Idiotic	35 years	Fits	36	Fem'le	do
TATE TOWNSHIP.						
George Robb	Deaf and dumb	36 do	Bald hives	40	Male	do
Andrew McCullum	Blind	25 do	From birth	25	do	do
William B. Smith	Deaf and dumb	31 do	do	31	do	do
Isaac Crane	Idiotic	15 do	Fits	17	do	do
Filena Rice	do	14 do	do	15	Fem'le	do
Alvin B. Randall	do	4 do	do	5	Male	do
Philip Quinlan	Blind	27 do	Hurt	31	do	do
Samuel Homan	Idiotic	9 do	Not known	63	do	do
Leonodus W. Homan	Blind	5 do	Catarrh	7	do	do
FRANKLIN.						
Edwin Tucker	Fits, Idiotic	30 do	Not known	48	do	do
Susan Parrell	Deaf and dumb	35 do	do	35	Fem'le	do
Mary Edwards	Fits	40 do	Fits	40	do	do
Aaron Stephens	do	45 do	do	45	Male	do
—— Plumer	do	From birth	do	17	do	do
WASHINGTON TOWNSHIP.						
Adalina Lewis	Idiotic	11 years	Unknown	11	Fem'le	do
John C. Barkley	Deaf and dumb	8 do	Neuralgia	12	Male	do
Rachael V. Cluse	Insane	6 do		18	Fem'le	do
Sarah Manning	Deaf and dumb	12 do	Fevers	16	do	do
MONROE.						
Sophia C. Clark	Dumb	10 do		10	do	do
William Anderson	Blind	4 do	Paralysis	60	Male	do
OHIO.						
Eliza Gellaskie	Deaf and dumb	17 do	Unknown	17	Fem'le	do
Simeon O. Swim	do do	From birth	From birth	7	Male	do
Ann E. Swim	do do	do	do	4	Fem'le	do
Henry Nash	Insane	12 years	Fits	23	Male	do
Sarah Dair	Deaf and dumb	44 do		44	Fem'le	do
Mary Hugh	Idiotic	32 do		32	do	do
Nancy Stump	Blind	7 do	By fevers	43	do	do
William Ferrece	Idiotic	28 do	Fits	28	Male	do
Smith Holladay	do	From birth	Not known	18	do	do
Jacob Hill	Insane	20 years	Study	70	do	do
Sarah Smith	Idiotic	From birth	Not known	18	Fem'le	do
Theodore Shradney	Deaf and dumb	5 years	Sickness	9	Male	do
George W. Harris	do do	35 do	do	40	do	do
Josiah Groves	do do	30 do	Unknown	30	do	do
James Garrison	Insane	50 do	do	50	do	do
Mary Powers	Deaf and dumb	20 do	do	40	Fem'le	do
John Clark	Insane	36 do	Convulsive Fits	36	Male	do
Margaret Hunter	Deaf and dumb	60 do		60	Fem'le	do
Mary Hunt r	do do	57 do		57	do	do
David Slymdtz	Idiotic	22 do		22	Male	do

41

in the County of Clermont, Ohio, on the second Monday of May, 1856.

Occupation.	Birth-place.	Educated or not.	Names of Parents.	Occupation.	Birth-place.	No. children.	No. afflicted.	Relationship of parents be fore marriage
None...	Ohio	Partly..	M. and Eliz. Black	Farmers ..	Ohio......	5	1	None.
do	do	Not	Unknown........	Unknown .	Unknown	4	1	Unknown.
do	do	do	John Gill........	do	do	..	..	do
do	kentucky ..	do	Unknown........	Farmers ..	do	..	1	do
....	....	Educated	do	Unknown .	do	..	..	do
....	....	do	do	do	do	..	..	do
cop'smith	Ohio	do	George & H. Emerson	Tradesman	Ver.& Mas.	4		Cousins.
None....	do	Not	Samuel and J. Homan	Farmers ..	New Jersey	7	1	None.
Cooper..	do	do	Moses & R. Robb	do	New York	6	1	do
None....	do	do	H. & H. M'Collum	do	N. J. & Pa.	8	1	do
do	do	do	T. & Mary South	do	do	8	1	Cousins.
do	do	do	Oliver & E. Crane..	do	N.J. & Ohio	6	1	None.
do	do	do	C.Rice &M. Henderson	Merchant .	Vt. & Ohio	10	1	do
do	do	do	M. Randall & J. Smith	Drayman..	Ohio......	6	1	do
do	do	do	John & C. Quinlan ..	Merchant .	Penna	1	1	do
Farmer .	New Jersey	Educated	A. Homan, E. Doughty	....	Ohio......	7	1	do
None....	Ohio	Not	....	....	do	7	1	do
Farming	Maryland	do	Richard Tucker	Farmer ..	Maryland .	8	1	do
Sewing..	Not known	do	Unknown........	....	....	..	..	Unknown.
do	Vermont ..	do	do	....	....	..	..	do
None....	do	do	Silsby Stephens......	Farmer....	Vermont ..	..	..	do
Farmer ..	Ohio......	do	Thomas Plummer....	do	do	..	..	None.
None....	do	do	Isaac & D. Lewis	do	Ohio......	8	1	do
do	do	Educated	J. & F. Barkley......	do	do	9	1	do
do	do	do	E. & Harriet Cluse ..	Mechanic .	Maryland .	8	1	do
At school	do		Squire Manning	Farmer ..	Ohio......	7	1	do
....	do		....	....	do	..	..	do
Farmer .	Not known	Unkno'n	....	....	do	..	..	do
Unkn'on	Ohio......	do	Rich. Clark, & E. Cox	Blacksmith	New York.	7	1	do
....	do	do	W & Nancy Swim....	Farmers ..	Ohio......	4	2	(No rela-
....	do	....	do do	do	do	..	..	tion s.
....	do	Educated	Henry & Sarah Nash .	do	do	10	1	no relation.
....	Germany..	Not	Matthew Dair........	do	Germany..	4	1	Cousins.
....	do	o	Frederick Hugh......	do	do	2	1	None.
H keeper	Ohio......	d o	....	....	Penna	2	1	Unknown.
None...	do	o	Isaac Terrace........	do	Unknown	..	1	do
do	do	do	Thomas & J Holladay	do	Ohio......	2	1	no relation.
Minister	S. Carolina	Educated	John & Elizabeth ...	do	Unknown .	6	1	do
None...	Ohio......	Not	David & Sarah......	do	Penna	8	1	do
do	do	do	George and Mary	Tailor	France....	6	1	do
Laborer .	New Jersey	do	William. and R.Harris	Glassblow'r	New Jersey	8	1	None.
Farmer .	Maryland .	do	John & Mary Groves	Farmer....	Maryland .	10	1	do
do	New Jersey	o	James & M Garrison	do	New Jersey	6	2	Cousins.
H. work.	Ohio......	do	T Powers & J Harris	do	do	6	1	Unknown.
Farmer .	do	Educated	Arthur & A. Clark..	do	N. J. & Pa.	7	1	do
....	Penna	....	William & M. Hunter	do	Irel'd & Pa.	8	2	
....	do	....	do do	do	Pa. & Ohio	7	1	
....	Ohio......	....	John & E. Slymdtz ..	do	do	8	1	

RETURN of the number of Deaf and Dumb, Blind and Idiotic

Names of Persons.	Nature of Affliction.	Duration of Affliction.	Cause where known.	Age.	Sex.	Color
OHIO.						
Benjamin Osborn	Idiotic	13 years		13	Male.	White.
John W. Patterson	do	8 do	Scarlet Fever	16	do	do
Phebe Cramer	Insane	10 months	Loss of friends	21	Fem'le	do
Elizabeth M'Conn	Idiotic	22 years	Sickness	1:	do	do
Sarah Brower	Insane	13 do	Abuse by hus'd	27	do	do

persons in the county of Clermont, Ohio—*Continued*.

Occupation.	Birth-place.	Educated or not.	Names of Parents.	Occupation.	Birth-place.	No. children.	No. afflicted.	Relational ip if parents before marriage.
....	Ohio......	....	John & Sarah Osborn	Farmer..	Va. & Ky.	3	1	Unknown
....	do	....	Ed. & M. Patterson ..	do	Ky. & Ohio	10	1	do
....	do	Educated	Samuel & E. Cramer	do	New Jersey	5	1	do
....	Penna	....	Bernard & A. M'Conn	do	Ireland ..	..	..	do
....	New Jersey	Educated	Ephraim & M. Pruden	do	New Jersey	12	1	do

RETURN of the Number of Deaf, Dumb, Blind, Insane and Idiotic persons in

Names of Persons.	Nature of Affliction.	Duration of Affliction.	Cause Where Known.	Age.	Sex.	Color.	Occupation.
UNION TOWNSHIP.							
William Flemming	Insane	35 years	Scull fractured	84	Male	White	Miller
Perry Dale	do	3 do	Epilepsy	30	do	do	Farmer
Robert G. Seal	do	2 do	Same	34	do	do	do
Mary Lisler	do	4 do	Not known	38	Fem'le	do	
Jane Darby	do	9 do	do	62	do	do	
Bridget Denlin	do	5 do	do	45	do	do	
William Scott	Idiotic	12 do	do	55	Male	do	Car'ge mk
Joseph Greene	do	16 do	do	24	do	do	Farmer
George Hobson	do	30 do	do	55	do	do	do
Jessee Townsend	do	15 do	do	33	do	do	do
Charles Cowgill	do	17 do	do	17	do	do	
Stacia Stafford	do	20 do	do	31	Fem'le	do	
Eleanor Scott	Insane	18 do	do	28	do	do	
John Jones	do	20 do	do	49	Male	do	Farmer
Julia A. Sullivan	Idiotic	15 do	do	33	Fem'le	do	
Margaret Black	do	35 do	do	25	do	do	
A. T. Sewell, Jr	do	20 do	do	35	Male	do	
Susanna Fisher	Insane	22 do	Fits	22	Fem'le	do	
George Wilson	Deaf and dumb	20 do	Not known	20	Male	do	
R. W. Sirrell	do do	21 do	do	21	do	do	Laborer
CHESTER TOWNSHIP.							
Mary E. Karnes	Deaf and dumb	From birth	Not known	16	Fem'le	White	Laborer
David H. Burton	Insane	9 years	Fits	22	Male	do	do
Elizabeth Williams	do	From birth	Not known	15	Fem'le	do	Cant work
B. D. Dakin	Deaf and dumb	From birth	do	21	do	do	Laborer
Lydia E. Dakin	Same	26 years	Affec'n of brain	33	do	do	Tayloress
Elizabeth Dakin	Same	From birth	Not known	17	do	do	Laborer
Matilda Ellis	Insane	From birth	Fits	26	do	do	Cantwork
Benj. McMillan	do	13 years	Fits	19	Male	do	do
GREENE TOWNSHIP.							
John Kirby	Insaue	4 years	Erysipelas	65	Male	White	Farmer
Eliza J. Hadgron	do	25 do	Spasms	26	Fem'le	do	
Harvey White	Idiotic	From birth	do	10	Male	do	Farmer
David Bashon	Insane	14 years	Not known	42	do	do	do
Clarissa Hanes	do	15 do	do	40	Fem'le	do	
RICHLAND TOWNSHIP.							
R. Brag	Deaf and dumb	From birth		11	Male	White	
LIBERTY TOWNSHIP.							
Lucy Bangham	Blind	12 years	Cataract	74	Fem'le	White	
VERNON TOWNSHIP.							
Mary Ackley	Idiotic	From birth	Fits	31	Fem'le	White	Farmer
John Jones	Insane	20 years		60	Male	do	do
CLARK TOWNSHIP.							
Aaron Smith	Deaf and dumb	48 years	Sickness	50	Male	White	None
Wm. D. Johnson	Deaf and dumb	20 do	Measles	55	do	do	Farmer
Jane Hinman	Blind	16 do	Sickness	70	Fem'le	do	
MARION TOWNSHIP.							
Hannah Garrison	Deaf and dumb	From birth		39	Fem'le	White	Weaver
Jeremiah Garrison	Deaf and dumb	From birth		38	Male	do	Farmer
Irwin Garrison	Deaf and dumb	From birth		20	Male	do	Farmer

45

the County of Clinton, State of Ohio, on the second Monday of May, 1856.

Birth place	Educated or Not	Names of Parents	Occupation	Birth-place	No. children	No. children thus afflicted	Relationship of Parents before marriage
Pennsylv'a	Educated	Not known	Not known	Not known		2	Not kno'n
Ohio	do	"	"	"		1	do
do	do	"	"	"		1	do
do	do	"	"	"		1	do
Virginia	do	"	"	"		1	do
Ireland	do	"	"	"		1	do
Ohio	do	"	"	"		4	do
do	Not	"	"	"		1	do
do	Educated	"	"	"		1	do
do	do	"	"	"		1	do
do	Not	"	"	"		1	do
do	do	"	"	"		1	do
do	do	"	"	"		1	do
do	Educated	"	"	"		1	do
do	Not	"	"	"		1	do
do	do	"	"	"		1	do
do	do	Amos T. and Sarah Sewell	Recorder	Virginia	6	1	do
Virginia	do	Not known	Not known	Not known		1	do
Ohio	Educated	Alexander Wilson and lady	Farmer	Ohio	7	1	do
do	do	Not known	Not known	"		1	do
Ohio	Educated	John and Elizabeth Karnes	Laborer	Virginia	6	1	Not kno'n
do	Not	David and Eliza Burton	Farmer	"	8	1	do
do	do	Peter and Rachel Williams	Carpenter	Pennsylv'a	7	1	do
do	Educated	Lewis and Eliza Dakin	Farmer	N.Y. C'y	9	3	do
do	do	Same	"	"			
do	do	Same	"	"			
do	Not	John and Mary Ellis	"	Pennsylv'a	9	1	do
do	do	Newton and Rachel McMillan	"	"	7	1	do
Virginia	Educated	John and Nancy	Farmer	N. Carolina	8	1	None.
Ohio	Not	Eleazer and Ann	"	"	9	1	do
do	do	John and Grace	"	Ohio	2	1	do
Virginia	Educated	John and Susan	"	Virginia	8	1	do
Ohio	do	John and Mary	"	N. Jersey	2	1	do
Ohio	Not						
Virginia	Educated	Zachariah and Mary	Farmer	Virginia	10	1	None.
Ohio	Not	Scoby and Margaret	Brick makr	Pa. & N.J.	11	1	None.
Penn	Educated	Thomas and Mary	Not known	Virginia		1	do
N. Carolina	Not	William and Margaret	Farmer	N.C. & Geo	6	1	None.
do	Educated	Ashley and Ursula	"	N. Carolina	8	1	do
Ireland	do				3	1	do
Ohio	None	Benjamin and Rebecca	Farmer	N. Jersey	12	3	Cousins.
do	Partly	Same					
do	do	Same					

46

RETURN of the Number of Deaf, Dumb, Blind, Insane and Idiotic persons in

Names of Persons.	Nature of Affliction.	Duration of Affliction.	Cause Where Known.	Age.	Sex.	Color.	Occupation.
WASHINGTON TOWNSHIP.							
Horace Lewis	Idiot	F'minɪ'ncy	Fits	18	Male	White	
Henry A. Richards	Blind	do	Fever	9	"	"	
WAYNE TOWNSHIP.							
Adon Linch	Deaf and dumb	From birth		27	Male	White	Farmer
Elizabeth Linch	" "	"		29	Fem'le	"	
Soloman Airheart	Idiot	"		9	Male	"	
ADAMS TOWNSHIP.							
John A. Headley	Idiot	F'minɪ'ncy	Unknown	17	Male	White	
Sarah A. Mooth	"	"	Scald 18 months	36	Fem'le	"	
WILSON TOWNSHIP.							
Hamilton Brown	Deaf and dumb	From birth	Unknown	30	Male	Black	F'rm hand
William Oliver	Blind	13 years	Affection of eye	36	"	White	Farmer
Joel Hunt	Insane	45 "	Unknown	65	"	"	"
Margaret Mills	Idiotic	42 "	Whoopi'g cough	42	Fem'le	"	

the County of Ashtabula, Ohio, on the second Monday of May, for the year 1856.

Birth-place	Educated or Not.	Names of Parents.	Occupation	Birth-place	No. children	No. children thus afflicted	Relationship of Parents before marriage
Ohio	Not	Jackson and Mary	Shoemaker	Ohio	8	1	None.
Kentucky .	"	Pierson and Elizabeth	Farmer ..	N. York ..	6		"
Virginia ..	Not	Linton and Sarah	Farmer ...	Virginia	11	4	None.
" ..	"	Same	" ..	"		1	"
Ohio	"	John and Mary....	" ..	" ..	9	1	"
Ohio	Not	William and Mary	Farmer ..	N. Carolina	3	1	None.
Pennsylv'a	"	Samuel and Elizabeth	Mechanic,	Penn.	4	1	"
Ohio	Not	....	....	....	..	1	....
N. Carolina	"	Joceph and Isabel	Farmer ..	N. Carolina	18	1	Cousins.
"	Educated,	Josiah and Ann	" ..	"	7	2	None.
Ohio	Not	James and Margaret	" ..	Maryland,	7	1	"

RETURN of the number of Deaf and Dumb, Blind, Insane and Idiotic persons

Townships.	Names of Persons.	Nature of Affliction.	Duration of Affliction	Cause where known.	Age.	Sex.	Color.
Liverpool..	Mary Blakely	Deaf and Dumb	16 years	Scarlet fever	21	Female	White
do	John C. Logan	Blind	4 do	Accid'nt with fork	15	Male	do
Middleton.	Samuel Baird	Deaf and Insane	42 do	Scalded	48	do	do
do	James Ward	Insane	7 do	Fits	17	do	do
Unity	James C. Taggart	Demented	4 do	Heredetary	55	do	do
Yellow cr'k	Daniel Frazer	Insane	10 do	Not known	35	do	do
do	Rebecca Martin	do	15 do	. do	45	Female	do
do	William M. Gilvery	do	8 do	do	26	Male..	do
Madison ..	James A. Curry	Deaf and Dumb	18 do	Scarlet fever	19	do	do
do	Jack. M. Laughlin..	Deaf	15 do	do	26	do	do.
do	Alex. & J. Wright..	Idiots	fr'm birth	Not known	13	do	do
do	John Robinson	do	do	do	26	do	do
do	Jane Noble	Blind	45 years	Overheated	62	Female	do
Elkrun ...	William Fout s.....	Idiot	f m inf'cy	Unknown	60	Male	do
Fairfield...	James S. Williams..	Deaf and Dumb	do	Cold when young.	33	do	do
do	Jabes Freet	Blind	30 years	Catarrh	35	do	do
do	Ruth Edmundson..	Insane	11 do	Not known	61	Female	do
Salem.....	James H. Patterson.	Idiotic	12 do	do	12	Male..	do
do	Daniel Hardman...	do	30 do	do	30	do	do
Franklin ..	Loneda Cooney....	Insane	f'm inf'cy	do	22	do	do
do	Sarah Linn	Idiotic	do	do	37	Female	do
do	Two Miss Linns....	Insane in part.	do	do	26	do	do
Hanover...	Charity Gallreath..	Insane	20 do	do	24	do	do
do	Lawrence Flood....	Blind	2 do	do	70	Male..	do
Butler.....	David Test	Insane	4 months	Inflam. of brain	30	do	do
do	Mary A. Kerr	do	26 years	Whooping cough.	28	Female	do
do	Mary Newburn	do	12 do		66	do	de
do	Thomas Kirklan....	do	15 do	Loss of property..	58	Male..	do
Perry.....	Sidney E. Pennock..	Idiotic	9 do	Measels	12	Female	do
do	John L Goulbourn..	Insane	8 do	Unknown	30	Male .	do
do	James Ford	Idiotic	17 do	do	17	do	do
do	Daniel Ireman	Deaf not Dumb.	7 do	From a cold	44	do	do
do	Amos Eldridge	Deaf and Dumb	4 do	Sickness	10	do	do
do	Ellen Davis	Idiotic	fr'm birth		16	Female	Mulatto
do	Robert Spencer	Deaf and Dumb	do		40	Male..	Black
Wit	Catherine Snook ...	Insane	f'm inf'cy	Cause unknown..	36	Female	White.
do	Elizabeth Hiveley..	Idiot	do	de	36	do	do
Knox	Rebecca Ickes....	Insane	10 years	Scarlet fever	25	do	do
Centre and Infirmary..	William Smoot	do	Unkno'n	Unknown	65	do	do
do	John Henry	do	do	do	28	do	do
do	Samuel Beans	do	do	do	57	do	do
do	Chalkley Kelley ...	Idiot			50	do	do
do	Adolphus Button...	Insane			65	do	do
do	Nathan Hatcher....	do	7 years	Unknown	34	do	do
do	John Taggart	do			31	do	do
do	Augustus Nail....	do	1 year..	Unknown	46	do	do
de	Janley M. Grew....	do	Unkno'n.	do	70	do	do
do	Yokley Wiley	Deaf and Dumb			45	do	do
do	John Irwin	Insane	Unkno'n.	Fever	45	do	do
do	Harrison Byrns.....	do	9 years.	Study	28	do	do
do	A.iam Extine	Insane	4 do	Unknown	30	do	do
do	George Howe	Idiot	Unkno'n.		50	do	do
do	Margaret Emeck....	do			50	Female	do
de	Martha Scott	do			40	do	do

in Columbiana County, State of Ohio, on the second Monday of May, 1856.

Occupation.	Birthplace.	Educated or not.	Names of Parents	Occupation.	Birthplace.	No. of Children	No. thus Afflicted.	Relationship of Parents before marriage.
....	Penn.....	Educated	J. S. and Jemima Blakely.	Manuf'er	Eng.& Pa.	4	1	None.
....	Ohio....	Not......	James and Scynthia Logan.	....	Ohio....	3	1	do
....	Penn.....	do....	Wm. and Mary Baird.....	Farmer..	do	3	1	do
....	Virginia..	do....	Unknown...............	do	do	3	..	do
Farmer..	Ohio....	Educated	J. Taggart & Rebec. Clark.	do	Penn.....	7	1	do
do	do	Com. ed.	Alex. and Marg. Frazer.....	do	Scotland..	4	1	do
do	....	do....	S. and Martha Swarenger..	do	....	8	1	Cousins.
do	Ohio....	do....	Daniel McGilvery........	do	....	6	1	None.
Tailor..	do	Educated	Joseph and Marg. Curry..	Blksmith	Penn.....	8	1	do
Farmer.	do	do....	Jas. & Ann McLaughlin..	Farmer.	Ohio....	..	..	....
....	do	Not.....	Geo. and Anne Wright....	do	do	11	3	1st cous.
....	do	do....	John and Eleanor Robinson	oo	Penn.....	5	1	....
....	Scotland.	Educated	Alex. & Jane Noble........	do	Scotland..	4	1	None.
....	Ohio....	Not......	Wm. and Elizabeth Toutts.	....	....	..	..	....
Labor r.	Penn.....	Partially.	Jesse and Mary Williams..	Tailor...	Penn.....	10	1	None.
bro'm mr	Ohio.....	do....	Geo. and Charlott Freed...	Farmer..	Virginia	8	4	do
....	Penn.....	Educated	....	do	do	7	1	do
None...	do	Not.....	J. H. & Margaret Patterson	Wh'right	Penn.....	9	1	do
do	Ohio.....	do....	Danl. & Hanna Hardman..	Farmer.	do	8	1	do
....	do	do ...	Thomas & Mary Cooney.	do	do	19	1	do
....	do	do....	Hugh and Ann Linn......	do	Ireland...	9	1	2d cousins
....	do	do....	do do	do	do	9	2	do
None...	....	do....	James Galbreath........	do	....	3	1	None.
do	....	Limited..	P. Flood & Cath. Plankard.	....	....	..	1	do
Farmer.	Ohio.....	Not......	Isaac and Hannah Test ..	Farmer.	....	7	1	....
....	do	do....	Wm. and Mary Kerr......	do	....	7	1	....
....	Penn.....	Educated	Enos Vanayoc,...........	....	....	..	1	....
Farmer..	England.	do....	R. and Dorothy Kirtland...	....	....	7	1	....
None....	Ohio.....	Not......	John and Sydney Pennock	Farmer.	America..	4	1	None.
out dr wk	Penn.....	Educated	J. and Rachel Goulbourn..	do	England..	5	1	do
None..	Ireland...	Not......	Jane Moore.............	Weaver.	Ireland...	2	1	do
Wheelri't	America...	Educated	H. and Christina Ireman .	Farmer.	America	12	1	do
None....	do	Not......	Enos and Sarah Eldridge..	do	Pa.& Eng.	9	1	do
H'se w'k	Ohio.....	do....	Edith Fisher, mother......	H'se w'k	Virginia..	3	1	do
Out d.wk	Virginia.	do....	N. and Elizabeth Spencer..	Out door	do	3	1	do
None....	Ohio.....	do....	John and Martha Snook...	Farmer...	Unknown	5	1	do
do	do	do....	John and Mary Hively....	do	Penn.	6	1	2d cousins
do	Penn.....	do....	George and Lydia Ickes....	do	....	8	1	....
Farmer .	....	Educated	Unknown................	....	....	..	1	....
Shoem'kr	Ohio....	do....	do	....	....	..	1	....
Ch'rnm'r	do	do....	do	....	....	..	1	....
Farmer...	....	....	....	....	....	..	1	....
None.....	Unknown	Educated	Unknown................	....	....	..	1	....
C'ragem'r	do	do....	do	....	....	..	1	....
Farmer...	Ohio....	do....	Jas. and Alice Taggart....	Farmer...	....	..	1	None.
Washer...	Germany.	do....	....	....	....	..	1	....
Millright	Penn.....	do....	Unknown................	....	....	..	1	....
None.....	Ohio....	do....	....	....	....	..	1	....
do	Unknown	do....	....	....	....	..	1	....
do	Ohio....	do....	John and Maria Byrns....	B'ksmith	Ohio....	3	1	None.
Contrac'r	Germany.	do....	....	....	....	..	1	....
....	Uuknown	....	....	....	....	..	1	....
....	Ohio....	....	Phillip and Marg. Enith ..	Weaver.	Penn.....	3	1	....
....	do	Educated	....	....	....	..	1	....

4—REP. SEC'Y. STATE.

RETURN of the number of Deaf and Dumb, Blind, Insane

Townships.	Names of Persons.	Nature of affliction	Duration of Affliction	Cause where known	Age.	Sex.	Color.
Centre and Infirmary..	Susan Way........	Idiot...........	....	....	35	Female	White..
do	Mary Beaumont....	Insane........	15 years	....	45	do	do
do	Isabella Williamson.	do	16 do	....	31	do	do
do	Ellen Williams.....	do	....	....	40	do	do

and Idiotic persons in Columbiana County, Ohio—Continued.

Occupation.	Birthplace.	Educated or not.	Names of Parents.	Occupation.	Birthplace.	No. of Children	No. thus afflicted.	Relationship of Parents before marriage.
....	Ohio	Educated	....	....	....	..	1	....
....	do	do	....	....	....	..	1	....
....	do	do	....	....	....	..	1	....
....	do	do	Joseph and Marg. Williams	Farmer.	....	..	1	....

RETURN of the number of Deaf and Dumb, Blind, Insane and Idiotic persons

Townships.	Names of persons.	Nature of Affliction.	Duration of Affliction.		Cause where known.	Age.	Sex.	Color.
Bedford...	Samuel McCullough	Insane	7	years.	Unknown	28	Male..	White
Clark.....	E. Purdy	Speechless	28	do	Fits	28	Fem'le	do
Adams...	E. Sherer	Deaf and Dumb	5	do	Unknown	15	do	do
do	M. A. Lewis	Lunatic	5	do	do	12	do	do
Jefferson...	— Stewart	Deaf and Dumb	2	do	do	..	do	do
....	— Elder	do do	11	do	do	..	do	do
Keene.....	George Bechtol....	Blind	6	do		86	Male..	do
do	Jas. McFetridge...	Insane	26	do		46	do	do
do	Susan Boyd	Deaf and Dumb	33	do		36	Fem'le	do
Millcreek..	Hannah Aultman...	Blind	22	do		67	do	do
do	Hosea Morehead...	Deaf and Dumb	..	..		15	Male..	do
Pike......	E. White..	do do	11	do		11	Fem'le	do
do	James Lake	Insane	20	do	Fits	35	Male..	do
Oxford....	E. Switzer	Blind	9	do	Weakness	55	Fem'le	do
White Eyes	David Sutton	Deaf and Dumb	10	do	Scarlet fever	12	Male..	do
do	John H. Little	Blind	35	do		44	do	do
do	Wm. A Gardner...	Deaf and Dumb	12	do		12	do	do
Washi'gton	Charles Crout	do do	22	do		22	do	do
do	Emanuel Pordue...	Idiot	..	..		30	do	do
do	George Smith	Insane	12	do	Fits	20	do	do
Virginia...	H. Davis	Deaf and Dumb	4	do	Not known	4	do	do
do	Margaret Davis....	do do	2	do	do	2	Fem'le	do
do	E Cornell	do do	47	do	Fever	48	do	do
Tuscaraw's	William Rambo....	Insane	7	do	Spinal affection	34	Male..	do
do	Ann Cresip	do	8	do	Epileptic	22	Fem'le	do
do	C. Grounizor	Idiot	17	do	Scarlet Fever	23	do	do
do	Sarah Mobley	Insane	5	do	Unknown	60	do	do
do	Frederick Harman..	Deaf and Dumb	25	do		25	do	do
do	M. Wells	Idiot	70	do		70	Male..	do
do	Joshua Wells	do	60	do		60	do	do

in the County of Coshocton, State of Ohio, on the second Monday of May, 1856.

Occupation.	Birth-place.	Educated or not.	Names of Parents.	Occupation.	Birth-place.	No. Children.	No. Children thus afflicted.	Relationship of parents before Marriage.
Farmer...	Delaware.	Educated	Wm. and J. McCullough.	Farmer ..	Unknown	7	1	Unkno'n
....	Ohio.....	Not.....	Josia and U Purdy....	do	Penn.....	4	1	2d cous.
....	Germany.	do.....	Jacob and Eliz. Sherer..	do	Germany.	6	1	Unkno'n
....	Ohio.....	do.....	Jas. and Mary Lewis	do	England.	4	1	do
None....	do	do.....	Andrew E. Stewart......	do	Ireland ..	3	1	do
do ...	do	do.....	John and E. Elder......	do	do ..	6	1	do
....	Penn.....	Educated	....	....	....	..	..	....
....	Penn.....	do	....	....	....	..	..	....
....	Maryland	do	....	....	....	..	..	....
....	Penn.....	....	Joseph Devorse..........	....	....	..	1	None ...
....	Ohio	....	Samuel and M. Morehead	Farmer ..	Ohio	.	1	Cousin..
....	do	Not.....	Lewis White.............	....	Virginia..	..	1	do ...
....	do	..,....	Spencer Lake............	....	Virginia..	9	1	....
....	Penn.....	Not.....	....	....	....	4	..	....
....	Ohio	Educated	Wm. E. Sutton..........	Farmer ..	Penn.....	..	1	None ...
....	Penn.....	Not.....	John and M. Little......	St'e mason	Ireland ..	4	1	do
....	Ohio	Educated	Adam and N. Gardner...	Miller....	Penn.....	9	1	do
Farmer..	....	Educated	Joseph Crout............	Farmer ..	....	6	1	....
do ..	....	Not...	....	....	....	..	..	....
....	....	Educated	James M. Smith.........	Farmer ..	....	..	1	....
....	Ohio	Not.....	Benj. and A. Davis......	Minor ...	Wales...	..	3	None ...
....	do	do.....	do do	do ...	do	..	3	do
....	Penn.....	do.....	Peter and L. Cornell.....	Smith....	Penn.....	6	1	do
Farmer..	Ohio	Educated	Unknown .... ,.	Farmer ..	Penn.....	12	1	Unkno'n
....	Ohio	do	James C. Cresip.........	Smith....	Unknown	5	1	do
...,....	Germany.	Not.....	Unknown	....	Germany.	..	1	do
Seamstr's	....	Educated	do	....	....	..	1	do
Farmer..	Germany.	Not.....	George Harman.........	Farmer ..	Germany.	2	1	None ...
....	Penn.....	do.....	C. D. and M. Wells....	do	Maryland	10	3	do
....	Penn.....	do.....	do do	do	Maryland	10	3	do

RETURN of the number of Deaf and Dumb, Blind, Insane and Idiotic persons

Townships	Names of Persons	Nature of Affliction	Duration of Affliction	Cause where known	Age	Sex	Color
Cranbery	John W. Kling	Deaf and dumb	5 years	....	5	Male	......
"	Thos. J. Davis	Dumb & Idiotic	7 "	....	7	"	......
"	Henry Orviler	Deaf and dumb	27 "	....	27	"	......
Auburn	Susan Hutchison	Idiotic	35 "	....	35	Fem'le	White.
Vernon	John Ribley	Blind	9 "	Unknown	44	Male	do
Polk	Polly Evans	Insane	35 "	"	58	Fem'le	do
"	John Brakaw	"	10 "	"	49	Male	do
"	Delila Hengst	"	5 "	Fits	7	Fem'le	do
"	Elizabeth Suttan	"	7 "	Sickness	53	"	do
"	Elizabeth Swisher	"	13 "	Diffic'y wth hus.	40	"	do
"	Benj. S. Straw	Deaf and dumb	41 "	....	41	Male	do
Sandusky	Wm. Torrence	"	½ "	Fever	29	"	do
"	Wm. Tustison	"	½ "	"	30	"	do
Chatfield	Elizabeth Shuga	Insane	5 "	Jealousy	50	Fem'le	do
"	Wm. Hatten	"	8 "	Unknown	45	Male	do
"	Henry Kinsel	Idiotic	20 "	Fits	23	"	do
"	Michael Casip	Insane	3 "	Unknown	46	"	do
"	Simon Presbee	Idiotic	33 "	"	33	"	do
"	Christian Pfleidera	"	28 "	Severe cold	2½	"	do
Whetstone	Margaret Melder	Deaf	66 "	Small pox	70	Fem'le	do
"	Wm. Woodling	Idiotic	5 "	Fits	15	Male	do
Bucyrus	Mary Cramea	Blind	7 "	Scarlet Fever	12	Fem'le	do
"	Maria Virgard	Idiotic	7 "	Not known	7	"	do
"	Mary Hammaker	Insane	2 "	Fright	26	"	do
Lykens	Thos. Burton	Dumb	19 "	Scarlet fever	23	Male	do
"	Mary Ann Lambert	Deaf and dumb	7 "	Unknown	7	Fem'le	do
"	Jeremiah Seery	Dumb	23 "	Hereditary	23	Male	do
"	August Serener	Insane	23 "	"	23	"	do
Tod	Savilla Shroll	Idiotic	21 "	Palsy and Fits	26	Fem'le	do
"	Elizabeth Dowland	"	9 "	Fever	12	"	do
"	John N. Dowland	"	3 "	....	3	Male	do

in the county of Crawford, State of Ohio, on the second Monday of May, 1856

Occupation	Birthplace	Educated or not.	Names of parents.	Occupation	Birthplace	No. children.	No. children thus afflicted.	Relationship of Parents before Marriage
....	Ohio	Not	Moses & Elizabeth Kling.	Farmer ..	Penn	7	1	None.
....	do	do....	James K. and Ann Davis.	Shoem'kr	do	3	1	do
....	do	do....	Lewis and Isabella Orviler	Farmer ..	do	4	1	do
....	do	do....	James & Nancy Hutchison	do	Maryland .	13	1	do
Farmer.	Germany.	Educated	Casper and Mary Ribley..	do	Germany..	4	1	do
None ..	Penn	do....	James & Elizabeth Evans.	do	Pa & N. J.	10	1	Uunkn'n
Farmer.	Ohio	Not.....	Abram & Margaret Brakaw	do	Penn	12	4	None.
None ..	Penn	do....	Jacob & Justina Hengst ..	Laborer ..	do	7	1	do
"	do	do....	David E. and Mary Evans	Farmer ..	do	6	2	do
"	do	Educated	J. and Elizabeth Garbrich.	do	do	10	1	do
Carp'tr	N. Hamp.	do....	Benj. and Ruth Straw	do	N. Hamp..	5	1	do
Farmer	Ohio ..	do....	N. and Christina Torrence	do	Penn	16	1	do
"	do	do....	Nelson and Jane Tustison.	None	Den. & Pa.	11	1	do
....	Germany.	do....	....	....	Germany..	2	1	do
Tailor .	Penn	do....	Wm. & Catharine Hatten..	Farmer ..	Penn	6	1	do
None ..	do	Not.....	David & Catharine Kinsel.	do	do	11	1	do
Farmer.	do	Educated	Philip and Sarah Casip ..	do	do	..	..	....
None ..	do	Not.....	John and Hannah Presbee	Carpenter	Penn	8	1	None...
"	Germany.	do....	O. and Barbara Pfleidera..	Farmer ..	Germany..	5	1	do
Seams't	do	Educated	Michael & Barbara Melden	do	do	2	1	do
....	Ohio	Not.....	Father of this boy a lunatic	....	....	..	..	....
None ..	do	Educated	John & Catharine Cramea	Shomaker	Germany..	8	1	None...
"	do	Not.....	Jacob & Christina Virgard,	Farmer ..	do	6	1	do
"	Penn	Educated	David & Sarah Hammaker	do	Penn......	8	1	do
Farmer	Ohio	Not.....	Benj. & Catharine Burton.	do	do	7	1	....
....	N. Jersey	do....	Emanuel & Marg Lambert	Bl'ksmith	do	3	1	....
....	Ohio	do....	Sol. & Magdalena Seery ..	Farmer ..	do	11	1	....
....	Germany.	do....	Michael & Mary Serener..	do	Germany..	4	1	....
....	Ohio	do....	Daniel and Mary Shroll..	do	Not known	13	1	None...
....	do	....	Wm. and Rebecca Dowland	....	....	7	2	do
....	do	....	do do	....	Ohio	..	..	do

RETURN of the number of Deaf and Dumb, Blind, Insane and Idiotic persons in

Townships.	Names of persons.	Nature of Affliction.	Duration of Affliction	Cause where known.	Age.	Sex.	Color.
Cleveland 2d Ward...	Wm. S. Smyth..	Deaf and Dumb	46 years	....	46	Male.	White.
2d do	Mary F. Smith...	do do	......	....	40	Feml'e	do
4th do	Oscar F. Phelps..	do do	29 years	....	29	Male..	do
4th do	Mrs. O. F. Phelps	do do	28 do	....	28	Feml'e	do
4th do	One Child......	do do	1 do	....	1	......	do
4th do	Allie Mell......	do do	6 do	Sickness..........	8	Feml'e	do
5th do	Cath. Shumway	Ch. Inf. Brain	11 do	Organic...........	30	do	do
5th do	Hannah Hopfer...	Deaf and Dumb	13 do	....	13	do	do
5th do	Rosannah Kopfer	do do	10 do	....	10	do	do
5th do	Henry Stump...	Mania........	38 do	By a fall.......... [him..........	40	Male .	do
7th do	Peter Wintz.....	Idiotic........	8 years	Hovel fallling on	29	do	do
Rarma	Louisa Bliss.....	Blind.........	36 do	Unknown.........	36	Feml'e	do
do	Lawrind Lane..	Idiotic........	18 do	Epileptic Fits......	18	do	do
do	Jane F. Thompson	Idiotic........	22 do	A fall 4 months old [ment of the brain	22	do	do
do	Margaret Scriber.	Idiotic........	8 years	Fever and derange-	13	do	do
Newburgh .	Jeremiah Priffing	Blind.........	3 do	Unknown.........	50	Male .	do
do	S. Volmar......	Insane........	3 do	....	59	do	do
Euclid.....	Horace King....	Idiotic........	30 do	Unknown.........	30	do	do
Dover......	Noah Cooly.....	Deaf and Dumb	45 do	Natural	45	do	do
Strongsville	Hen B. Saunders	do do	12 do	....	12	do	do
Independc'e	Wm. Gowdy....	do do	....	Sickness..........	18	do	do
Middleboro'.	Henrietta Titus..	Blind	18 years	Inflammation......	20	Fem'le	do
do	Mr. Lewis.......	Insane........	8 do	....	40	Male .	do
do	Angelina Brown.	Deaf and Dumb	12 do	....	12	......	do
Olmstead ..	Anna Annis....	Blind	3 do	Unknown.........	44	Fem'le	do
do	Wm. Sims......	do	2 do	....	60	Male .	do
Mayfield ...	Harry P. Straight	Insane........	2 do	....	65	do	do
do	Mary Battle.....	Insane........	1 do	....	30	Fem'le	do
do	Alfred Jinks....	Deaf and Dumb	23 do	....	23	Male .	do
do	Nath. Dennon....	Idiotic........	....	....	43	do	do
Orange	John Burton	Idiotic........	32 years	Fits	33	do	do
Royalton...	Enoch E. Scovel.	Idiotic........	11 do	Fits	21	do	do
do	Wm. Scoval.....	Idiotic........	12 do	Fever.............	16	do	do
do	Drusilla Scoval..	Idiotic........	10 do	Fever and Ague....	14	Fem'le	do
do	John Stewart....	Deaf and Dumb	17 do	Unknown	17	Male .	do
do	Phebe Stewart ..	do do	13 do	do	13	Fem'le	do
do	Wm. Miller......	do do	20 do	Scarlet Fever......	24	Male .	do

the county of Cuyahoga, State of Ohio, on the second Monday of May, 1856.

Occupation	Birth-place.	Educated or not.	Names of Parents.	Occupation.	Birth-place.	No Children.	No. Children thus afflicted.	Relationship of Parens before marriage.
Cabn't Maker	Mass...	Educat'd	Elisha and Mrs Smith	Farmer...	Pa. & Mass.	9		Unkn'n
Seamstress..	Ohio....	Educat'd	John and Sarah Bean	Magistrate.	N. Hamp..	9		
....	....	Educat'd	....	....	....			
....	Ohio....	Not....	....	....	....			
None.......	N. York	Educat'd	L. B & M. A. Shumway	Car'gmak'r	N York...	2	1	None.
do	Germany	Not....	John and Anna Hopfer	Laborer...	Germany..	2		
do	do	Not....	John and Anna Hopfer	do	do			
do	do	Not....	Harvy and C. Stump.	Farmer....	....			
de	do	Not....	Peter and Eliza. Wintz	do	Germany..	2	1	None.
Sewing.....	Ohio....	Educat'd	Wm. & Cinthia Bliss	Silversmith	Ct. & N. Y	5	1	do
None.......	do	Not....	John and Eliza. Lane	Farmer...	Penn.....	9	1	do
do	Conn...	Not....	Wm. & M. Thompson	do	Scotl.& Irel.		1	do
do	Germany	Not....	Geo. and Eliza. Scriber	do	Germany..	8	1	do
Farmer.....	Conn...	....	....	....	....			
do	Germany	Educut'd	Charles Volmar.....	Minister..	Germany.	8	1	None.
None........	Ohio.....	Not....	Polador and L. King	Farmer....	N. Y......		1	do
Farmer.....	Mass....	Educat'd	A. and Lydia Cooly	do	Mass.....	10	1	do
....	Ohio...	Not....	James & C. Saunders	....	England..	4	2	Cousins
Farmer.....	Ireland.	....	Wm. Gowdy........	Farmer....	Ireland...	8	1	......
Needle Work	....	Educat'd	....	....	....			
For'ly J.Peace	Ohio...	do	....	....	....			
....	....	do	....	....	....			
Farmer.....	N. Hamp	do	Webster & Mar. Annis	Farmer....	N. Hamp.	9		Unkn'n
Laborer.....	England	Not....	Wm. and Mrs. Sims	Laborer...	England..	8		
Farmer.....	N. York	Educat'd	Unknown..........	....	....			
....	do	do	Luther and Mrs. Battle	Farmer...	N. Y.....	10		
Farmer.....	Ohio...	do	Lindus and Mrs. Jinks	do	Massachus.	7		None
....	N. York.	....	E. S. and Mrs. Dennon	do	do	5		......
....	Ohio....	Not....	Jedediah & P. Burton	do	Vermot...	6	1	None.
None.......	do	do....	Enoch and E. Scovel	Cooper....	N. Y....	10	3	Cousins
....	do	do....	do	do	N. Y....			Cousins
None.......	Mich...	do....	....	....	....			
Farmer.....	Ohio....	Educat'd	John and H. Stewart	....	....	6	2	None.
Seamstress..	do	do	do	do	....			None.
Farmer.....	England	do	Unknown..........	....	....	3	1	Unkn'n

RETURN of the number of Deaf and Dumb, Blind, Insane and Idiotic persons

TOWNSHIPS.	Names of Persons.	Nature of affliction.	Duration of affliction.	Cause where known.	Age.	Sex.	Color.
York	Rebecca Hercules	Insane	10 years	Scarlet fever	11	Female	White
(Omitted)	John Jackanaw	Insane & helpl's	30 "	Fits	35	Male	"
Franklin	Elizabeth Winterow	Blind	15 "	By cold	26	Female	"
Richland	Faith T. Pessinger	"	15 "		73	"	"
Patterson	Nelson Taylor	Insane	10 "	Fits	15	Male	"
Twin	Mary E. Hausbrook	Idiotic	14 "	Unknown	14	Female	"
do	Febyunus Hausbrook	"	16 "	"	7	"	"
do	Henry Fourmen	"	12 "	"	16	Male	"
(Omitted)	Levi Hart	"	20 "	"	12	"	
do	Rosanna Hart	"	"	"	20	Female	
do	Margaret Hart	"	26 "	"	26	"	
do	Annetta Brice	"	18 "	"	18	Male	
Allen	Salena Barnhart	Insane	7 "	Hereditary	40	Female	White
Van Buren	Philip Trowbridge	Idiotic	15 "		15	Male	"
Butler	Rebecca Bloom	Blind	3 "		80	Female	"

in the county of Darke, State of Ohio, on the second Monday of May, 1856.

Occupation.	Birth-place.	Educated or not.	Names of Parents.	Occupation.	Birth-place.	No. Children.	No. children thus afflicted.	Relationship of parents before marriage.
....	Ohio	Not	David & Eliz. Heroules..	Farmer ..	....	5	1	....
....	France...	"	John & Mary Jackanaw .	" ..	France....	2	1	None.
....	Ohio	"	Dan. and R. Winterrow..	Farming .	Penn	8	1	"
Farmer .	Penn	Educated	....	....	....	..	..	....
None	Ohio	Not	Esom and Eliz. Taylor..	....	Kentucky .	..	1	Cousins
"	"	"	Arcable Hausbrook	Farming .	America ..	3	2	None.
"	"	"	do do	" ..	" ..	..	..	"
"	"	"	Geo. & Cath'rine Fourman	" ..	Americans	4	1	"
....	....	....	Dennis and Jane Hart...	....	....	1	1	"
....	....	....	do do do ...	....	....	1	1	"
....	....	....	do do do ...	....	....	1	1	"
....	Ohio	....	Geo. and Mary Brice	....	Penn	..	..	"
None	"	Educated	....	....	....	..	..	....
....	Penn	Educated	J. and Marg. Trowbridge	....	Virginia ..	9	1	None.
....	Penn	Educated	Silas Gere.............	Farmer ..	Connectic't	4	1	....

RETURN of the number of Deaf and Dumb, Blind, Insane and Idiotic persons

Townships.	Names of Persons.	Nature of Affliction.	Duration of Affliction.	Cause where known.	Age.	Sex.	Color.
Hicksville..	Henry Thomas	Idiotic	From birth.		52	Male	White.
Richland..	James R. Gerves	Insane	20 years.	Hereditary	55	"	White.
Farmer...	Michael Glaspie	"	27 do	Epilepsy	35	"	White.
....	George W. Hill	"	21 do	Fits	22	"	White.
Tiffin.....	Elizabeth A. Moon	"	11 do	Hereditary	45	"	White.
Tiffin.....	David Russell	Idiotic	23 do	Hereditary	23	"	White.

in the county of Defiance, State of Ohio, on the second Monday of May 1856.

Occupation.	Birthplace.	Educated or not.	Names of Parents.	Occupation.	Birthplace.	No. children.	No. children thus afflicted.	Relationship of Parents before Marriage
None..	Penn....	Not.....	John and Barbara Thomas	Farmer.	United S..	9	1	Unknown
Farmer.	Penn....	Educated	Unknown........	....	....	..	..	....
None..	Virginia.	Educated	J. M. & Dorcas Glaspie...	"	Virginia..	6	1	None....
Farmer.	Ohio....	Not......	D. M. F. & Permelia Hill..	"	Pa. & N. J.	8	1	None....
....	Virginia.	Educated	Wm. and Sarah Wiles....	"	Unknown.	12	1	Unknown
....	Ohio....	Not.....	Saml. & Margaret Russell.	"	Virginia..	8	1	....

RETURN of the number of Deaf and Dumb, Blind, Insane and Idiotic persons in

TOWNSHIPS.	Names of Persons.	Nature of affliction.	Duration of affliction.	Cause where known.	Age.	Sex.	Color.
Delaware..	Frederick Antoni	Deaf and dumb	20 years	.. Not known....	20	Male..	White
do ..	Rosanna Antoni	" "	15 "	.. " "	15	Female	"
do ..	Albert Antoni	" "	3 "	.. " "	3	Male..	"
do ..	Jarvis B. Harris......	Insane & dumb	12 "	.. Fits...........	14	" ..	Black
Troy	Sudy Delia Welch....	Deaf and dumb	22 "	.. Gath'g in head	23	Fema'e	White
do	Thomas Main........	Blind	13 "	.. Inflammation..	50	Male..	".
do	John Campbell	Idiotic........	20 "	....	2	" ..	"
do	Edward Campbell....	"	18 "	....	18	" ..	"
do	Henry Campbell	"	16 "	....	16	" ..	"
Brown	Nancy Beckwith.....	Blind	16 "	.. Cataract	60	Female	"
do	Mary A. Thrall......	"	3 weeks	.. Scarlet fever ..	18	"	"
Trenton ..	Marion Day	Idiotic........	9 years	....	9	Male..	"
do ..	Eliza J. Edminster...	Deaf and dumb	15 "	.. Not known....	15	Female	"
do ..	Charles Ridgway	Idiotic........	24 "	.. " "	24	Male..	"
do ..	Ellen Boston	Blind	....	.. " "	..	Female	"
do ..	Minerva Boston......	"	....	.. " "	..	"	"
Thompson .	John Minter	"	5 years	.. " "	75	Male..	"
Berlin	Justus Cook	Deaf.........	41 "	.. Whoop'g cough	4t	" ..	"
Orange....	Thomas McCloud....	Blind	18 "	.. Sore eyes......	82	" ..	"
do	Nancy Baker........	"	16 "	.. Not known....	73	Female	"
do	William H. Spooner ..	Idiotic........	13 "	.. " "	13	Male..	"
Scioto	Lanslot Maze........	"	23 "	.. Sickness	25	" ..	"
Radnor ...	Georgia Ellen Clark..	"	12 "	.. Not known....	12	Female	"
Concord...	Marion Fultz	Insane........	....	.. Fits	21	Male..	"
do ..	William C. Harris....	"	6 "	.. "	9	" ..	"
Oxford....	Joseph Chadwick	Idiotic........	13 "	.. Not known....	13	" ..	Dark.
do	Dorsey.............	Insane........	1/2 "	.. Hereditary	43	" ..	"

the county of Delaware, State of Ohio, on the second Monday of May, 1856.

Occupation	Birth-place	Educated or not	Names of Parents	Occupation	Birth-place	No. Children	No. children thus afflicted	Relationship of parents before marriage
Brewer ..	Ohio	Educated	Fred. and Ros' Antoni..	Brewer ..	France..	5		3 Cousins.
....	"	"	" " "	....	" ..			
....	"	....	" " "	....	....			
None	N. Carol'a	Not	Jac. and Ch'lotte Harris	Mason ...	N. Carolina	10	1	None.
"	Ohio	Educated	Hiram and Nancy Welch	Farmer ..	New York	16	1	"
Farmer .	Virginia .	"	Sabeers and H. Main ..	" ..	" "	13	1	"
....	New York	....	Jno. and Ellen Campbell	" ..	Ireland ...	10	3	"
....	" "	....	" " "	" ..	" ...	10	3	"
....	Ohio	....	" " "	" ..	" ...	10	3	"
....	Penn	Can read	Thomas and Eliz'h Gray	Weaver ..	Penn'a....			"
....	Ohio	Educated	M. C and Sarah Thrall	Bl'cksm'h	Conn	13	1	"
....	"	Not	Jane Day................	....	Ohio......	1	1	Not mar.
....	"	Educated	P. and S. S. Edminster	Farmer ..	New York	1	1	Cousins.
....	" ...	Not ...	William Ridgway.....	....	Delaware..	1	1	None.
....	Maryland.	"	William Boston.........	....	Maryland .	8	4	Cousins.
....	"	"	" "	....	" .	8	4	"
Farmer ..	Virginia..	Educated	John and Eliz'h Mintei	Farmer ..	Virginia ..	7	1	Not k'wn
H'rn'ss mr	Conn	"	John and Mary J. Cook	....	Conn	6	1	None.
Farmer ..	....	....	....	....	....			....
....	....	....	Jas. and Mary Spooner	Shoemak	....	6	1	None.
....	Oh o	Not	John and Sarah Maze..	Farmer ..	Penn'a....	8	1	"
....	"	"	G W. and Ellen J. Clark	" ..	....	1	1	"
....	....	"	John and Mrs. Fultz....	" ..	....	5	1	Strang'rs
....	Ohio	"	Wm. and Maria Harris..	" ..	Va. & Ohio	6	1	"
....	"	"	Jos. and Jane Chadwick	" ..	....	5	1	None.
Farmer ..	Penn	Educated	....	....	....	12	3	"

RETURN of the number of Deaf and Dumb, Blind, Insane and Idiotic persons

Townships	Names of Persons.	Nature of Affliction.	Duration of Affliction.	Cause where known	Age.	Sex	Color.
Milan	David Abbott........	Blind	5 years ..	Unknown	9	Male .	White.
....	Andrew J. Raymond.	do	20 "	"	20	"	White.
....	Clarisa Jane Raymond	do	12 "	"	12	Fem'le	White.
....	Sarah Ann Raymond .	do	10 "	"	10	"	White.
....	Martha Pierce	Insane........	9 "	Hereditary	36	"	White.
Berlin	Sally Fisk	Idiotic........	30 "	Measles	32	"	White.
....	Josephine Falmon....	Deaf..........	4 "	Sickness	8	"	White.
Vermillion.	Charlotte C. Neeb....	Blind..........	17 "	Mal-practice ..	18	"	White.
"	Christiana Cumpton..	do	34 "	Inflammation ..	62	"	White.
"	James H. Wilson.....	Idiotic........	28 "	Fits	28	Male .	White.

in the county of Erie, State of Ohio, on the second Monday of May, 1856.

Occupation.	Birthplace.	Educated or not.	Names of Parents.	Occupation.	Birthplace.	No. children.	No. children thus Afflicted	Relationship of Parents before Marriage
....	Ohio ...	Not.....	Benj. & Laurena Abbott	Farmer .	Ohio	3	1	None.....
Wood Sa'r.	New Y..	"	Geo. & S. A. Raymond	Laborer.	New Ycrk.	11	4	" .....
Mu. teacher	Ohio ...	"	" "	....	N. Jersey .	..	..	....
Learn'g mu	Ohio ...	"	" "	....	....	..	..	....
....	New Y..	Educated	Rufus and Betsy Perry.	Farmer .	New York.	13	3	None.....
....	R Island	Not.....	Richard & Abigal Fisk	"	R. Island .	10	1	Cousins...
....	France..	Educated	Jos. and Rose Falmon.	Carpen't.	France....	4	1	None.....
Mu. teacher	Ohio ...	"	John and Mary Neeb...	Landl'rd	Germany..	2	1	" .....
....	Penn ...	"	Geo. and Mary Sherod.	Farmer .	Penn.....	14	1	" .....
....	U. C ...	"	M. and Rachel Wilson.	"	U. Canada.	5	1	" .....

5—SEC. OF STATE.

RETURN of the number of Deaf and Dumb, Blind, Insane and Idiotic persons

Townships.	Names of Persons.	Nature of Affliction.	Duration of Affliction.	Cause where known.	Age.	Sex.	Color.
Clear Creek	Nathaniel Moore	Deaf and dumb	7 years	Gath'rng in he'd	7	Male	White.
"	Levi Hedges	Blind	54 "	Fever	60	"	"
Amanda	Kesiah Hardesty	Insane	4 "	....	79	Fem'le	"
"	John F Lear	Blind	13 "	Accident	29	Male	"
"	Christian Hege	Mute	14 "	Scarlet fever	15	"	"
"	Jemimah Norris	Mute	33 "	Measels & ty fev	34	Fem'le	"
Bloom	James Baley	Deaf and Dumb	45 "	....	45	Male	"
"	Francis Chaney	"	2 "	Medicines	4	"	"
Violet	Catharine Rice	Insane	25 "	....	60	Fem'le	"
"	Adam Leonard	Blind	23 "	Fever	25	Male	"
"	Joseph Williamson	"	8 "	"	24	"	"
"	Harvey Bish	n sa.e	23 "	Sickness	24	"	"
"	Jacob Houser	Deaf and Dumb	4 "	Whooping c'gh	4	"	"
Liberty	I. J. Messerley	Deaf	24 "	....	24	"	"
Greenfield	Caroline Shanholzer	Blind	11 "	Scarlet fever	12	Fem'le	"
Hocking	Wm. S. Levering	Idiotic	19 "	Sickness	19	Male	"
"	Hester Miller	"	42 "	....	42	Fem'le	"
"	William Fricker	Deaf and dumb	48 "	....	48	Male	"
Lancaster	Susan Fricker	"	30 "	....	30	Fem'le	"
"	John Gilbert	Blind	5 "	....	44	Male	"
"	Mary E. Louck	Insane	.. "	....	30	Fem'le	"
"	M's. Julia Ann Cook	Lunatic	20 "	Domes. trouble	45	"	"
"	William Baird	Insane	.. "	....	..	Male	"
"	Susanna Knepper	Idiotic	40 "	....	40	Fem'le	"
"	Henry Shackleford	Insane	15 "	Frac. of skull	30	Male	Blk
"	Jane Shackleford	Idiotic	22 "	....	22	Fem'le	"
"	Margaret Davis	Deaf and dumb	48 "	Sickness	50	"	White.
Madison	Jacob F. Glanner, jr.	Insane	5 "	....	35	Male	"
"	John Turner	"	13 "	....	36	"	"
"	Hester Herrin	Blind	29 "	Fever	50	Fem'le	"
"	Susanna Moore	Deaf and dumb	24 "	....	24	"	"
"	Elizabeth Moore	"	20 "	....	20	"	"
Berne	Sarah Jane Blazer	"	22 "	....	22	"	"
"	John Cogan	"	7 "	....	7	Male	"
"	Emanuel Rudolph	Idiotic	23 "	....	23	"	"
"	Lawrence Strayer	Insane	6 "	Study	67	"	"
Pleasant	John Rice	Idiotic	30 "	....	30	"	"
"	Rebecca Rice	"	28 "	....	8	Fem'le	"
"	Sarah Rice	"	26 "	....	26	"	"
"	Joseph Arnold	"	40 "	Hereditary	40	Male	"
"	Jacob Arnold, Sr.	"	1 "	"	77	"	"
"	Thomas Anderson	Blind	10 "	Sickness	70	"	"
"	Henry Black	Insane	35 "	Hereditary	42	"	"
"	Eve Black	Blind	5 "	Sickness	73	Fem'le	"
"	Nancy Ann Beall	"	30 "	....	78	"	"
"	Daniel Stemen	Idiotic	.. "	....	38	Male	"
"	James Baldwin	Insane	.. "	....	22	"	"
"	Mary Krus	"	.. "	....	37	Fem'le	"
"	Hanna Bennet	"	.. "	....	60	"	"
"	Phœbe Bower	Blind and dumb	.. "	....	20	"	"
"	Elizabeth Smith	Insane	.. "	....	16	"	"
"	Mary Blauser	"	.. "	....	57	"	"
"	Jane Baker	"	.. "	Fits	22	"	"
"	Ann Daugherty	"	.. "	....	35	"	"
"	—— Frances	"	.. "	....	50	"	"
"	—— Sufflicia	"	.. "	....	65	"	"
Walnut	Nancy Jeffries	"	5 "	Fever	10	"	"

in the county of Fairfield, State of Ohio, on the second Monday of May, 1856.

Occupation	Birthplace	Educated or not.	Names of Parents.	Occupation	Birthplace.	No. children	No. children thus afflicted	Relationship of Parents before Marriage
with parent	Ohio	Not	Eli and Sarah Moore	Farmer		6		None
....	Virginia	"	Mathias & M. A. Hedges	do	Maryland	14	1	do
Housewife.	"	Educated	Richard and Nancy Low	do				
Farmer	Penn	"	John and Nancy Lear	do	Ger. & Eng	4		None
"	Ohio	"	Peter and Mary Hege	do	Penn	10		do
Housewife.	"	Not	John and Mary Norris	Laborer	Eng.& Md.	14		do
Laborer	"	Educated	James and Sarah Baley	Farmer				
"	"		Jas. and Caroline Chaney					
....	Virginia	Educated	Jas. & Jon. Looker	Farmer	Virginia	16	1	None.
....	Ohio	Not	A. & Elizabeth Leonard	do	Ohio	6	1	do
Br'm mak'r	"	Educated	Geo. & Isabel Williamson		do	1	1	do
....	"	Not	Dewalt & Mary Bish	None	do	12	1	do
....	"	"	Peter and Marg. Houser	Farmer	do	6	1	do
Stone cutter	"	Educated	Michael & Eliz. Messerly					
At School.	"	"	P. & Susan Shanholzer	Blk'smth	Va. & Ohio	10	1	None.
....	"	Not	Maris & E Jane Levering	Farmer	Maryland	4	1	do
....	Penn	"	Henry & Catharine Miller	Carpn'tr	Penn	10	1	do
Laborer	Ohio	Educated	Thomas Fricker	Farm'r				do
Housewife.	"	"	same	Hatter	Penn	6	4	
Cooper	Canada	Limited		Potter	France	4		None.

In co. jail..

Housewife.	Dist. Col.	Educated	Wm. & Margaret Davis	pap'r m'r		10	1	None.
Farmer	Europe	"	J. F. & Margaret Glanner	Farmer	Europe	9	1	do
Sch. teach'r	Ohio	"	S. Turner & M Pinkstock	do	Virginia	8	1	do
....	Penn	Not	Jacob Herrin & H. Roof	do	Penn	12	1	do
House work	Ohio	Educated	Jeremiah Moore & Nancy	do	Ohio	9	2	do
....	"	"	Buzzard	do				
....	"	Not	Geo & Mary Blazer	do	Ohio	4	1	None.
....	"	"	John & Elizabeth Cogan	do	Ireland	2	1	do
....	"	"	Peter & Cath. Rudolph	do	Ohio	7	1	do
Farmer	Penn	Limited	Jacob & Elizabeth Strayer	do	Penn	6	1	
....	Maryland	Not	John C. & Sarah Rice	do	Maryland	6	3	Cousins.
....	"	"	do					
....	"	"	do					
....	Ohio	"	Jacob & Rachel Arnold	Farmer	Maryland	8	1	None.
Farmer	Maryland	Educated						
"	Virginia	"						
....	Ohio	Not	John & Eve Black	Cooper	Maryland	8	1	None.
....	Virginia	Educated	do					
....	Maryland	"						
....	Ohio	Not...						
....	"	"						
....	Virginia	"						
....	Ohio		} In County Infirmary.					
....	"	Edu'td						
....	France							
....	Germany							
....	Ohio	Not	James & Mary Jeffries	Farmer	Virginia	5	1	None

RETURN of the number of Deaf and Dumb, Blind, Insane

Townships.	Names of Persons.	Nature of Affliction	Duration of Affliction	Cause, where known	Age.	Sex.	Color.
Walnut	Benjamin Artz	Insane	12 years	Gravel	70	Male	White.
"	Susan Greek	"	33 "		33	Fem'le	"
Richland	Ann Beaver	Idiotic	23 "		23	"	"
"	Cornelia Reid	Deaf and dumb	45 "		45	"	"
"	John G. Turner	Blind	25 "	Cold	34	Male	"
Rush Creek	Mary Black	"	5 "	Old age	95	Fem'le	"
"	Elizabeth Everitt	Insane	22 "	Sickness	24	"	"

and Idiotic persons in Fairfield county, Ohio—Continued.

Occupation.	Birth place.	Educated, or not.	Names of Parents.	Occupation.	Birth-place.	No. Children.	No. Children thus afflicted.	Relationship of Parents before marriage.
Farmer ..	Virginia .	Not	Henry & Christina Artz..	Farmer ..	....	9	1	None.
....	Ohio	"	Frederick & Polly Greek .	Carpenter	Penn & Va.	7	1	"
....	"	"	John & Elizabeth Beaver.	Farmer ..	Virginia ..	4	1	....
....	Ohio	Not	Basil & Elizabeth Turner.	....	Maryland .	7	..	Cousins
....	Ireland ..	....	....	....	....	..	..	....
....	Ohio	Not	Abel and Eliza Everitt ..	....	....	..	..	....

RETURN of the number of Deaf and Dumb, Blind, Insane and Idiotic persons

Names of persons.	Nature of affliction.	Duration of affliction.	Cause where known.	Age.	Sex.	Color..	Occupation.
Harriet Thompson	Insane	10 years	Not known	12	Fem'le	White	None
Jesse McKay	Blind	24 "	Rickets	26	Male..	"	"
R. A. Nuckels	Deaf and Dumb	Life	Not known	30	"	"	"
Margaret Shafer	Idiotic	12 years	"	35	Fem'le	"	"
Catharine Millikan	Deaf	7 "	Scarlet Fever	14	"	"	"
Wm. Coil	Idiotic	Life	Not known	28	Male.	"	"
Wm. Bush	"	"	"	10	"	"	"
Mary Turnipsed	"	"	"	23	Fem'le	"	"
Henry Delaney	"	"	"	34	Male..	"	"
Jackson Grady	"	"	"	28	"	"	"
Thos. Bonner	"	"	"	26	"	"	"
Wm. Bonner	Insane	12 years	"	40	"	"	"
Rebecca Todhunter	"	10 "	"	20	Fem'le	"	"
Jane Todhunter	"	5 "	"	65	"	"	"
Caroline Ellis	Deaf and Dumb	18 "	"	20	Male..	"	"
Moses Geller	"	8 "	Sickness	12	"	"	"
Wm. Buzard	Idiotic	Life	"	50	"	"	"
Wm. Devault	Deaf	Life	Not known	16	"	"	"
Rebecca Bowmin	Blind	10 years	"	40	Fem'le	"	"

in the County of Fayette, State of Ohio, on the second Monday of May, 1856.

Birth-place.	Educated or not	Names of Parents.	Occupation	Birth-place.	No. Children	No. Children thus afflicted	Relationship of parents before marriage.
Ohio	None	James and R. Thompson	Farmer	Virginia	12	1	None.
"	"	Jesse and M. McKay	"	"	4	1	"
"	Moderate	S. and M. Nuckels	"	"	8	1	"
"	None	James and C. Shafer	"	Unknown	7	2	First Cousins.
"	"	Curran and C. Millikan	Miller	Ohio	4	1	None.
"	"	John and Mary Coil	Farmer	Va	12	1	"
"	"	Daniel and S. Bush	"	Va	9	1	"
"	"	Not known	Not known	Unknown	..	..	Not known.
Penn	"	"	"	"	..	..	"
Ohio	"	"	"	"	..	..	"
"	"	Wm. and S. Bonner	Farmer	Penn	8	2	First Cousins.
"	"	"	"	"	..	..	"
"	Moderate	A. and J. Todhunter	"	Va	7	1	"
Va	None	Not known	Unknown	Unknown	..	..	Not known.
Ohio	"	John and Rebecca Ellis	Farmer	Pensylvan.	10	1	None
"	"	John and S. Geller	"	"	6	1	"
Va	"	Wm. and S. Buzard	"	Virginia	12	1	"
Ohio	"	W. and S. Devault	"	"	6	1	First Cousins.
Kentucky	"	J. and S. Bowmin	"	"	14	1	None.

RETURN of the Number of Deaf and Dumb, Blind, Insane, and Idiotic Persons

Names of persons.	Nature of Affliction.	Duration of Affliction.	Cause where known.	Age.	Sex.	Color.
William Dixon	Deaf and dumb.	23 years	Scarlet fever	31	Male	White
Jane C. Ware	Insane	2 "	Ill health	23	Fem'le	"
D. F. Sawhill	Deaf and dumb.	Childhood	Bealing ears	26	Male	"
Margaret Sawhill	" "	"	Not known	20	Fem'le	"
J. M. A. Donovan	Blind	15 years	By accident	21	"	"
Michael Fisher	Deaf and dumb.	Born		25	Male	"
Charles Edw'd Rankin	" "	"		9	"	"
Plumb M. Park	" "	35 years	Swelling under ears	39	"	"
Charlotte Park	" "	38 "	" "	40	Fem'le	"
James M. Park	" "	4 "	" "	4	Male	"
Mary J. Fitzpatrick	" "	19 "	Whooping cough	23	Fem'le	"
John Fish Chandler	Insane	3 "	Masturbation	27	Male	"
Robert McCoy	Blind	14 "	Scarlet fever	25	"	"
Henry Francis	Idiot	Since born.		25	"	"
Mary Ann Francis	"	" "	Unknown	27	Fem'le	"
Fritz Henry	Insane	18 years	"	30	Male	"
Jane Ann Moore	Blind	From birth.		20	Fem'le	"
Adam Bear	Fits	12½ years.	Inflamation of brain	13	Male	"
Thomas J. Miller	Nervous affect'n	3 "	Unknown	6	"	"
Phebe Adaline Cooley	Fits	11 "	Chills and fever	17	Fem'le	"
James Smith	Idiotic	Unknown.	Unknown	10or12	Male	"
Milton Hand	"	From birth.	"	6	"	"
Rachel Seuder	"	" "	"	20	Fem'le	"
Frederick Field	"	32 years	Cold leprosy of matter.	32	Male	"
Mary Kiner	Insane	6 "	Typhoid fever	22	Fem'le	"
James C. Isenbarg	Deaf and dumb.	From birth.	Unknown	23	Male	"
Jacob Evins	Idiotic	" "	"	45	"	"
Samuel D. Mecord	Blind	1 year	Purulent opthalmia	27	"	"
Horace Case	"	13 "	Inflammation	15	"	"
George A. Cowan	"	23 "	Cold in the eyes	34	"	"
Henry Peck	Idiot	18 "	Supposed to be fits	20	"	"
Martha B. Watson	Dumb	From birth.		6	Fem'le	"
Enos Leib	"	"		29	Male	"
Amos Wilcox	Deaf and dumb.			80	"	"
Hiram Chandler Lee	Blind	3 years	Scrofulous	6	"	"
Martha Walcutt	Insane	27 "	Unknown	38	Fem'le	"
Samuel W. Flanegan	Deaf and dumb.	6 "		37	Male	"
Mary Flanegan	" "	34 "	Accident	36	Fem'le	"
Henry Dennison	" "	14 "	Fall from horse	14	Male	"
Mahala Reed	Insane	35 "	Sickness	55	Fem'le	"
Charlotte Sandy	Deaf and dumb.	32 "	No cause	32	"	"
Cynthia Ann Yates	Dumb	45 "	Unknown	45	"	"
Mary C. Porter	"	8 "	Medicine	8	"	"
David Beatty	Deaf	50 "	Born	50	Male	"
Charles W. Hedges	"	20 "	Scarlet fever	20	"	"
Percival Pursel	Deaf and dumb.	28 "	Fever	31	"	"

in the county of Franklin, State of Ohio, on the second Monday of May, 1856.

Occupation.	Birthplace.	Educated or not.	Names of parents.	Occupation.	Birthplace.	No. of child'n	No. of child'n thus afflicted.	Relationship of parents before marriage.
Laborer...	Franklin co.	Not...	John & Eliz. Dixon...	Farming.			2	None
None......	Columbus..	Ed'cted	Robert & Jane Ware..	Merchant				
Farmer....	Penn......	"	Neeley & Marg. Sawhill	Farmer..	Penn......	6	3	Cousins,
Seamstress.	"	"	do do	do	Penn......	6	3	do
Music t'cher.	Ireland....	"	D. & Eliz. Donovan..	....	Ireland ...	5	...	....
Laborer....	Bavaria....	Not...	Mich'l & Marg. Fisher.	....	Bavaria ..	4	1	....
....	Springfield.	"	William Rankin.....	....	Maryland.	3	1	Unknwn
Teacher....	Akron.	Ed'ted	John Park..........	Farmer...	New York.	1	1	None
Consort....	New York..	Not...	Sarah Park..........	....	do	4	1	do
None.....	Columbus..	"	P. M. & Charl'te Park.	Teacher..	Ohio&N.Y.	4	1	do
....	Mass......	Ed'ted	J. & Cath. Fitzpatrick.	Farming.	Ireland ...	9	1	do
Farmer....	Maine.....	"	F. & Esther Chandler.	....	Maine	8	1	do
Broommaker	Ohio	Not...	Rob't & Nancy McCoy	Farming.	Penn......	8	1	do
None......	"	"	Thomas & Jane Francis	do	Virginia ..	6	2	do
"	"	"	"	do	do	6	2	do
"	"	"	M. & Cath. Henry....	do	Germany..	2	1	Unknwn
"	Franklin co.	Ed'ted	Jos. & Rosanna Moore.	do	Penn......	9	1	None
"	"	Not...	Adam & Nancy Bear..	do	Virginia ..	9	1	do
"	Licking co.	"	A. & Amanda Miller..	do	Licking co.	6	1	2d cous.
"	Knox co....	"	Fanny & Clark Cooley.	Shoemker	Ohio.....	4	1	None.
"	Franklin co.	"	Elias & Polly Smith..	Farming .	New Jersey	2	1	do
"	"	"	Charles & Jane Hand.	do	do	7	1	do
"	Virginia ...	"	M.&Magdalena Souder	do	Virginia ..	9	1	dc
....	Athens co..	"	Walter & Mary Field.	do	N. Y.& Pa.	9	1	do
....	Coshocton co	"	C. & Elizabeth Kiner..	do	Penn.....	10	1	do
Farmer....	Penn	Ed'ted	J. Isenbarg & M. Canan	do	Penn......	1	1	do
None.....	Virginia ...	Not'...	C.Evins&E.C.Weddell	do	Penn	3	1	do
Farmer....	Penn......	Ed'ted	H.Mecord&E.Ferguson	do	Penn	5	1	do
None......	Sharon tp.	Not...	J. N. & E. Case	do	Sharon tp.	8	1	do
Prof'r music.	New York..	Ed'ted	....	....	....	...	...	....
None	Clinton tp..	Net...	S. & Prudy Peck	Farmer ..	New York.	5	1	None.
"	Blenden tp.	"	D. & Marg. C. Watson.	do	Conn.....	3	...	....
"	Fairfield co.	"	Dan'l & Barbara Lieb.	Miller ...	Penn	14	1	do
....	Rhode Isl'd.	"	....	....	....	...	...	....
....	Franklin co.	"	E. Hiram & S. A. Lee.	Farmer...	Penn	4	1	do
....	Ross co....	Ed'ted	J. & Mary Walcutt...	do	Ohio	11	1	do
Farmer....	Franklin co.	"	S. G. & E. Flanegan..	do	Penn	9	1	do
....	Portage co..	"	G. & Laura Bradley..	Hatter ..	Beston....	6	3	do
Farmer....	Perry co ...	Not...	J. & Hannah Dennison.	Farming.	Perry co...	2	1	do
House work.	Maryland ..	Ed'ted.	....	....	....	...	...	....
Seamstress.	Franklin co.	"	J. & Delilah Sandy...	Seamstres	....	...	...	....
....	Ross co....	Not...	Morris and Mary Yates	Mason...	Not known	9	9	None
....	Licking co .	"	A. and Eliz. Porter...	Mason ...	....	2	1	do
Farmer	Virginia ...	Partly	D. & Mary A. Beatty.	Miller ...	Virginia ..	3	2	do
"	"	"	Don't know.........	Unkn'wn	Virginia ..	4	1	do
Shoemaker.	Franklin co.	Ed'ted	J. and Susan Pursel ..	Farmer ..	Penn	9	1	do

74

RETURN of the number of Deaf and Dumb, Blind, Insane and Idiotic persons

Names of Persons.	Nature of affliction.	Duration of affliction.	Cause where known.	Age.	Sex.	Color.	Occupation
Lemuel Whitten	Deaf and dumb	From birth	....	43	Male..	White.	None ...
George Kupley	Blind	10 years	Inflam'n of eyes	68	" ..	"	" ..
Alex. Jonath'n Standish	Deaf and dumb	....	....	10	" .	"	Farmer.
Moses Gunn	Insane	14 years	Death of mother	29	" ..	"	" ..
Harriet Reachard	Deaf and dumb	From birth	....	19	Female	"	....
Jonathan Hampton	Blind	2 years	....	60	Male..	"	Farmer.
James Darrough	Deaf and dumb	From birth	....	62	" ..	"	Shoem kr
Mary McCutchen	"	"	7 m. after b	Dropsy in head	25	Female	"	At school
Daniel Johnson	Blind	10 years .	Inflammation..	19	Male..	"	Do chores
Anne Louisa Watson	Deaf and dumb and blind 1 eye	Blind 3 yrs df & d fr. b	Blind fr'm ac'dt sup'sd d'b fr fits	5	Female	"	....
Conrad Hart	Idiot	From birth	....	22	Male..	"	....
Elizabeth Dougherty	Idiotic	"	....	27	Female	"	Knit, &o.
John W. Struble	Nearly df & db	about 24 yr	Inflam'n of head	30	Male..	"	Carpent'r
Simon Carr	Insane	6 years	ac'dtl mansl'ter	30	" ..	"	....

in the county of Fulton, State of Ohio, on the second Monday of May, 1856.

Birthplace.	Educated or not.	Names of Parents.	Occupation.	Birth-place.	No Children.	No. ch'ldren thus afflicted	Relationship of parents before marriage.
New York	Not......	Archilaus and Betsy Whitten..	Blacksmith	Ct. & N. Y.	13	..	1 None.
Penn'a....	Educated.	....	....	....	..	..	....
Indiana...	Not	Phineas and Emeline Alexander	Farmer ...	Ohio.....	7	..	1 None.
Ohio	Educated.	Henry and Sarah Gunn......	"	..Massach'tts	8	..	1 2d cous.
"	....	Charles and Sarah Reachard ..	"	..Ohio.....	6	..	1 None.
....	....	....	....	....	..	..	....
Penn's....	8 mo at Col	Eph. and Deborah Darrough ..	Tailor	....	7	..	3 None.
"	5 ys at Col	James and Jane McCutchen..	Farmer ...	Penn'a....	10	1	"
Ohio	Not......	John and Catharine Johnson ..	"	..Ohio.....	11	1	"
"	"	William and Elizabeth Watson	Laborer ...	England ..	5	1	"
Germany..	....	John Hart...............	Farmer ...	Germany..	3	1	"
Penn'a....	Not......	John and Julia Ann Dougherty	"	..Penn'a....	10	5	"
Ohio	Educated.	....	....	....	7	6	....
....	....	....	....	....	..	..	....

RETURN of the number of Deaf and Dumb, Blind, Insane and Idiotic persons

Townships.	Names of Persons.	Nature of affliction.	Duration of affliction.	Cause, where known.	Age.	Sex.	Color.
Chester...	Jacob Whiting.....	Blind.........	4 years	Cateract........	78	Male..	White..
do ..	Harriet Chilson.....	Deaf and Dumb	12 do	Unknown.......	12	Female	do
Auburn...	Almeda Webster....	Idiotic........	F'm brth	do	26	do	do
Newburg..	Rosella Shaw	Deaf and Dumb	8 years	Rickets in head..	9	do	do
Munson...	Abigail Hovey.....	Insane........	11 years.	Unknown.......	42	do	do
do ..	L. F. Robinson.....	Idiotic.......	F'm brth	do	34	Male..	do
Chardon...	Martin Newell.....	do	18 years.	Scrofula	18	do	do
do ..	Rhoda Newell.....	do	9 do	do	9	Female	do
Hambden .	Timothy Andrews..	Blind	11 do	Cataract........	74	Male..	do
do ..	R. Stebbins	Idiotic........	F'm brth	Unknown.......	20	do	do
Parkman..	Laney Owen.......	Deaf and Dumb	do	do	59	Female	do
do ..	Edwin Pidd.......	Idiotic........	do	do	31	Male..	do
Huntsb'rge	Almon Brooks......	Blind....	do	do	16	do	do
do	Allen Brooks......	do	do	do	27	do	do
do	Belsey Ann Smith..	do	do	Fits............	38	Female	do
do	Jonathan Green....	Deaf and Dumb	Not rept.	Under water spout	38	Male..	do
Thompson.	Amolena Murphy...	do do	F'm brth	Unknown.......	33	Female	do
do	Harriet Wilber.....	Insane........	15 years	do	34	do	do
do	Dexter Scott.......	Idiotic........	F'm brth	do	14	Male .	do
do	Eliza Beher........	do	do	do	9	Female	do

in the County of Geauga, State of Ohio, on the second Monday of May, 1856.

Occupation	Birthplace	Educated or not	Names of Parents	Occupation	Birthplace	No. of child'n	No. of child'n thus afflicted	Relationship of parents before marriage
Farmer	Canada	Educated	Not reported.............	Not rep.	.....	..	..	
None...	N. York	do	Velorus Chilsen..........	Mech'nic	New York	4	1	None
do	Ohio....	do	Joseph and Sally Webster.	Farmer.	R. Island	12	2	Cousins
do	do	do	Alvin and Louis Shaw....	do	Vt. & O.	2	1	None
Unkno'n	Vermont.	do	E. Foster................	do	do	3	2	do
None...	do	Not.....	C. Robinson.............	do	Mass.....	5	1	Unknown
do	Ohio....	do	Fred. and Julia Newell....	do	New York	7	2	None
do	do	do	do do	do	do	7	2	do
Farmer.	Unknown	Educated	Not known.............	do	do	..	..	do
do	do	do	do	do	do	..	..	do
do	Mass.....	Not.....	Daniel and Rachel Owen..	do	Conn.....	6	1	do
None...	Ohio....	do	Joseph and Mary Pidd....	Carpent'r	Mass.....	5	1	do
do	N. York.	Partially.	Aron P. Brooks..........	Farmer.	Vermont..	6	2	do
do	Vermont..	do	do do	do	do	6	2	do
do	N. York.	do	Martin and Parmilia Smith	do	Conn.....	9	1	do
Farmer.	Penn.....	do	Unknown	do	do	..	..	do
Hse w'rk	Ohio....	do	Moses and Lucy Murphy..	do	New York	10	1	do
do	N. York.	Educated	Solomon and Marth Wilber	do	Vermont..	5	1	do
None...	Ohio....	Not.....	Ahial and Rosana Scott..	do	Germany.	5	1	do
do	do	do	John and Henrietta Beher..	do	do	7	1	do

RETURN of the number of Deaf, Dumb, Blind, Insane and Idiotic persons

Names of Persons.	Nature of Affliction.	Duration of affliction.	Cause where known.	Age.	Sex.	Color.
F. Heaton	Deaf and dumb	58 years	Born	58	Male	White.
Cynthia Heaton	do do	64 "	do	64	Fem'le	do
Patty Lemon	Idiotic		Unknawn	50	do	do
Joe Spismesser	do		do	29	Male	do
Jacob F. Myers	Blind	5 years	Injury from leg	43	do	do
Sarah Thomas	do	17 "	Fever	32	Fem'le	do
Samuel Stewart	Deaf and dumb	9 "	do	15	Male	do
Sarah White	Insane	1 "	Unknown	24	Fem'le	do
Enoch Massey	Idiotic	60 "	Born	60	Male	do
Esther Thorn	Insane	27 "	Unknown	44	Fem'le	do
Joseph Mercer	Idiotic	29 "	do	29	Male	do
Caleb Mercer	do	17 "	do	17	do	do
Samuel Savill	Deaf and dumb	33 "	do	33	do	do
John Harness	Insane	7 "	do	52	do	do
Phillip Harness	do	2 "	do	24	do	do
John Melross	Idiotic	Born	do	14	do	do
Chalkley Thomas	Insane	7 years	Abolitionism	37	do	do
Rachael J. Arnold	do	17 "	Tape worm	17	Fem'le	do
Stacy Templar	Blind	15 months	Unknown	74	Male	do
Thomas Turner	Deaf and dumb	Born			do	do
Alexander Gowdy	do do	"		65	do	do
Francis Dyer	Blind	4 years	Blowing rocks	35	do	do
Benjamin Manor	Dumb and Idiotic	18½ "	Fits	20	do	do
Mary Abercrombie	do do	40 "	Born	40	Fem'le	do
King Alington	Insane	16 "	Unknown	45	Male	do
Matilda Stout	Deaf and dumb	29 "	Born	29	Fem'le	do
Susan Stout	do do	27 "	do	27	do	do
Lewis Snowden	Idiotic	36 "	Sickness	36	Male	do

in Greene County, State of Ohio, on the second Monday of May, 1856.

Occupation	Birth-place	Educated or not	Names of Parents	Occupation	Birth-place	No. chil'ren	No. afflicted	Relationship of parents before marriage
Carpen'r	Penna	Not						
....	do	do						
....	do	do						
....	Ohio	do						
Farmer	Virginia	Educated	Michael T. Myers	Farmer	Virginia		1	None.
do	Ohio	do	Francis & A. Thomas	do	do		1	do
do	do	Not	Samuel & M Stewart	do	Penna		1	do
do	do	Educated	James & D Sallsbury	do	North Caro	2	1	Related.
do	do	Not	H. & Jane Massey	do	Virginia	14	4	1st Cous'ns
None	do	ducated	W. & Rachael Thorn	do	do		1	None
do	Virginia	Not	J. & Rebecca Mercer	do	do	15	2	do
do	do	do	do do	do	do	15	2	do
Farmer	do	Educated	Samuel & Ann Savill	do	do	12	2	1st Cous'ns
do	Ohio	do	M. and Susan Harness	do	do	7	1	None.
do	do	do	J. & Nancy Harness	do	do	5	1	do
....	do	do	J. & Cath. Mellross	do	Scot.&Ohio	8	1	do
Student	do	do	Jesse & Ann Thomas	do	Penna	2	1	2d Cour'ns.
....	do	Not	J. & Rachael Arnold	do	Ohio	2	1	None.
....	Virginia	do	J. & Martha Tempiar	do	N. J. & Pa		1	do
Farmer	Ohio	Educated	A. & Eleanor Thomas	do	Carolina		1	2d Cou'ins.
do	Virginia	Not	John Gowdy	do	Unknown		1	Unknown.
Laborer	Ireland	do	Bartholomew Dyer	Unknown	Ireland		1	do
None	Ohio	do	G. & Elizabeth Manor	Farmer	Virginia	8	1	None.
do	do	do	J. & Jane Abercrombie	do	Penna	13	2	1st Coun.
do	Penna	Educated	W. & Franc. Allington	do	do		1	Unknown.
do	Ohio	Not	J. & Rebecca Stout	do	Ohio	3	2	None.
do	do	do	do do	do	do	3	2	do
do	do	do	J. & Mary Snowdon	do	N. J. & Va.	4	1	do

RETURN of the number of Deaf and Dumb, Blind, Insane and Idiotit

Names of persons.	Nature of affliction.	Duration of affliction.		Cause where known.		Age.	Sex.	Color	Occupation.
Joseph White	Idiotic	14	years	Caused by fever		36	Male	White	Tailor
Joseph Wilson	Deaf	44	"	"	"	50	"	"	Shoemake
John Welsh	Deaf and Dumb	3	"	Not known		23	"	"	
Ann Welsh	"	"	18	"	"	18	Fem'le	"	Asylum..
Catharine Findley	Insane	20	"	"	...	66	"	"	Farmer ..
Susan Frame	"	Not known		"	....	75	"	"	
Lavina Fuller	"	"		"	....	26	"	"	
Jane Meskimins	"	"		"	....	36	"	"	
Rosana Dueher	"	"		"	....	35	"	"	
Thomas Ligman	"	"		"	....	13	Male.	"	
Joseph Riddle	"	"		"	....	33	"	P't Ind	
Agnes Kimble	"	"		"	....	24	Fem'le	White	
Martha Story	"	"		"	....	60	"	"	
Susana Shiply	"	23	years	So born	....	23	"	"	None
Hanah Barton	Dumb & Idiotic	15	"	"	....	15	"	"	"
John Donahoo	Insane	3	"	Sickness	....	65	Male.	"	Farmer ..
Wm. Hall	"	10	"	Unknown	....	30	"	"	"
Joshua McCoy	"	10	"	So born	....	10	"	"	None
Samuel J. Brown	Deaf and Dumb	12	"	Scarlet fever	...	14	"	"	"
Angeline Gibson	" "	20½	"	Bealing in head		21	Fem'le	"	"
Milton Gibson	" "	2	"	So born	....	2	Male.	"	"
Wm. Gallaher	" "	23	"	"	....	23	"	"	"
Mary Molden	Idiot	Life		Not known	....	42	Fem'le	"	Tailoress
John Collins	Deaf and Dumb	25 years		Sickness	....	30	Male.	"	Farmer ..
Thomas Ferguson	Idiot	Life		Not known	....	33	"	"	Laborer..
James Kid	Insane	2	years	"	....	55	"	"	Physician
Susanah Wallace	Deaf	2	"	Scarlet fever	..	9	Fem'le	"	None
Benjamin Ratliff	Idiot	5	"	Fits	....	7	Male.	"	"

persons, in the County of Guernsey, Ohio, on the second Monday of May, 1856.

Birth-place.	Educated or Not.	Names of parents.	Occupation.	Birth-place.	No. Children.	No. Children thus afflicted.	Rerationship of Parents before Marriage.
Cambridge	Not	Joseph White...........	Tailor......	Penn....	11	1	None.
Penn	Not	James Wilson...........	Farmer.....	Not kno'n	9	1	"
"	Educat'd	Robert Welsh...........	"	Penn.....	6	2	"
"	"	"	"	"	6	....	"
"	"	....	....	....	..	....	....
"	"	Not known	....	....	..	....	....
"	"	"	....	....	..	....	....
"	"	"	....	....	..	....	....
Ohio.....	"	"	....	....	..	....	....
"	Not	"	....	....	..	....	....
"	"	"	....	....	..	....	....
"	"	"	....	....	.	....	....
Pa	"	"	....	....	..	....	....
Maryland.	"	A. Shipley.............	Farmer.....	Maryland.	4	1	None.
Ohio.....	"	Alexander Bartin........	"	Ireland...	13	1	"
Ireland...	Educat'd	Arthur Ducher..........	Weaver.....	" ...	6	1	Not known.
Virginia..	"	Samuel Hall	Farmer ..	" ...	4	1	None.
Ohio	Not	Benj. McCoy.......	"	Pennsylva.	10	1	"
"	"	Moses Brown............	"	Ireland...	10	1	"
"	"	James Gibson............	"	Ohio.....	8	2	"
"	"	"	"	"	..	....	"
"	"	John Galaher............	"	Ireland...	4	1	"
....	"	Jacob Molden............	"	....	..	2	
Pennsylva.	"	John Collins	"	....	3	1	"
Ohio.....	"	Thomas Ferguson........	"	Ireland...	10	1	"
Ireland...	Educat'd	Not known..............	....	....	..	....	
Ohio.....	Not	Wm. Wallace............	Farmer.....	Ohio.....	5	1	"
"	"	Wm. Ratliff............	"	Va........	8	1	"

6—REP. SEC'Y. STATE.

RETURN of the number of Deaf and Dumb, Blind, Insane and Idiotic persons

Names of Persons.	Nature of affliction.	Duration of affliction.	Cause where known.	Age.	Sex.	Color.	Occupation.
Mary Collins	Chronic mania	6 years	Nostalgia	32	Female	White.	Domestic
Mary F. Hughs	"	3 "	Disap'd affect'n	21	do	do	S,amst's
Mary Kennedy	Dementia	3 "	Domestic afflc'n	45	do	do	Domestic
Sarah Black	Chronic mania	13½ years	Unknown	58	do	do	Housek'r
Catharine Tague	Dementia	Unknown	"	32	do	do	Domestic
Magdalena Hillman	"	3½ years	Masturbation	23	do	do	Seamst's
Winford Daily	Chronic mania	11½ "	Grief	65	do	do	House k'r
Catharine Schananver	Imbecile	18 "	Congenital	20	do	do	Domestic
Philipena Holstein	Chronic mania	Unknown	Unknown	57	do	do	House k'r
Margaret Boby	"	11 years	Disap'd affect'n	30	do	do	Domestic
Sarah Baker	"	8 "	Unknown	49	do	do	House k'r
Mary Pierce	"	Unknown	"	34	do	do	Domestic
Bridget Dolan	"	7 years	"	36	do	do	House k'r
Mary Spence	"	5 "	Doms'c Trouble	38	do	do	"
Eliza Davidson	"	Unknown	Unknown	63	do	do	Unknwn
Margaret Boyland	"	2 years	Intemperance	39	do	do	House k'r
Louisa Brockman	Dementia	10 "	Disap'd affect'n	30	do	do	Domestic
Mary Ulry	"	Unknown	Unknown	43	do	do	"
Margaret Nugent	Chronic mania	6 years	Nostalgia	33	do	do	"
Barbara Loeh	"	2 years	Doms'c Trouble	39	do	do	House k'r
Elizabeth Hummel	"	Unknown	Nostalgia	28	do	do	Domestic
Jane Davison	Dementia	"	Epilepsy	30	do	do	None
Catharine Herwig	Chronic mania	"	Unknown	31	do	do	Domestic
Martha Thompson	"	9 years	"	40	do	do	"
Eleanor Dinsmore	"	2½ "	Grief	50	do	do	House k'r
Henrietta Schultz	"	1 "	Domes'c trouble	29	do	do	Seamst's
Charlotte Myer	"	2 "	Disap'd affect'n	27	do	do	Domestic
Mary Lefevin	"	3 "	Poverty	41	de	do	House k'r
Catharine Brohner	"	1 "	Nostalgia	37	do	do	"
Mary Long	Dementia	Unknown	Unknown	21	do	do	Domestic
Amelia Wolonman	"	"	"	25	do	do	"
Mary Croty	Chronic mania	3 years	"	41	do	do	House k'r
Mary Drychans	Dementia	4½ "	Nostalgia	34	do	do	"
Honora Walsh	Chronic mania	2 "	Typhus fever	29	do	do	Domestic
Anna Finstewald	"	Unknown	Unknown	20	do	do	"
Mary McDonald	"	2½ years	Loss of child	47	do	do	House k'r
Nancy Tanner	"	Unknown	Unknown	22	do	do	Domestic
Regina Weddel	Melancholy	1½ years	Fever	40	do	do	House k'r
Hannah Tresset	Chronic mania	1½ "	Family trouble	40	do	do	Domestic
Catharine Muligan	"	3 "	Domes'c trouble	26	do	do	"
Maria Winkler	Monomania	4½ "	Loss of child	35	do	do	House k'r
Mary Snelbaker	Chronic mania	4½ "	Masturbation	35	do	do	"
Mary McCann	"	Unknown	Unknown	35	do	do	"
George Rapp	"	25 years	"	51	Male	do	Tailor
James Cowen	Imbecility	22 "	Congenital	22	do	do	None
Antoine Padovain	Chronic mania	2 "	Unknown	42	do	do	Peddler.
Solomon Michael Baker	"	Unknown	"	36	do	do	"
Joseph Doolan	"	15 years	"	42	do	do	Laborer
Philip Ottis	Dementia	2½ "	Disease of brain	29	do	do	Boatman.
Charlotte Beckman	"	1½ "	Jealousy	4	Female	do	House k'r
Margaret Kennedy	Chronic mania	2 "	Unknown	43	do	do	"
Barbara Beck	Monomania	1½ "	Seduction	19	do	do	Domestic
Sophia Bultman	Periodic'l mania	1½ "	Injury of head	29	do	do	"
Louisa Stiles	Dementia	2 "	Domes'c trouble	47	do	do	"
Mary Everhart	Melancholy	9 months	Supr'sd menses	28	do	do	Seamst's
Mary Smith	"	4 years	Unknown	29	do	do	Domestic
Catharine Welsh	"	9 months	Jealousy	35	do	do	House k'r
Julia Gleason	Monomania	1 year	Ungov'd temper	18	do	do	Domestic

in the county of Hamilton, State of Ohio, on the second Monday of May, 1856.

Birth-place.	Educated or Not.	Names of Parents.	Occupation.	Birth-place.	No. children.	No. children thus afflicted.	Relationship of parents before marriage.
Ireland .	Unknown	Unknown................	Unknown .	Unknown	..	..	....
Penn	read & wrt	"	"	"	..	..	....
Ireland ..	Unknown	"	"	"	..	..	....
Penn	"	"	"	"	..	..	....
Ireland ..	Not	"	"	Ireland ...	..	..	....
Germa y.	read & wrt	"	"	"	..	..	....
Ireland ..	"	"	"	"	..	..	....
Germany.	"	Istel and Margaret Schananver	Baker.....	Germany..	5	1	....
"	"	Unknown...............	Unknown .	Unknown..	..	..	....
"	"	"	"	"	..	..	....
Ohio	Unknown	"	"	"	..	..	....
Missouri .	Not	Daniel and Elizabeth Pierce..	Farmer....	New York.	3	1	....
Ireland ..	Can read.	Morris and Catharine Dolan..	"	Ireland ...	9	1	....
Scotland .	Educated	Unknown...............	Unknown .	Scotland ..	..	..	....
Ohio	Unknown	"	"	Unknown ..	..	..	....
Scotland .	Educated	"	"	"	..	..	....
Germany.	Unknown	"	"	"	..	..	....
Ireland ..	"	"	"	"	..	..	....
"	Not	Edward and Bridget Nugent .	Farmer....	Ireland ...	6	1	....
Germany.	read & wrt	Unknown...............	Unknown .	Unknown..	..	..	....
"	Unknown	"	"	"	..	..	....
Ohio	"	"	"	"	..	..	....
Germany.	read & wrt	Law'nce and Magdalena Steinle	Shoemaker	Germany..	12	1	....
Penn	"	Joshua J. and Ann Thompson	"	Pennsylv'ia	11	1	....
"	Unknown	Unknown...............	Unknown .	Unknown..	..	..	....
Germany.	read & wrt	"	"	"	..	..	....
"	Unknown	"	"	"	..	..	....
"	read & wrt	Henry and Elizabeth Wesling	Carpenter .	Germany..	..	..	....
"	Can read.	Jacob and Philipena Tobias..	Laborer ...	"	10	..	....
"	Unknown	Unknown...............	Unknown .	Unknown..	..	..	....
"	"	"	"	"	..	..	....
Ireland ..	read & wrt	John and Catharine Quinton ..	Farmer....	Ireland....	11	1	None ....
Germany.	Unknown	Unknown...............	Unknown .	Unknown..	..	..	....
Ireland ..	Can read.	John and Catharine Welch....	Farmer....	Ireland....	10	1	None ...
Germany.	Unknown	Unknown...............	Unknown .	Unknown..	..	..	....
Ireland ..	"	"	"	"	..	..	....
England .	Can read.	John and Hannah Tanner.....	Shoemaker	England ..	8	1	....
Germany.	"	Unknown...............	Unknown .	Unknown..	..	..	....
"	"	Christian and Magdal'a Tusset	Butcher ...	Germany..	5	1	....
Ireland ..	"	Unknown...............	Unknown .	Unknown..	..	..	....
England .	Educated	"	"	England ..	..	..	....
Ohio	"	"	"	"	..	..	....
Ireland	Not......	Peter and Elce McCann	Farmer ...	Ireland...	..	..	....
Germany.	Educated	George and Christine Rapp....	Tailor	Germany..	4	1	....
Ohio	Not.	Unknown...............	Unknown .	Ireland ...	1	1	....
France...	Educated	"	"	Unknown ..	..	..	....
Germany.	read & wrt	Samuel M. and Sarah Baker..	Peddler ...	Germany..	5	1	....
Ireland ..	Can read.	Unknown...............	Unknown .	Ireland....	..	..	....
Germany.	read & wrt	"	"	Germany...	..	..	....
"	Not	"	"	"	..	..	....
Ireland ..	"	"	"	"	..	..	....
Germany.	read & wrt	Frederick and Maria Beck	Weaver ...	"	10	1	....
"	Not	Henry and Dora Bultman....	Gardener ..	"	8	1	....
Virginia .	"	Unknown...............	Unknown ..	Unknown ..	..	..	....
Germany.	read & wrt	John and Castinia Everhart..	Shoemaker	Germany..	4	1	....
Penn	"	Henry and Mary Smith......	Farmer....	Ohio......	15	1	....
Ireland ..	"	Andrew and Ellen Heite......	Tailor	Ireland....	1	1	....
"	Can read.	James and Mary Gleason......	Stonemas'n	"	10	1	

RETURN of the number of Deaf and Dumb, Blind, Insane and Idiotic persons

Names of Persons.	Nature of Affliction.	Duration of Affliction.	Cause where known.	Age.	Sex.	Color.
Sophia Gardner	Chronic mania	Unknown	Unknown	78	Fem'le	White.
Mary Mayher	"	7 months	"	50	do	"
Mary Cook	Melancholy	Unknown	"	30	do	"
Gette Stanbury	Monomania	2 years	Disap. affection	23	do	"
Catharine B. Schwartz	Dementia	Unknown	Unknown	65	do	"
Mary Ettenson	Acute Mania	5 months	Jealousy	30	do	"
Jane Han	Periodic'l mania	9 "	Yellow Fever	43	do	"
Louisa Epmyer	Acute mania	2 "	Loss of son	56	do	"
Mary Eshelby	Chronic mania	7 years	Religion	42	do	"
Mary Ann Dain	"	10 "	Fever	30	do	"
Jane Gratefenk	Melancholy	2 months	Disap. affection	30	do	"
Mary Household	Periodic'l mania	6 years	Tyhus Fever	11	do	"
Elizabeth H. Smith Tuton	Monomania	4 "	Intemperance	53	do	"
Mary Rhinehart	"	5 or 6 "	Unknown	56	do	"
Mary Hillman	Melancholy	5 "	"	25	do	"
Caroline Susan Peters	Chronic mania	2½ "	Injury of head	28	do	"
Wilemena Promitz	"	3½ "	Nostalgia	26	do	"
Judy Day	Imbecility	2½ "	Tyhus Fever	19	do	"
Mary Martin	Dementia	2½ "	Grief	30	do	"
Mary Morris	Chronic mania	5 "	Nostalgia	23	do	"
Catharice Solor	"	7½ "	Crief	48	do	"
Hannah Green	"	4½ "	Disap. affection	45	do	"
Mary Murphey	"	3 "	Grief	33	do	"
Catharine Snider	"	23 "	Unknown	50	do	"
Martha B. Kemper	"	10½ "	Domest. trouble	42	do	"
Elizabeth Ryan	"	5½ "	Unknown	32	do	"
Amelia Westermaker	"	6½ "	Disap. affection	35	do	"
Frederika C. Ranshart	Idiotic	18 "	Congenital	18	do	"
Deborah Van Curwin	"	23½ "	Injury of head	37	do	"
Margaret Kunreel	Dementia	4½ "	Nostalgia	23	do	"
Mary Ann Bolinger	Chronic mania	11½ "	Domest. trouble	44	do	"
Rebecca Matton	Idiotic	24 "	Congenital	24	do	"
Ursula Watson	Chronic mania	15 "	Domest. trouble	41	do	"
Mary Heavin	Dementia	6½ "	Unknown	21	do	"
Mary Ann Boland	Chronic mania	5½ "	Domest. trouble	40	do	"
Elizabeth Parker	Servile mentia	13¼ "	Religion	64	do	"
Elizabeth Mulally	Periodic'l mania	24½ "	Epilepsy	32	do	"
Louisa Hollford	"	11½ "	Jealousy	39	do	"
Ann Walker	Chronic mania	9½ "	Fever	54	do	"
Mary Fenner	"	4½ "	Grief	32	do	"
Arthur Fergurson	Imbecility	19½ "	Congenital	54	Male	"
Thomas Callahan	Chronic mania	13½ "	Unknown	53	do	"
Henry Schott	"	2½ "	"	27	do	"
Daniel Spooner	"	8½ "	Religion	31	do	"
Joseph Satir	"	2 "	Intemperance	27	do	"
Elias Santzinger	"	4½ "	Unknown	41	do	"
Edward Garvey	"	16½ "	"	43	do	"
John B. Messiast	"	9½ "	"	32	do	"
Joshua W. Hill	Dementia	11 "	Masturbation	37	do	"
Augustus Funkin	"	4 "	Unknown	32	do	"
Morris Francis	Chronic mania	4½ "	"	45	do	"
Jacob Poleff	"	4½ "	"	24	do	"
Christian Muller	"	3 "	Domest. trouble	58	do	"
Patrick Conroy	"	5½ "	Nostalgia	24	do	"
John H. Marvin	Dementia	14½ "	Unknown	47	do	"
Conrad Estel	"	8 "	Epilepsy	28	do	"
Owen Calvin	Chronic mania	5 "	Loss of money	38	do	"
Frederick Bierman	"	Unknown	Unknown	37	do	"
Allen Perry	"	7½ "	"	34	do	"

in the county of Hamilton, State of Ohio, on the second Monday of May, 1856.

Occupation.	Birth-place.	Educated or not.	Names of Persons.	Occupation.	Birth-place.	No. children	No. afft tied	Relationship of Parents before marriage.
Domestic	Germany..	re'd &wrt	No more history.....					
"	Ireland...	Unkn'wn	Unknown...........	Unknown.	Unknown.			Unknown.
"	"	Not	"	"	Ireland ...			"
"	Germany..	re'd &wrt	"	"	Unknown.			"
"	"	"	"	"	"			"
House k'r	"	"	J. & Cath. M. Ettenson	Farmer ...	Germany..	13	1	None. ....
Domestic	Ireland ...	Not	F. & Cath. Kreskadden	"	Ireland ...	7	1	Unknown.
House k'r	Germany..	"	— and Anna Meyer...	"	Germany..	1	1	"
"	Ireland ...	Educated	A. and Mry Drennen	Book bindr	Ireland ...	14	2	"
Domestic	Ohio	Not	Julias and Mary Dain	Laborer...	New York	8	1	"
"	Germany..	re'd &wrt	C. & Mary Gtratefenk	Farmer ...	Germany..	3	1	None. ....
None ...	Pennsylva.	Unkn'wn	Unknown........	Unknown.	Unknown.			Unknown.
House k'r	England ..	Educated	J. & Elizabeth Paul	"	England ...		1	"
Seamst's	Pennsylva.	Can read	B. & Sarah Rhinehart	Carpenter .	Pennsylv'a	7	1	None. ....
Domestic	Germany..	re'd &wrt	Unknown.........	Unknown.	Unknown.			Unknown.
"	New York	Can read	John & Mary Peters	Merchant .	New York	6	1	"
Seamst's	Germany..	re'd &wrt	Unknown........	Unknown.	Unknown.			"
Domestic	Ireland ...	Not	James and Mary Day	Laborer...	Ireland ...	6	1	"
"	"	re'd &wrt	Unknown.........	Unknown.	Unknown.			"
"	"	Can read	"	"	"			"
"	Germany..	Not	"	"	"			"
Seamst's	England ..	re'd &wrt	"	"	"			"
Domestic	Ireland .	"	"	"	Ireland ...			"
"	Germany..	"	Cath. & Eliza. Snider	Baker	Germany..	12	1	"
House,k'r	Mass.	"	B. & Hannah Wood.	Merchant .	Ohio	7	1	None. ....
Domestic	Ireland ...	Unkn'wn	Unknown....	Unknown	Unknown.			Unknown.
Seamst's	Germany..	re'd &wrt	"	"	"			"
None ...	"	"	"	"	"			"
Domestic	Ohio	"	"	"	"			"
"	Ireland ...	"	T. & Mary Kennedy	Steward ..	Ireland ...	4	1	"
House k'r	Germany..	Not	Unknown....	Unknown.	Unknown.			"
None ...	"	Unkn'wn	"	"	"			"
House k'r	Kentucky .	"	"	"	"			"
Domestic	Ireland ...	"	"	"	"			"
House k'r	"	"	"	"	"			"
"	New Jersey	"	"	"	"			"
Domestic	Ireland ...	"	"	"	"			"
House k'r	Germany..	re'd &wrt	"	"	"			"
"	Virginia ..	"	"	"	"			"
"	Pennsylva.	Unkn'wn	"	"	"			"
Laborer .	Scotland ..	Not ..	"	Farmer ...	Scotland ..			"
"	Ireland ...	re'd &wrt	W. & Christia Calaban	"	Ireland ...	10	1	"
Tailor ..	Germany..	"	Unknown....	Unknown.	Unknown.			"
Laborer .	Ohio. ...	"	"	"	"			"
Tailor ..	Germany..	"	J. S. & Catharine Satir	Stone cuttr	Germany..	5	1	"
Machn'st	Switzerla'd	"	E. & Barba. Santzinger	Clerk	Switzerla'd	4	1	"
Laborer .	Ireland ...	"	Unknown....	Unknown.	Unknown.			"
Tanner .	France....	Unkn'wn	"	"	"			"
Tobac'ist	Virginia ..	re'd &wrt	"	"	"			"
Cook ...	Germany..	Unkn'wn	"	"	"			"
Minister	"	"	"	"	"			"
Tailor ..	"	re'd &wrt	"	"	"			"
Laborer .	"	Can read	"	"	"			"
"	Ireland ...	re'd &wrt	"	"	"			"
Farmer .	Ohio.	Can read	"	"	"			"
Laborer .	Germany..	re'd &wrt	"	"	"			"
"	Ireland...	Not	"	"	"			"
"	Germany..	re'd &wrt	"	"	"			"
Farmer .	Ohio	Ukno'wn	"	"	"			"

RETURN of the number of Deaf and Dumb, Blind, Insane and Idiotic persons

Names of Persons	Nature of affliction.	Duration of affliction.	Cause, where known.	Age.	Sex.	Color.	Occupation.
Herman Theus	Idiotic	17 years	Congenital	20	Male	White	None
John Schuderman	do	4 do	Unknown	22	do	do	Tailor
James Davy	Imbecility	40 do	Congenital	40	do	do	do
John Hatt	Chronic mania	8½ do	Unknown	57	do	do	Soldier
Manuel Stiltz	Dementia	3½ do	Masturbation	22	do	do	Laborer
Jost Mulifer Buhlman	do	2 do	Unknown	32	do	do	Tailor
Solomon Heacht	Chronic mania	1½ do	Disap'nted love	30	do	do	Peddlar
Michael Hany	do	1½ do	Intemperance	32	do	do	Butcher
William Barker	Idiotic	Unknown	Unknown	24	do	do	None
Norval Kelso	Chronic mania	do	do	41	do	do	Farmer
Martin Welsh	Dementia	do	do	26	do	do	Laborer
John Peters	Chronic mania	10 years	Injury of head	52	do	do	Farmer
Christian Hinks	Idiotic	Unknown	Unknown	33	do	do	None
Lewis Mephord	do	15 years	Congenital	15	do	do	do
Frederick C. Verner	Chronic mania	16 do	Typhoyd fever	44	do	do	Clerk
Patrick McIntire	do do	3 do	Intemperance	36	do	do	Laborer
Josiah Morehead	do do	12 do	Injury of head	26	do	do	Moulder
Frederick Henn	Demented	6 do	Domestic tro'ble	41	do	do	Soldier
William J. Murry	do	7 do	Masturbation	33	do	do	Merch'nt
John Haddler	Imbecility	21 do	Congenital	22	do	de	Laborer
Martin Christopher	Chronic mania	Unknown	Unknown	41	do	do	do
Edward O'Conner	do do	2 years	Injury of head	46	do	do	do
Nicholas Spevnly	do do	Unknown	Unknown	57	do	do	Farmer
Martin Beminger	do do	3½ years	Intemperance	43	do	do	Boatman
Simon Steigler	do do	6 months	do	34	do	do	Cooper
Hezekiah Woodson	Periodic'l mania	15 years	Epilepsy	20	do	do	Cook
John Murry	Chronic mania	2 do	Intemperance	37	do	do	Laborer
William A Lattle	Servile dem'ntia	Unknown	Unknown	80	do	do	do
Michael McLaughlin	Chronic Mania	do	Loss of property	64	do	do	Merchant
Hubert Kirchner	Periodic'l mania	1 year	Epilepsy	44	do	do	Tailor
Evan Jones	Servile dem'ntia	10 months	Spiritualism	72	do	do	Farmer
Peter Flinn	Chronic Mania	Unknown	Unknown	40	do	do	Laborer
John Hughs	do do	9 months	Injury of head	70	do	do	Merchant
Mason Perry	Periodic'l mania	8 years	Epilepsy	30	do	do	Laborer
Hamilton Johnston	Acute mania	5 months	Unknown	25	do	do	do
William Dawson	Chronic mania	3 years	Hereditary	50	do	do	do
Firman Hatt	Periodic'l mania	2 do	Epilepsy	26	do	do	Saddler
Isaac Perkins	Dementia	12 do	do	20	do	do	None
Peter McMillen	Menancholia	4 months	Unknown	45	do	do	Laborer
Robert Coffee	do	4 years	Injury of head	26	do	do	do
David Russell	Periodic'l mania	31 do	do do	46	do	do	do
Mathias Biber	Chronic mania	9 do	Unknown	36	do	do	do
David Burns	Acute mania	Unknown	do	78	do	do	Tailor
Nicholas Geisler	do	do	do	37	do	do	Unkno'n
Daniel Rian	Blind	do	Blasting rock	45	do	do	Co inf'ry
Edward Carigan	do	16 years	Unknown	17	do	do	None
James Tap	Insane	11 do	do	25	do	do	do
Asa Colegate	Idiotic	40 do	do	40	do	do	do
William Thompson	Blind	2 do	do	58	do	do	do
Jacob Michael	do	Unknown	do	80	do	do	do
Michael Shely	Deaf and dumb	17 years	do	17	do	do	do
George Shelby	do do	11 do	do		do	do	do
Elizabeth Bower	Blind	Unknown	Sickness	21	Fem.	do	Unkno'n
Nancy Wernkle	Insane	12 years	Unknown	13	do	do	None
Caroline Hopman	Deaf and Dumb	23 do	From infancy	23	do	do	Sewing
Margaret Jane McGache	Deaf	2½ do	Severe cold	7	do	do	None
Jacob Frech	Blind	8 do	Cholera	38	Male	do	Laborer
Ann Hagerty	Idiot	14 do	Sickness	16	Fem'le	do	None

87

in the County of Hamilton, State of Ohio, on the second Monday of May, 1856.

Birth place.	Educated or not	Names of Parents.	Occupation.	Birth-place.	No. children	No. of child'n thus afflicted	Relationship of parents before marriage
Germany..	Partially	Unknown.................	Unknown.	Unknown.			Unknown.
do	Unkno'n	do	do	do			do
England..	Partially.	Wm. and Bridget Davy.......	Tailor....	England..	7	2	do
France....	Can read	Unknown.................	Unknown.	Unknown.			do
Indiana...	do	do	do	do			do
Germany..	Partially.	M Jost and Louisa Buhlman..	Weaver...	Switzerl'nd	4	1	do
do	do	Unknown..................	Peddlar...	Germany..	2	1	do
do	do	John and Elizabeth Haney....	Baker....	do	5	1	do
Ohio.....	Unkno'n	Unknown.................	Unknown.	Unknown..			do
Kentucky.	Partially.	John and Francis Kelso.......	Cabinetm'r	Virginia...	4	1	do
Ireland....	Not.....	Unknown.................	Unknown.	Unkown...			do
Vermont.	Unkno'n	do	do	do			do
Germany..	do	do	do	do			do
Ohio.....	do	do	do	do			do
Germany..	Educated	do	do	do			do
Ireland...	Not.....	do	do	do			do
Ohio......	do	do	do	do			do
Germany..	do	do	do	do			do
Ohio......	Educated	Abram and Mary Murry......	Carpenter.	Louisiana.			do
Germany..	Not.....	Unknown..................	Unknown.	Unknown..			do
do	do	do	do	do			do
Ireland...	Partially.	Ed. and Bridget O'Conner....	Farmer...	Ireland..	9	1	do
Germany..	do	Sapher and Catherine Spevnly	do	Germany..	3	1	do
do	do	Martin and Mary Beminger...	do	do	8	1	do
do	do	Unknown..................	Unknown.	Unknown..		6	do
Kentucky.	do	H and Julia Ann Woodson..	Farmer...	Kentucky.	8		do
Ireland....	Not.....	Ed. and Mary Murray........	Laborer...	Ireland....	8	1	do
N. Jersey..	Unkn'wn	Unknown..................	Unknown.	Unknown..		1	do
Ireland....	Educated	Michael and Sibby McLaughlin	Farmer...	Ireland..	9		do
Germany..	Partially	Robert and Julianna Kirchner.	Clerk.....	Germany.	1	1	do
Wales....	do	Wm. and Martha Jonees......	St'ne cutter	Wales....	10	1	do
Ireland...	do	Wm. and Oner Flinn.........	Farmer...	Ireland..	8	1	do
N. York...	do	Richard and Elizabeth Hugh..	do	do	4	1	do
Ohio......	do	James and Mary Perry........	Laborer...	N. Jersey..	4	1	do
Ireland....	do	Robert and Sarah Johnston....	Farmer...	Ireland..	7	1	do
do	do	Jas. and Catherine Dawson....	do	do	7	1	do
Ohio......	do	Kinnet & Lear Hatt..........	Cooper....	Ohio....	4	1	do
do	do	J N and Elizabeth Perkins...	Merchant.	do	4	1	do
Scotland..	do	David and Agnes McMillen..	Farmer...	Scotland..	8	1	do
Ireland...	Not.....	Robt. and Catherine Coffee....	Soldier...	Ireland...	2	1	do
Kentucky..	Can read	John and Rebecca Russell....	Potter....	Unknown.	3	1	do
Germany..	Not.....	John & Mary Biber..........	Farmer...	France....	16	1	do
N. Jersey..	Unkn'wn	Unknown..................	Unknown.	Unknown..			do
Germany..	do	do	do	do			do
Ireland....	Not....	do	do	do			do
Cincinnati.	do....	John Mary Carigan..........	Tailor....	Louisiana.	3	1	None.
Ohio......	Educated	Noel and Sarah Sap.........	Grocer....	Germany..	5	1	do
do	Not....	Unknown.................	Unknown	Unknown..			Unknown
Penn......	Educated	do	do	do			do
Kentucky..	do....	do	do	do			do
Ohio......	Not....	do	do	Germany..			do
do	do	do	do	do			do
Unknown..	Unkn'wn	do	do	do			do
Oldenberg.	Not....	John Wenkle................	Unknown.	do	4	1	None
Germany..	Not....	Berman Hopman............	Laborer...	do	7	1	do
Penn......	do	Andrew & Mary McGache....	Unknown.	Penn......	8	1	do
Germany..	Educated	Philip Frech................	Gardner..	Germeny..	7	1	do
U.N. States	Not....	Ann Hagerty................	Unkoown.	do	3	1	do

RETURN of the Number of Deaf and Dumb, Blind, Insane and Idiotic persons in

Names of Persons.	Nature of Affliction.	Duration of Affliction.	Cause, Where Known.	Age.	Sex.	Color.	Occupation.
Anna G. Tomas	Blind	4 years	Unknown	56	Fem'le	White	H's keep'r
Wm. C. Vankirk	Blind	12 "	Strain	60	Male	do	Tailor
William Totton	Deaf and dumb	Unknown	Unknown	23	Fem'le	do	Laborer
Sarah Huff	Blind	"	"	77	"	do	
Michael Crow	Deaf and dumb	From birth	"	21	Male	do	None
Adam Crow	" "	" "	"	17	"	do	"
Stephen V. Day	" "	56 years	Sickness	59	"	do	Farmer
James Wilder	Deaf	26 "	Unknown	70	"	do	"
Prudence Keller	Insane	1 "	"	76	Fem'le	do	
M. B. Mundell	Blind	19 "	Scarlet fever	21	Male	do	None
Daniel Hosbrook	Blind	14 "	Unknown	72	"	do	Surveyor.
Joseph Leming	Deaf and dumb	6 months	"	½	"	do	None
Muller Peter	Deaf	55 years	Fits	60	"	do	Tailor
Martin Frech	Blind	22 "	Measles	24	"	do	Br'shm'kr
Andrew Sterrits	Insane	11 months	Unknown	31	"	do	Merchant,
Martha Youmans	Insane	From birth,	"	17	Fem'le	do	None
Mathilda Tennemann	Deaf and dumb	"	"	5	"	do	"
Victory Gasser	" "	" "	"	35	"	do	Houskeep
Caroline Fensebeck	" "	8 y's 3 mo's	Sickness	9	"	do	None
Julia Fensebeck	" "	6 " 3 "	"	7	"	do	"
Joseph Barandt	Dumb	10 years	Cutting teeth	11	Male	do	"
Baily Guard	Deaf and dumb	9 "	Measles	11	"	do	"
Mary Ellen Guard	" "	4 "	Fever	6	Fem'le	do	"
Salina Frazee	Idiotic	Fr'm inf'cy	Unknown	18	"	do	"
John Schoenlaub	Deaf and dumb	Unknown,	"	8	Male	do	"
Adam Kaufman	" "	" "	"	12	"	do	"
Charles Dyen	Blind	Fr'm inf'cy	Sickness	41	"	do	Grocer
Catharine Bend	Deaf and dumb	" "	Unknown	40	Fem'le	do	None
Rebecca Martin	Blind	16 years	Affect'n of head	24	"	do	"
Andrew Martin	"	Fr'm inf'cy	Spasms	20	Male	do	"
Charles Jacobs	Idiotic	"	Unknown	51	"	do	"
Anna Hubbard	"	"	"	23	Fem'le	do	"
Ann Armstrong	Blind	2 years	Sickness	3	"	do	"
Anthony Miller	Insane	7 "	Religion	60	Male	do	
Ellen Francis Rice	Idiotic	13 "	From birth	13	Fem'le	do	
Robert Corry	Blind	32 "	Accident	65	Male	do	
Mary A Tranley	Deaf and dumb	8 "		8	Fem'le	do	None
John Case	" "	7 "		7	Male	do	"
Thomas Sutton	" "	9 "		9	"	do	"
Peter Fagley	Idiotic	24 "	Fright	24	"	do	"
Mary Danes	Insane	12 "		31	Fem'le	do	"
Hannah Solomon	Blind	4 "		82	"	do	"
Allice Williamson	Deaf and dumb	9 "	Unknown	11	"	do	None
Nancy Stillwell	Blind	2 "	"	2	"	do	"
Susan Allingham	Insane	3 "	Loss of children	43	"	do	"
Hiram Thorp	Idiotic	30 "	Unknown	30	Male	do	"
Eda Alfeld	Deaf and dumb	Fr'm inf'cy	"	22	Fem'le	do	H'sekeepr
James Glass	" "	" "	"	27	Male	do	None
Martin Waber	Blind	15 years	Cutting teeth	17	"	do	"
Ann Sophia Broksmith	Deaf and dumb	5 "	Inflam. of head	6	Fem'le	do	"
James McClelland	Blind	12 "	Cataract	58	Male	do	Farmer
Catharine April	Deaf and dumb	33 "	Sickness	35	Fem'le	do	None
Sarah May	Blind	4 "	Unknown	61	"	do	"
Frank Catley	Deaf and dumb	Fr'm inf'cy	"	11	Male	do	"
George Hoffman	" "	21 years	"	21	Male	do	"
Aaron Olark	Deaf	30 "	"	40	Male	do	Shoem'kr

the county of Hamilton, State of Ohio, on the second Monday of May, 1856.

Birth-place.	Educated or Not.	Names of Parents.	Occupation	Birth-place	No. children.	No. children thus afflicted.	Relationship of Parents before marriage
Penn	read & wrte	Richard and Mary Dill	Mason	Ireland	10	2	None.
"	" "	Thomas and Mary Vankirk	Tailor	N. Jersey,	2	1	"
Ohio	" "	Joseph and Phoebe Totten	Farmer	"	6	1	"
Penn							
Germany.	Educated	Nicholas and Margaret Crow	Farmer	Germany	4	2	None.
"	"	" " " "	"	"			"
N. Jersey,	Not	Wm. J. and Sarah Day	"	N. Jersey,	7	1	"
R. Island,	Educated,						
Ohio	"						
"	Partly edu	Levi and Elizabeth Mundell	Merchant,	Ohio	1	1	None.
Virginia	Educated,				3	1	"
Ohio	Not	Joseph Leming	Tailor	Germany	1	1	"
Germany	Educated,		Unknown,	Unknown,			
"	"	Martin Frech	"	Germany	3	1	None.
"	"	J. L. and S. Duffield	Insur'ce agt	"	6	1	"
Ohio	Limited	John Youmans	Chair makr	N. Jersey,	5	1	"
"	Not	J. H. Tennemann	Farmer	Germany,	1	1	"
Switzl'nd,	"	Anton Gasser		Switz'land,	13	1	"
Ohio	Limited	John Fensebeck	Laborer	Germany	6	2	"
"	"	" "	"	"			"
Germany.	Not	Joseph Barrandt	Tailor	"	1	1	"
Ohio	"	Alexander and Eliza Guard	Farmer	Indiana	6	2	{3d cousins.
"	"	" " " "	"	"			None.
"	"	Jonas and Sarah Frazee	Pensioner	N. Jersey,	8	1	None.
Cinn., O.,	"	Adam Schoenlaub	Laborer	Germany	5	1	"
Germany.	"	Barbara Kaufman	None	"	3	1	"
Maine	Educated,	David and Abigal Dyen	Carpenter,	Maine	10	3	"
Germany,	Not			Farmer	Germany	15	1	"
Cinn, O.,	Educated,	Sarah and Thomas Martin	F'ndryman	Ireland	13	2	"
"	"	" " " "	"	"			"
Ohio	Not				6	1	"
"	"	Thomas and Elizabeth Hubbard	Farmer	Maryland,	21	1	"
Cinn., O.,	"	John and Mary Armstrong	Blacksmith	Ireland	2	1	"
Germany,						1	
Penn		John and Susan Rice		Pennsylv'a	10	1	None.
						1	"
Ohio	Not	Domian and Elizabeth Tranly	Gardner	Germany	1	1	"
Penn	"	Joseph and Elizabeth Case	Miller	"	3	1	"
Ohio	"	James and Elizabeth Sutton	Sawyer	Kentucky	2	1	"
"	"	Edwd. and Ann Maria Fagley				1	"
"	Educated,	Julius and Mary Danes				1	"
N. Jersey,						1	"
Ohio	Not	David and Agnes Williamson	None		2	1	"
"	"	James and Catharine Stilwell	Boatman	Unknown	3	1	"
Ireland	Educated		Not known	Ireland	5	1	"
Ohio	Not		"	"		1	"
Germany,	Educated	Henry and Catharine Shepner,	Laborer	Germany	4	1	"
Ohio	"	Wm. and Elizabeth Glass	Board'g h's	U. States,	1	1	"
Germany,	Not	Martin and Margaret Weber	Laborer	Germany	3	1	"
Ohio	"	Henry and Mary Brocksmith	Cooper	"	2	1	"
"	Educated	James and Jane McClelland	Farmer	Ireland	10		
New Yo'k	Not	John J. and Catharine April	Butcher	Germany	8	1	Cousins.
Ireland	Educated						
Vermont,	Not	Jonathan and Catharine Cotley,	Laborer	Ireland	1	1	None.
Germany,	"	Geo. and Catharine Hoffman					
Ohio	Educated	Ichabod and Susanna Clark	Farmer	N. Jersey,	6	1	None.

RETURN of the Number of Deaf, Dumb, Blind, Insane and Idiotic persons in

Names of Persons.	Nature of Affliction.	Duration of Affliction.	Cause Where Known.	Age.	Sex.	Color.	Occupation.
Ann Clark	Deaf and dumb,	....	Unknown	28	Male..	White.	None....
Danforth Ward	Idiotic	Unknown,	"	17	do ..	do	do ..
George Thompson	do	....	....	22	do ..	do	do
B. G. Turrill	do	Unknown,	Unknown	54	do ..	do	do
Albert Mann	do	....	"	14	do ..	do	do

the County of Hamilton, State of Ohio, on the second Monday of May, 1856.

Birth-place.	Educated or Not.	Names of Parents.	Occupation	Birth-place	No. children.	No. children thus afflicted.	Relationship of parents before Marriage
Ohio	Educated	John and Mary Emmons	Farmer	N. Jersey,	4	1	None.
"	Not	Morris and Polly Ward	....	"	3	1	"
"	"	Wm. and Fanny Thompson	Unknown	Not known	8	2	....
"	"	Jared and Hannah Turrill	....	"	4	1	None.
"	"	J. B. and Catharine Mann	Farmer	Ohio	7	1	"

RETURN of the number of Deaf and Dumb, Blind, Insane and Idiotic persons in

Names of persons.	Nature of Affliction.	Duration of Affliction.	Cause where known.	Age.	Sex.	Color	Occupation.
John W. Hagerman	Blind	7 years	Inflamation	11	Male	White	
Catharine Barst	Insane	8 months	Sickness	36	Fem'le	"	Farmer
Martha Curren	"	10 years	Trouble	64	Fem'le	"	
Peter Shoemaker	Deaf and Dumb	Life	Unknown	70	Male	"	Farmer
John V. Hineline	" "	"	"	32	Male	"	Farmer
Sarah Ann McGowan	" "	"	"	24	Fem'le	"	

the county of Hardin, State of Ohio, on the second Monday of May, 1856.

Birthplace.	Educated or not.	Names of Parents.	Occupation.	Birth-place.	No. Children	No. Children thus afflicted.	Relationship of Parents before marriage.
Richl'd co.	Not	Samuel Hagerman	Farmer	Ohio	9	1	None.
Penn	Educat'd	John and Elizabeth Liaper	Laborer	Unknown..	5	1	None.
Maryland .	Educat'd	....	....	....	..	..	
Virginia ..	Not	....	....	Virginia ..	12	6	
"	Partially	Redding Hineline........	Farmer	N. Jersey .	12	1	None.
Ohio	"	George & Rebecca Butcher	"	Virginia ..	6	3	None.

RETURN of the number of Deaf and Dumb, Blind, Insane and Idiotic persons in

Names of Persons.	Nature of Affliction.	Duration of Afflietion.	Cause where known.	Age.	Sex.	Color.	Occupation.
Transina Arnold	Blind	28 years	Nervous affec'n	80	Fem'le	White	Ordinary
James Smith	Idiotic	22 "	From birth	22	Male	do	None
George Smith	Idiotic	20 "	"	20	do	do	None
Ruth Ford	Dumb	12 "	By fever	20	Fem'le	do	None
Rachel Walker	Idiotic	18 "	By fits	26	do	do	None
Sophia Furney	Dumb		Not known	43	do	do	None
Mary Gillison	Deaf and dumb	From birth	"	42	do	do	Needlewk
William Hollowell	Idiotic	From inf'cy	Fits	27	Male	do	None
Robert C. Carrick	Dumb	"	Not known	9	do	do	None
Benjamin Blackwell	Deaf and dumb	From birth		21	do	do	Farming
Benjamin Ruby	Deaf and dumb	"		70	do	do	Farming
Thomas Jones	Blind	"		28	do	do	None
Mary Gutshall	Idiotic	5 years	Not known	55	Fem'le	do	Ordinary
Mary Dunlap	Idiotic	6 "		22	do	do	None
Samuel Dickerson	Idiotic	5 "	From a fall	10	Male	do	None
Benjamin Leizure	Insane	From birth		9	do	do	None
Martha Lowmiller	Insane	"		25	Fem'le	do	None
Benjamin Brindley	Insane			45	Male	do	None
Elizabeth McCullough	Idiotic	2 years	Not known	45	Fem'le	do	Milliner
Amos Hines	Idiotic	6 "	Not known	24	Male	do	Farming
Benjamin Conoway	Insane	From birth	From birth	35	do	do	

the County of Harrison, State of Ohio, on the second Monday of May, 1856.

Birth-place	Educated or not	Names of Parents	Occupation	Birth-place	No. Children	No. Children thus Afflicted	Relationship of parents before marriage
New York.	Educated	Timothy & Elizabeth Davis....	Farming ..	New Jersey	10	1	None ....
Ohio	Not.....	Wm. & Mrs. Smith...........	"	England ..	..	....	....
Ohio	Not.....	Wm. & Mrs. Smith...........	"	England ..	2	2	None ....
Ohio	Not.....	Lewis & Rebecca Ford........	"	Ohio	7	1	None ....
Ohio	Not.....	Wesley & Susan Walker	"	Ohio	5	1	"
Harrison co	Not.....	Patrick & Deborah Furney....	"	Maryland .	7	1	"
Virginia ..	Educated	Amos & Hannah Gillison	"	Virginia ..	5	1	"
Penn......	Not.....	Benjamin & Sarah Hollowell...	"	Penn......	9	1	"
Penn......	Not.....	James & Sarah Carrick ......'.	"	Penn......	10	1	"
Harrison co	Not.....	Wm. & Catharine Blackwell...	"	Virginia...	1	1	"
Harrison co	Not.....	Benjamin & Constan Ruby	"	Penn......	..	1	"
Jefferson co	Not.....	Elisha & Martha Jones........	"	Jefferson co	4	1	"
Maryland .	In Ger'n	Names not known............	"	Maryland .	..	....	Unknown
Harrison co	Educated	Robert & Mary Dunlap	"	Not given.	6	1	None ....
Harrison co	Not.....	J. Dickerson (mother's not given	"	Not given.	6	1	"
Harrison co	Not.....	B. Leizure (mother's not given.	"	Not given.	3	1	"
Harrison co	Not.....	Henry & Eve Lowmiller	"	Not given.	.	1	"
Maryland .	Not....	Benjamin & Ellen Brindley....	Wheelright	Maryland .	11	2	Not given
Jefferson co	Educated	Thomas & Jane Patton........	Farmer ...	Penn......	7	1	None ....
Ohio	Can read	Jacob & Susannah Hines......	"	Penn......	8	1	"
Ohio	Not.....	Charles & Francis Conaway...	"	Baltimore .	12	1	"

RETURN of the number of Deaf and Dumb, Blind, Insane and Idiotic persons in

Townships	Names of Persons	Nature of affliction	Duration of affliction	Cause where known	Age	Sex	Color	Occupation
Liberty	T. W. Huggins	Insane	Not known	Fits	40	Male	White	Merchant
"	Wm. Farris	"	From boy	Fits	40	"	"	Farming
"	Reb. Ashenfetter	"	Not known	Not known	39	Fem'le	Col	None
"	Sara Watts	Idiot	From birth		56	"	White	"
"	Mary V. Crum	Insane		Fits	18	"	"	"
"	Mary McMillen	Blind	7 years	Fever	76	"	"	"
"	John W. Lucas	Deaf and dumb	From birth		27	Male	"	
"	Coonrad Baker	Insane	30 years		51	"	"	Shoemakr
"	Menerva Cattan	Idiot	From birth		21	Fem'le	"	
"	Sarah Barrett	"	"		18	"	"	
"	James Flinn	Insane			14	Male	"	
"	John Earle	Idiot	From birth		11	"	"	
"	Abner Sinclair	Insane	6 years		26	"	"	Farming
NewMark't	John Hunter	"	10 "		63	"	"	"
"	Thomas Hunter	Idiot	From birth		45	"	"	None
"			"		40	"	"	None
Paint	Sarah Clark	Fits	30 years	Fright	39	Fem'le	"	None
"	Susan Copas	Fits	38 "	From birth	38	"	"	None
Brush Cr'k	Phebe Butters	Blind	46 years	Cataract	49	Fem'le	Whit	
"	Susan Franklin	Idiot	30 "		46	"	"	
Union	Mary Hart	Idiot	From birth		36	Fem'le	White	None
"	Daniel Drace	Blind	"		13	Male	"	None
Concord	M.Hestheringt'n	Idiot	"		9	Fem'le	White	None
White Oak	Reuben Fisher	Deaf and dumb	"		38	Male	White	Carpenter
"	George Lance	" "	From birth		28	"	"	Farming
"	John Lance	" "	"		33	"	"	"
"	E. Hardyshell	" "	"		34	Fem'le	"	Housek'pr
"	Jas. A. Haslan	" "	2 years	Diseasof heart	3	Male	"	
"	David Haman	Idiot	From birth		52	"	"	None
"	Mary A. Fender	Deaf and dumb	23 years	Fever	16	Fem'le	"	None
Madison	Robert Smith	Deaf	20 "	Over heat	70	Male	"	Farming
	James Tuthill	Blind	6 "	Hard lifting	95	"	"	"
Marshall	Alfred Skeen	"	12 "		22	"	"	"
"	J. Furmp	Deaf and dumb	9 "		10	"	"	
Clay	M. L. Bratton	Fits and Insane	20 "	Fright	22	"	"	
"	Mary J. Powers	Insane	18 "		24	Fem'le	"	None
"	Elizabeth Hall	"	10 "	Epilepsy	22	"	"	"
"	M. J. Waterlake	"	12 "	Not known	13	"	"	"
"	Sarah Parker	Deaf and dumb	18 "		18	"	"	"
"	N. J. Bingham	Insane	4 "	Fits	9	"	"	
Penn	Geo. Peckman	Deaf and dumb	From birth		3	Male	"	
"	J. C. Dunham	Deaf and dumb	30 years	Sickness	40	"	"	Shoemakr
"	Elen Crew	Idiot	From birth		9	Fem'le	"	

the County of Highland, State of Ohio, on the second Monday of May, 1856.

Birthplace.	Educated or not.	Names of Parents.	Occupation.	Birth-place.	No. Children.	No. children thus afflicted.	Relationship of parents before Marriage.
Brown co.	Educated	Not known					
Highl'd co.	"	E. Farris and Mary E. Mills.	Farming.	Va.& Irel'd	6	1	
Ross co...		G. Claybaugh and E. Becket	"	Virginia...	15	1	
S. Carolina	Educated	John Watts and Jane Arnold			7	4	
Highland.	"	John Crum		Virginia...		1	
Pa				Penn'a...			
Highland.	Not	A. Lucas and Sarah Kindle.	Farmer..	Highland.	8	1	First Cousins
	"	Jacob Baker & Susan Weyer	Shoemakr		5	2	
Highland.		John Cattin and Polly Woods	Merchant.		4	1	
		Thomas Barret	Farming.				
	Educated			Ireland...			
Highland.					1	1	
Butler co..	Educated						
Bedford Va	"	Elizabeth Sinclair	Farming.		8	..	None.
Ohio		Robert Hunter	"	Penn'a...	5	2	
"		Elizabeth Hunter	"	Penn'a...			
"	Not	Hosea and Sarah Clark	"	Virginia...			
"	"	Isaiah and Sarah Copas	"	"			Cousins.
Va	"	John and Sarah Butters	"				
Ohio	"	A. Franklin & Mary Nelson	"				
"	"	Joel and R. Hart	"	N. Carolina	8	1	Second Cous.
"	"		"	Kentucky.	7	1	Not related.
"	"	C. Hetherington	"	Ireland...	7	1	Cousins.
"	"	Peter and Dolly Fisher	Cabi'tmkr	Virginia..	6	2	Not known.
"	"	Not known			..	..	"
"	"						
"	"	Peter and Dolly Fisher	Cabi'tmkr	Virginia...			"
"	"	John and Elizabeth Haslen..	Wag.makr	Ohio	1	1	No relation.
"	"						
"	"	John and Catharine Fender..	Farming.	Ohio	9	1	No relation.
Penn	Educated	Wm. and Catharine	"	Penn'a...	10	..	"
Jersey	"	Daniel and Mary	Farming.		2	..	"
Highland.	Not	James and Elizabeth	Farming.	Virginia..	9	1	"
"	"	Joseph and Mary	Farming.	Delaware.	9	1	"
"	"	Joshua and Sarah Bratton...	"	Ohio & Va.	10	1	"
"	"	J. W. Powers	"	Virginia..	9	1	"
Brown, O.	Partly	Patrick and Mary Hall	"	"	10	1	"
"	Not	Walter Waterlake	"	Brown co.	7	1	"
N. Carolina	Not	James Parker	"	Europe...	6	1	"
Highland.	Not	S Bingman	"	Brown co.	5	1	"
"	Not	Peter and Maria	Shoemakr	Virginia..	9	1	"
Va	Educated	James F. Dunham	Black s'ith	"	7	1	
Highland.	Not	Nancy Crew		Ohio	5	1	Not known.

7—SEC. OF STATE.

RETURN of the number of Deaf and Dumb, Blind, Insane and Idiotic persons

Names of Persons.	Nature of Affliction.	Duration of Affliction.	Cause where known.	Age.	Sex.	Color.	Occupation.
Charles Lance........	Dumb.........	8 years..	Born.........	8	Male.	White.	None....
Gust. Fricker........	Deaf and dumb	25 do	do.........	25	do	do	t'lor & b'kr
Thomas Woltz........	do	43 do	do.........	43	do	do	Carpenter.
Elmira Smith........	Blind.........	17 do	Fright........	17	Fem'le	do	None....
Lucinda Garret.......	Idiotic........	16 do	Fits..........	16	do	do	do
Lawrence Bensonhaver.	do	30 do	do.........	30	Male.	do	None....
Rachel Bensonhaver...	do	34 do	do.........	34	Fem'le	do	do....
Joseph C. Moore......	Dumb........	20 do	Sickness......	28	Male.	do	Farming.
Margaret Swalley.....	do	16 do	do	16	Fem'le	do	None....
James Angle.........	Blind.........	53 do	Inflammation..	56	Male.	do	cab'nt mkr
Miss Silber..........	Idiotic........	17 do	Unknown.....	17	Fem'le	do	None....
H. F. Sisco..........	do	10 do	Fits..........	22	Male.	do	do....
Elizabeth Reel........	Deaf and dumb	34 do	Unknown.....	34	Fem'le	do	house w'rk
Frederick Shannich ...	Blind.........	8 do	do	65	Male.	do	None....
Peter Heft...........	do....	2 do	Old age.......	76	do	do	do

in the County of Hocking, State of Ohio, on the second Monday of May, 1856.

Birth-place.	Educated or not.	Names of Parents.	Occupation.	Birth-place.	No. children.	No. children thus afflicted.	Relationship of parents before marriage.
Ohio	Not	John Lance	Farmer	N. Jersey	5	1	None
do	Educated	——— Fricker	do	Ohio	5	3	Unknown
Virginia	Not	George Woltz	Jeweler	Virginia	7	1	None
Ohio	do	R. H. Smith	Farmer	Unknown	6	1	do
do	do	Isaac Garret	None	do	1	1	do
Germany	do	Lawrence Bensonhaver	Farmer	Germany	7	2	do
do	do	do	do	do	7	2	do
Ohio	Educated	Robert Moore	do	Penn	10	1	do
do	Not	John Swalley	do	do	9	1	do
Virginia	Educated	Henry Angle	Weaver	Germany	13	1	do
Germany	Not	John G. Silber	Farmer	do	6	1	do
Ohio	do	A. F. Scisco	do	Ohio	5	1	do
Germany	do	Henry Reel	Deceased	Germany	6	1	do
do	Educated	Unknown	do	do	..	1	do
Penn	do	do	do	Penn	..	1	do

RETURN of the number of Deaf and Dumb, Blind, Insane and Idiotic Persons

Townships.	Names of Persons.	Nature of affliction	Duration of Affliction.	Cause where known	Age.	Sex.	Color.
Walnut Creek	Susannah Miller...	Deaf..........	12 years...	Cold.........	14	Fem'le	White
"	Moses Hershberger.	Insane........	13 "	Unknown.....	35	Male..	do
"	Aaron Miller......	Deaf..........	40 "	Fits..........	43	do	do
"	Catharine Spicher..	Insane........	75 "	Fever.........	79	Fem'le	do
"	Johh Brenman.....	do	20 "	Unknown.....	49	Male..	do
Prairie.....	Dennis Beall......	Blind.........	16 "	Hurt by knife..	19	do	do
Paint.......	Simon Walpoldt ...	do	4 "	Fever.........	68	do	do
"	Margaret Koley....	Insane........	20 "	Unknown	44	Fem'le	do
Berlin	Rebecca Miller	do	16 "	Fever.........	19	do	do
Washington.	William Watchtel..	Idiotic........	20 "	Fits..........	24	Male..	do
Mechanic ...	John Wade	do	F'm inf'cy.	I'tempr'te father	35	do	do
"	Margaret Conrad...	Deaf and Dumb	"	Unknown.....	13	Fem'le	do
Killbuck ...	Jonn Canahan.....	Blind.........	49 years...	Sickness	50	Male..	do
"	Elizabeth Fortune..	Insane........	21 "	Unknown.....	21	Fem'le	do
Knox.......	Samuel Vance.....	do	22 "	"	61	Male..	do
"	James Jones	do	10 "	"	31	do	do
"	Frederick Kalar....	Idiotic........	23 "	....	23	do	do
Monroe	Eliz. Hutchinson ..	do	From birth	Fits	28	Fem'le	do
"	Easter Allison.....	Insane........	"	Unknown.....	33	do	do
"	Isabella Sansom ...	do	20 years...	"	74	do	do
"	William Sansom...	do	From birth	"	41	Male..	do
"	Jane Sansom......	do	"	"	38	Fem'le	do
"	Sarah Sansom	do	"	"	31	do	do
German	Christopher Barret.	Deaf and Dumb	"	"	40	Male	do
"	Cath'rine Levengood	Idiotic........	"	"	50	Fem'le	do
"	Jonathan Utzie	do	"	"	20	Male .	do
"	Barbara Utzie.....	do	"	"	18	Fem'le	do
"	Wm. Kline.........	do	"	"	6	Male .	do
"	A. McCormick.....	do	"	"	35	do	do
"	Elizabeth Burger ..	do	"	"	35	Fem'le	do
"	Sarah Olinger.....	do	"	"	50	do	do
"	Magdalena Lake...	Insane........	22 years..	Accouchment..	56	do	do

in the county of Holmes, State of Ohio, on the second Monday of May, 1856.

Occupation.	Birthplace.	Educated or not.	Names of Parents.	Occupation.	Birthprace.	No. children	No. children thus afflicted	Relationship of Parents before Marriage.
House work	Holmes co.	Not	Yost Miller..........	Farming ..	Holmes co.	1	1	....
Farmer ...	Ohio	Not	Christian Hershberger.	Farming ..	Penn	..	1	....
Shoemaker	Penn	Not	Daniel Miller........	Farming ..	Penn	7	1	....
House work	Penn	Not	Samuel Spicher......	Broomm'kr	Penn	1	1	....
Farmer ...	Europe ...	Not	Peter Brenman	Farming ..	Europe ...	7	1	....
Broomm'kr	Holmes co.	Educated	A. D. & Irena Beall	....	....	..	1	....
None	Germany..	Educated	S. and Roller Wolpoldt	Manufact'r.	Germany..	4	1	None.
"	Penn	Educated	J. and Susan Barkey..	Farming ..	Penn	15	1	"
"	Holmes co	Not ...	J. & Eliz. Miller......	Farming ..	Penn	3	1	....
"	Holmes co.	Not	Geo. & Mary Wachtel.	Farming ..	....	5	1	....
"	Maryland .	Not	B. and Rachel Wade.	Farming ..	Maryland .	4	, 1	....
"	Holmes co.	Not	J. C. & R. Conrad....	Farming ..	Penn	5	1	....
Farming ..	Virginia ..	Not	J. & Mary Canahan ..	Farming ..	Unknown .	6	1	None.
None	Ohio	Not	J. & Eliz. Fortune....	Farming ..	Penn.	4	1	"
Farming ..	Penn	Educated	John & Sarah Vance..	....	....	..	1	....
"	Ohio	Educated	John & Susan Jones..	Farming ..	Maryland .	6	1	None.
"	New York.	Not	H. & Melaney Kalar..	Farming ..	Germany...	..	1	"
None	Penn	Not	J. & Susan Hutchinson	Farming ..	....	..	1	"
"	Penn	Not	E. & Mary Allison ...	Farming ..	Pa. andMd.	9	1	"
"	Ireland ...	Educated	....	....	....	7	4	"
"	Penn	Not	....	....	....	..	..	....
"	Ohio	Not	....	....	....	..	..	....
"	Ohio	Not	....	....	....	..	..	....
Shoemaker.	Penn	Not	Not known..........	....	....	..	1	None.
None	Penn	Not	John Levengood......	Farming ..	Penn	11	1	"
"	Holmes co.	Not	Peter Utzie..........	Farming ..	Unk'own }	3	2	"
"	Holmes co.	Not	Peter Utzie..........	Farming ..	" }			
"	Holmes co	Not	John & Rosy Kline...	Farming ..	Holmes co.	4	1	None.
"	Holmes co.	Not	Jas. & Eliz McCormick	Not known	Penn	..	1	"
"	Holmes co	Not	Dan'l & Cath'e Burger.	Farming ..	Penn	10	1	"
"	Penn	Not	Christopher Olinger ..	Farming ..	Penn	..	1	"
"	Penn	Educated	Not known..........	Farming ..	Penn	..	1	"

RETURN of the number of Deaf and Dumb, Blind, Insane and Idiotic persons

Townships.	Names of persons.	Nature of Affliction	Duration of Affliction.	Cause where known	Age.	Sex.	Color.
Clarksfield.	John W. Vanator	Blind	10 years	Hard labor	32	Male.	White
	William Hunter	do	15 "	Unknown	22	do	do
	Thomas W. Justice	do	27 "	From birth	27	do	do
	Susan Justice	do	14 "	"	14	Fem'le	do
	Anda Anders'n Justice	do	9 "	"	9	Male.	do
Greenfield..	Albert Knapp	Idiotic	20 "	Fits	22	do	do
	James Jack	do	40 "	Unknown	40	do	do
	Westley Easter	do	21 "	Rickets	23	do	do
Hartland ..	William Carter	Blind	40 "	From birth	40	do	do
	Charles Bills	Deaf and dumb	9 "	"	9	do	do
	William Searls	do	46 "	"	46	do	do
	Harmon Bundy	Idiotic	17 "	"	17	do	do
New Haven	John Dubois	do	16 "	Fits	20	do	do
New London	James McClave, Jr., &	Deaf and dumb	31 "	Dropsy on brain	33	do	do
	his wife Elizabeth	do	19 "	Scarlet Fever	22	Fem'le	do
Norwalk...	William H. Powers	Idiotic	20 "	Unknown	22	Male.	do
	Angeline Peck	Deaf and dumb	44 "	Whoop'g cough	46	Fem'le	do
	Sophia Smith	Insane	30 "	By a fall	70	do	do
	Paul Slater	do	6 "	Liquor	67	Male.	do
	Henry Tompkins	do	6 "	Unknown	38	do	do
	Thomas Tillrow	do	5 "	"	27	do	do
	Inmate of co infirmary	do				do	do
	Luzetta Sampson	Idiotic	28 "	From birth	28	Fem'le	do
	Ella Ann Benham	do	15 "	"	15	do	do
	Luther Manahan	Blind	9 "	Inflammation	33	Male.	do
	Smith Jones	Idiotic	43 "	From birth	43	do	do
Norwich ...	Sally Ann Robinson	do	20 "	"	20	Fem'le	do
	Margaret Van Liew	Blind	10 "	Inflammation	59	do	do
	Esther Gregory	Insane	11 "	Unknown	38	do	do
	John W. Rice	Idiotic	8 months	Fits	14	Male.	do
	Alvin Friler	Insane	Unknown	Unknown		do	do
Peru	Jacob Stong	do	12 years	"	38	do	do
	Jacob Beverick	do	15 "	"	57	do	do
Richmond .	Charles Thompson	do	7 "	By fits	21	do	do
	William Davis	do	25 "	By rickets	35	do	do
	Mary Ann Slater	do	24 "	From birth	24	Fem'le	do
Ridgefield..	David Bennett	Deaf and dumb	19 "	"	19	Male.	do
	Henry Lewis	do	12 "	"	12	do	do
Ripley	Elizabeth Jones	Blind	15 "	"	15	Fem'le	do
	Samantha Jones	Partly blind	13 "	"	13	do	do
	Jacob Truxell	Deaf	7 "	Blow on head	60	Male.	do
	Frances B. Austin	Idiotic	23 "	From birth	23	Fem'le	do
Sherman...	Earnest Guyer	Deaf and Dumb	17 "	"	17	Male.	do
	Christian Guyer	do	15 "	"	15	do	do
Townsend .	William Babcock	Blind	25 "	Cataract	87	do	do
	Harry Kellog	Deaf and dumb		Unknown	57	do	do
	Mary G. Kellog his wife	do	46 years	Sickness	47	Fem'le	do

in the County of Huron, State of Ohio, on the second Monday of May, 1856.

Occupation	Birth-place	Educated or not	Names of Parents	Occupation	Birth-place	No. children	No. children thus affl'cted	Relationship of parents before marriage
Blacksm'h	Ohio	Educated	Ben. and S. Vanator	Farmer	Penna	2	1	None.
None	"	Not	Levi and A. Hunter	do	New York	9	1	do
"	"	do	Peter and L. Justice	Carpenter	Penna	9	3	do
"	"	do	do do	do	do	9	3	do
"	"	do	do do	do	do	9	3	do
"	"	do	Alfred and S. Knapp	Farmer	New York	5	1	2d cous.
"	Austria	do	Wm. and Mary Jack	Weaver	Sc'd & Ge'y	4	1	None.
"	"	do	—— Easter	Unknown	Ireland			do
Peddler	Vermont	Educated	John S. Carter & wife	Minister	Conn	7	1	
Unknown	Ohio		E. Bills and Wife	Farmer	do	6	1	
Farmer	Massa'etts	Educated	John Searls and wife	do	Massach'tts	4	1	
None	Ohio	Not	James Bundy and wife	do	Unknown	3	1	
"	"	do	Thos. J. and S. Dubois	do	N. Y. & Va	9	1	None.
Shoemak'r	New York	Educated	James and P. McClave	do	New York	10	1	de
"	"	do	Robert and L. Jackson	Merchant	do			
Unknown	Ohio		George and S. Powers	Farmer	Ct. and Pa.			
Dressmker	New York	Educated	Abijah and Polly Peck	Unknown	Ct.& N. Y.			
Unknown	Unknown		Unknown	do	Unknown			
Blacksm'h	Rh. Island	partly	do	do	do			
Farmer	New York	do	I. Tompkins and wife	Farmer	do			
"	Ohio	do	Thos. Tillrow and wife	do	do		2	
	Unknown		Unknown	Unknown	do			
Unknown	"	Not	do	do	do			
"	Ohio	do	Illegitimate	do	do			
Peddler	New York	Educated	Unknown	do	do			
Farmer	Connect'ot	partly	Nathan and C. Jump	do	do			
Unknown	New York	Not	E. and Ruth Robinson	Farmer	New York	4	1	Cousins.
Housekpr	"	Educated	Jacob and Maria Post	do	New Jersey	1	1	None.
"	"	do	Daniel and Mary Ellis	do	Unknown	9	1	do
Unknown	Ohio	Not	Hiram and Mary Rice	do	Vt. & N. Y.	5	1	do
Shoemakr.	Conn	Educated	Unknown	Unknown	Unknown.			
Farmer	Germany	do	do	do	do			
"	"	do	do	do	do			
None	Ohio	Not	Fred and M. Thompson	Farmer	do	9	1	None.
Wo'd ch pr	Penn	do	D. and Barbara Davis	Unknown	Penn a. \ .	5	1	do
Unknown	Ohio	do	John Slater and wife	do	Unknown			
"	"	Educated	John and S. Bennett.		Penn'a	9	1	None.
"	"	Not	Martin Lewis	do	Unknown.			
"	"	do	Sterling and P. Jones	Farmer	Connecticut	6	2	Cousins.
"	"	do	do do	do	do	6	2	do
Farmer	Penn	do	Wm. Truxell & wife	do	Penn'a			
Unknown	Ohio	do	Timothy Austin & wife	do	Mass	16	1	
Farmer	Germany	do	Christian & Eve Guyer	do	Germany	5	2	
"	"	do	do do	do	do	5	2	
"	Conn	do	Elijah and E. Babcock	Merchant	Connecticut	8		None.
"	Vermont	do	O. and Esther Kellog	Farmer	Unknown.	9		Cousins.
Unknown	"	Educated	N. and M. W. Griswold	do	Ct. & Mass	6	1	None.

RETURN of the number of Deaf and Dumb, Blind, Insane and Idiotic persons

Names of Persons.	Nature of Affliction.	Duration of Affliction.	Cause where known.	Age.	Sex.	Color.	Occupation.
Samuel Aten	Blind	3 years	Not known	50	Male	White	None
Margaret J. Evans	Deaf and dumb	16 "	Born so	16	Fem'le	do	"
Margar·t Davis	Deaf and dumb	16 "	Born so	16	"	do	"
James Davis	Idiotic	30 "	Born so	30	Male	do	"
Mary Price	Idiotic	45 "	Born so	45	Fem'le	do	"
John Rhadabaugh	in Tendency	6 "	Hereditary	21	Male	do	"
Henry Variann	Blind	1 "	Unknown	66	"	do	Farming
Charles B. Horton	Idiotic	8 "	Sickness	8	"	do	None
Margaret Buckley	Deaf	15 "	Sickness	29	Fem'le	do	"
Thomas J. Hale	Deaf and dumb	11 "	Not known	11	Male	do	"
Demson Steffler	Insane	14 "	Not known	18	"	do	"
David Williams	Blind	4 "	Cataract	24	"	do	"
David Mines	Deaf and dumb	25 "	Unknown	26	"	do	Farming
Hannah Crabtree	Deaf and dumb	45 "	Cold plague	47	Fem'le	do	None
Rosanna Wishon	Deaf and dumb	13 "	Not known	13	"	do	"
Robert H. Ford	Idiotic	15 "	Not known	15	Male	do	"
Sarah Ford	Idiotic	From birth	Not known	17	Fem'le	do	"
Wm. Steele	Deaf	4 years	Measels	7	Male	do	"
John Harding	Blind	16 "	Fever	53	"	do	Bookseller
Sarah Scott	Dumb and lame	From birth	Unknown	14	Fem'le	do	None
David Storer	Idiotic	8 years	Sickness	21	Male	do	"
Wm. W. Thorn	Deaf	17 "	Scarlet fever	23	"	do	"
Jane Martin	Deaf and dumb	50 "	Not known	70	Fem'le	do	"
Seline Craig	Blind	21 "	Infla'n of brain	22	"	do	bead work
Hamilton Stephenson	Deaf and Dumb	36 "	Unknown	36	Male	do	None
Ephraim Nickell	Blind	11 "	Sore eyes	14	"	do	"
Nancy Hawk	Insane	7 "	Unknown	40	Fem'le	Black	"

in the county of Jackson, State of Ohio, on the second Monday of May, 1856.

Birth-place	Educated or not.	Names of Parents.	Occupation.	Birth-place	No. Children.	No. Children thus Afflicted	Relationship of parents before marriage.
Penn......	Educated	Samuel Aten & Marga't Carmon	Farming..	Penn-.....	10	1	None ....
Ohio	Not	David & Mar. Evans..........	"	Wales			
Ohio	"	Morgan & Mary Davis........	"	Wales			
Ohio	"	Samuel & Elizabeth Davis.....	"	Virginia ..			
Wales	"	James & Latilda Price........	"	Wales			
Ohio	"	Geo. & Mary Rhadabaugh.....	"	Virginia..			
Germany..	"	....	....	Germany..			
Ohio	"	Lewis & Anna Horton	Farming..	Ohio	8	1	1st cousi's
Ohio	Educated	Wm. & Elizabeth Buckley.....	"	Virginia ..	10	1	None ....
Ohio	Not	G. W. & Mary Hale...........	"	Virginia ..	12	1	" ....
Ohio	Not	Paul & Mary Steffler.........	"	Ohio	9	1	" ....
Wales	Educated	Thomas & Eliza Williams.....	"	Wales	5	1	" ....
Ohio	"	Robert & Anna Mines.........	"	Virginia ..	7	1	" ....
Ohio	Not	Jas. & Hannah Crabtree......	"	Penn.......	3	1	" ....
Ohio	"	Wm. & Olive	"	Ohio	3	1	" ....
Kentucky .	"	R. H. Ford	Shoemaker	Virginia ..	4	2	" ....
Kentucky .	"	Sarah Ford..................	"	Virginia ..			
Ohio	"	Wm. B. & Julia Steele........	Farmer ...	Virginia ..	6	1	None ....
England ..	Educated	....	"	England ..	7		
Penn......	Not	J. Scott Vesey	"	Penn.......	5	1	None ....
Ohio	Educated	....	....	....	7	1	
Ohio	"	....	..-.......	....	5	1	
France....	"	....	....	....	4	1	
Ohio	"	Martha & S. Craig...........	....	Virginia ..	7	1	
Ohio	Not	Jas. & Margaret Stephenson....	Farmer ...	Virginia ..	8	1	None ....
Ohio	"	Alex. & Phœbe Nickell........	"	Virginia ..	6	1	
Virginia...	"	....	....	....			

RETURN of the number of Deaf and Dumb, Blind, Insane and Idiotic persons

Names of Persons.	Nature of Affliction.	Duration of Affliction	Cause where known.	Age.	Sex.	Color.	Occupation.
Benjamin T. Shaw...	Deaf and Dumb	11 years	Sickness......	12	Male	White	None......
Francis R. Shaw	do	3 do	Unknown.....	3	do	do	do
Mary Kelly........	Blind.........	9 do	Inflammation..	9	Female	do	do
Ann Jane Braden	do	25 do	Str'ck wth stone	30	do	do	do
Eve Myers..........	do	17 do	Cataract......	90	do	do	do
Alexander Scott	Idiot	18 do	Unknown.....	23	Male..	do	do
James Carman	Insane........	3 months	do	53	do	do	Shoemaker..
Dorsey Crail........	do	16 do	Medicine......	18	do	do	do
Samuel Holmes......	Deaf and Dumb	60 years	Unknown.....	60	do	do	Grocer......
Perry Kirkpatrick....	Insane........	10 do	do	34	do	do	None ......
Cutler Salmon	do	17 do	Intoxication....	54	do	do	Butcher ....
William T. McAdams.	do	7 do	Fits...........	8	do	do	None ......
David Laughlin......	Blind..........	6 do	Cataract	77	do	do	Farmer .....
James Norton........	Insane........	45 do	Unknown.....	60	do	do	do
Margaret Campbell ...	do	26 do	do	26	Female	do	None......
Edward Price........	do	48 do	do	48	Male.	do	Farmer.....
Jane Price..........	do	50 do	do	50	Female	do	None......
Benjamin M. Markle..	do	25 do	do	25	Male..	do	do
Calvin Close........	Blind.........	17 do	....	24	do	do	Broom maker
George Close........	do	5 do	....	10	do	do	None......
Mary Hamilton.......	Insane........	25 do	Fits..........	28	Female	do	do
Robert Mills.........	do	21 do	Unknown.....	80	Male..	do	Farmer.....
James McClain......	Deaf and Dumb	33 do	Fever.... ..	40	do —	do	do
Robert Cameron......	Idiot.........	23 do	....	23	do	do	None......
Achsah Cole........	do	26 do	....	40	Female	do	....
Homer Douglass	do	8 do	....	8	Male..	do	do
Dorcas Rutledge	Blind.........	2 do	....	55	Female	do	do
Martin Twaddle	do	43 do	....	43	Male .	do	Miner.....
Andrew Twaddle....	do	45 do	....	45	do	do	Farmer ....
Phœbe Ann Taylor...	do	23 do	....	23	Female	do	....
Benjamin Taylor	do	19 do	....	19	Male..	do	Farmer....
John Twaddle......	do	49 do	....	49	do	do	do
Reuben Carpenter	Insane........	5 months	....	43	do	do	Tailor......
Rachel Ann Clark....	Blind........	5 years..	....	9	Female	do	None......
William Paisley	Idiot	33 do	....	33	Male..	do	do
Joseph D. Bates......	Deaf and Dumb	60 do	Fever........	65	do	do	Farmer.....
Martha McCormack ..	Insane........	14 do	....	60	Female	do	....
Joshua Shoenesee	do	9 do	Nervous Fever.	34	Male..	do	Farmer.....
Samuel Jones........	do	27 do	Fits..........	33	do	do	....
Drusilla Wheeler	do	2 do	Unknown.....	44	Female	do	....
Elizabeth Laird......	do	Unkno'n.	do	64	do	do	....
Kinsey Scott	Deaf and Dumb	4 years	do	4	Male..	do	....
John Scott..........	do	34 do	do	45	do	do	Farmer.....
Alex. McConnell	Insane........	20 do	do	35	do	do	None......
Joshua Bennett......	do	10 do	Epilepsy......	35	do	do	Tailor......
Susannah Watkins ..	do	f'm inf'cy	Fright........	40	Female	do	....
Thomas Lewis	Idiot	12 years.	Unknown......	12	male..	do	....
Elizabeth Barrett.....	Blind.........	12 do	do	79	Female	Black.	....
William Lekins......	Idiot.........	23 do	do	24	Male..	do	Farmer.....
Israel Cox..........	do	20 do	do	20	do	White.	None......
Wm. J. Taylor......	Deaf and Dumb	14 do	Fits..........	16	do	do	Farmer.....
James Ekey	Idiot..........	16 do	Sickness......	17	do	do	....
Samuel Tubble......	do	9 do	Intemperance..	47	do	do	Farmer.....
Ann Jones..........	do	15 do	....	65	Female	do	....
Abner England......	do	35 do	....	35	Male..	do	....
Henry Ross	do	....	....	22	do	do	....
Owens Merrill	do	....	....	38	do	do	....
Reeoe Lupton........	do	....	....	24	do	do	....

in the County of Jefferson, State of Ohio, on the second Monday of May, 1856.

Birthplace.	Educated or not.	Names of Parents.	Occupation.	Birthplace.	No. of child'n	No. of child'n thus afflicted	Relationship of parents before marriage.
Ohio	Not	Alfred and Rachel Shaw	Sadl.tr. m'r	Ohio & Va.	4	2	None.
do	do	do do	do	do	4	2	do
do	do	James and Mary Kelly	Cabinetm'r	Ohio	4	1	do
Penn.	Educated	Samuel and Sarah Braden	Farmer	Penn.	1	1	do
Delaware	do	Jacob and Belijah Figley	do	Ger. & Del.	11	1	do
Ohio	Can read	John and Nancy Scott	do	Penn.	10	1	1st cousins
do	Not	Nath. and Elizabeth Carman	Saddler	New Jersey	8	1	None.
do	Educated	Joseph and Elleanor Crail	Shoemaker	Ohio	9	1	do
Ireland	do	John Holmes	Farmer	Ireland	3	1	Not known
Ohio	do	Samuel and Mary Kirkpatrick	Carpenter	New Jersey	9	1	None.
Virginia	do	Samuel and Catherine Salmon	Farmer	Unknown	9	1	do
Ohio	Not	John and Hannah McAdams	Carpenter	Ohio	15	1	do
Ireland	Educated	Robert and Mary Laughlin	Farmer	Ireland	8	3	do
Penn.	do	Thomas and Sarah Norton	do	do	10	2	do
Ohio		Alex. and Elizabeth Campbell	do	America	3	1	do
Penn.	Not	Edward and Nancy Price	do	Ireland	7	2	do
do	do	do do	do	do	7	2	do
Ohio	do	Abram and Rachel Markle	do	Penn.	15	1	do
do	Educated	Jacob and Mary Close	Carpenter	Ohio & Md.	6	2	do
do	Not	do do	do	do	6	2	do
do	do	Wm. and Mary Hamilton	Farmer	Penn.	6	1	do
Penn.	Educated	Unknown			5	1	
Ohio	do	James and Clarissa McLain	Farmer	N. J. & Pa.	12	1	None.
Virginia	Not	David and Elizabeth Cameron	Hotel ke'pr		2	1	do
Ohio	Educated	Thomas Cole	Farmer	Maryland		1	Unknown.
do	Not	Thompson Douglass	Gunsmith	Ohio		1	None.
do	Educated	Unknown	Farmer	do			
do	Not	John and Mary Twaddle	do	Penn.	10	6	None.
do	do	do do	do	do	10	6	do
do	do	Edward and Jane Taylor	do		5	2	1st cousins
do	do	do do	do		5	2	do
do	do	John and Mary Twaddle	do	Penn.	10	6	None.
England	Educated	Daniel and Sophia Carpenter	Clothier	England	6	1	do
Ohio	Not	James and Rachel Clark	Farmer	Ohio	11	1	1st cousins
do	do	Simon and Nancy Paisley	Cooper	Penn.	1	1	None.
Virginia	Educated	James and Ann Bates	Farmer		5	1	
Penn.	do	Robert and Mary McCormack			4	1	
Ohio	do	Jas. and Rebecca Shoeneesee					
do	Not	Joseph and Jane Jones					
do	Educated	Thos. and Rose Ann Wheeler			5	1	
Unknown	do	Benjamin Wheeler					
Ohio	Not	Levi and Levina Scott	Farmer	Maryland	16	1	
Ireland	Educated	Unknown					
Penn.	Not	do					
Ohio	Educated	Samuel and Rebecca Bennett					
Virginia	Not	John W. and Susannah Watkins	Farmer	Virginia	7	1	
Ohio	do	Griffin and Elizabeth Lewis	do	Ohio	6	1	None.
Penn.	Educated						
Ohio	Partly	Jacob and Susan Lickens	Farmer	Maryland	2	2	None.
do	Not	Israel and Margaret Cox	do	Ohio	12	1	do
do	do	Hiram and Eliza Taylor	do	do	11	1	do
	do	Peter and Margaret Ekey	do				do
Penn.	Educated				6	1	
Maryland	do						
Ohio		Israel and Ann England	Farmer	Ohio			None
do							
do							
do		Henry and Achsah Lupton	Farmer				

RETURN of the number of Deaf and Dumb, Blind, Insane and

Names of Persons.	Nature of Affliction	Duration of Affliction.	Cause where known	Age.	Sex.	Color.	Occupation.
Barney Mathers	Idiot	....	....	12	Male .	White.	....
Robert Fielding	do	....	....	13	"	do	....
Betsey Bell	do	....	....	16	Fem'le	do	....
Peter Barnet	Deaf	....	....	65	Male .	Mulat.	....
John Carter	Idiot	....	....	..	....	Black.	....
Haley Simmons	do	....	....	20	Fem'le	White	....
Alexander Scott	do	....	....	23	Male	do	....
Jane Boyd	do	9 years ..	....	28	Fem'le	do	....

Idiotic persons in the County of Jefferson, State of Ohio,—Continued.

Birthplace.	Educated or not.	Names of Parents	Occupation.	Birthplace.	No. of child'n	No. thus Afflicted.	Relationship of parents before marriage.
Ohio							
do		Joseph Fielding					None.
do							
Virginia							
Ohio							
do							
do		John Scott					Cousins.
do							

RETURN of the Number of Deaf and Dumb, Blind, Insane and Idiotic persons

Townships	Names of Persons.	Nature of Affliction.	Duration of Affliction.		Cause Where Known.	Age.	Sex.	Color.
Jackson	Charles Sargeant	Insane	9	years	Fits	11	Male	White.
"	Jonathan Phillips	"	12	"	"	13	"	do
Union	Jacob Hartman	"	6	"	"	7	"	do
"	Margaret Dunlap	Blind	20	"	Sickness	31	Fem'l.	do
"	Mi ton Stull	Insane	10	"	Fits	14	Male	do
Brown	Sarah Jane Keim	Deaf and dumb	13	"	Scarlet Fever	16	Fem'le	do
"	Peggy Bluebaugh	Idiotic	56	"	Unknown	50	"	do
Clay	Elizabeth Conway	"	F'm infau'y		"	29	"	Fair.
"	Esther Barnes	Deaf and dumb	"		"	36	"	White.
Harrison	Molly Welker	"	"		"	70	"	do
"	Charlotte Welker	"	"		"	60	"	do
"	Anna Welk+r	"	"		"	55	"	do
"	Barbara Welker	"	"		"	40	"	do
Monroe	Leonora Daymude	Partly deaf	8	years	"	13	"	do
"	James Vian	Idiotic	20	"	Supposed Fits	20	Male	do
"	James Carter	"	13	"	"	14	"	do
Pike	Wm. Whisler	"	23	"	Fever	23	"	do
"	Elizabeth Hammel	Deaf	20	"	"	20	Fem'le	do
"	Jacob Long	"	14	"	"	17	Male	do
"	George Pealer	Dumb	13	"	Unknown	13	"	do
Berlin	Isaiah Mock	Deaf	22	"	Scarlet Fever	30	"	do
Morris	Sanford P. Durbin	Idiotic	8	"	Unknown	9	"	do
Clinton	Elizabeth Webb	Deaf and dumb	F'm Infan'y		"	39	Fem'le	do
Mt. Vernon	Daniel G. Johnson	"	Unknown		"	41	Male	do
"	Eliza Johnson	"	"		"	39	Fem'le	do
"	Alexand r Elliott	"	"		"	37	Male	do
Milford	Washington Read	Idiotic	28	years	Affliction	32	"	do
"	Eli Ford	"	23	"	Unknown	62	"	do
"	James W. Donally	Dumb	6	"	Affliction	6	"	do
"	Andrew Atherton	Insane	6	months	"	50	"	do
"	William Bishop, jr	Idiotic	14	years	"	24	"	do
"	Sarah Ports	Insane	1	"	"	5	Fem'le	do
"	Anna Long	"	20	"	Unknown	68	"	do
"	Anna E. Coe	Idiotic	17	months	Affliction		"	do

in the County of Knox, State of Ohio, on the second Monday of May, 1856.

Occupation.	Birth-place.	Educated or not.	Names of Parents.	Occupation.	Birth-place.	No. Children	No. Childre. thus afflicted	Relationship of parents before marriage.
None	Musking'm	Not	George Sargeant,	Farmer	Champain	6	1	Not rela.
do	Knox co	"	Moses Phillip	"	Not given	12	1	"
do	Holmes co.	"	John and Hester Hartman	"	Germany.	7	1	"
Nd'le wk	Knox co	Educat'd	Joseph and Sarah Dunlap	"	Maryland	9	1	"
None	"	Not	Samuel Stull,	Gun smith	Ohio	9	1	"
At scho'l	"	Educat'd	D. Keim & Catha. Candle	Farmer	Pennsyl'a	9	1	2d Cous.
None	Maryland	Not	J. Bluebaugh & A Legston	Shoemak'r	Maryland	10	1	Not rela.
do	Knox co	"	Sam. & Lucinda Conway	Farmer	New York	3	1	"
Seamst's	Coshocton	"	H. and Esther Barnes	Far & m'c.	Ireland	8	3	"
do	Virginia	"	Wandal Welker)					
do	"	"	and					
do	"	"	Mary Welker.)	Farmer	Unknown		4	Not giv.
do	"	"						
None	Knox co	Educat'd	H. and Hannah Daymude	Farmer	Virginia	5	1	Not rela.
do	"	Not	William and Jane Vian	"	Maryland	14	1	Cousins.
do	"	Educat'd	John Carter	"	"	8	1	2d Cous.
do	Michigan	Not	Samuel & Hannah Whisler	"	Pennsyl'a	12	1	Not rela.
do	Stark co	"	Joseph and Sarah Hammel	"	"	3	1	"
do	Ohio	"	David and Margaret Long	"	"	11	2	"
do	"	"	Samuel and Sarah Pealer	"	Michigan	1	1	"
Laborer	Knox co	"	J. hn and Mary Mock	"	Pennsyl'a	8	1	"
None	"	"	John and Sarah Durbin	"	Ohio & Pa	13	1	"
Tailoress	Adams co	Educat'd	Osborn & Elizabeth Webb	"	N. J. & Pa	12	1	"
Baskt mr	Unknown	"	Not given	Not given	Not given	4		Not giv.
Housewk	"	"	"	"	"			"
Painter	"	"	"	"	"			"
None	Ohio	Not	H. and Elizabeth Read	Farmer	N. J. & Pa	12	1	"
do	Connecticut	Educat'd	Eli and Maraba Ford	"	Con. & Pa.	3	1	"
do	Ohio	Not	W. D. & Letty Donnelly	Mechanic	Ohio & Pa	5	1	Not giv.
Not gv'n	Pennsylva	Educat'd	F. and Nancy Atherton	Farmer	Not given	5	1	Cousins.
do	Ohio	"	Arnold & Matilda Bishop	"	R. I. & Va	10	1	Not rela.
do	Maine	"	Arenia and Sarah Knight	"	Maine	15	1	"
do	Unknown	Not	Not given	"	Unknown			
do	Ohio	"	David & Elizabeth Coe	"	Maryland	5	1	Cousins.

RETURN of the number of Deaf and Dumb, Blind, Insane and Idiotic persons

Names of Persons.	Nature of affliction.	Duration of affliction.	Cause where known.	Age.	Sex.	Color.	Occupation.
Phœbe Winters	Idiotic	32 years	Fits	33	Fem'le	White	None
E. M. Wood	Deaf and dumb	13 do	Measles	14	do	do	do
Ichabod Adams	Blind	22 do	Ulcers	29	Male	do	Br'm mk'r
Hannah Burns	Idiotic	30 do	Fits	36	Fem'le	do	None
Caroline Cole	do	17 do		17	do	do	do
W. Hitchcock	Deaf and dumb	19 do		19	Male	do	do
Nathan Whipple	do	62 do	Canker rash	64	do	do	do
James O. Jacobs	Blind	5 do	Inflammation	61	do	do	Peddler
Polly Walker	Insane	30 by spells	Not known	59	Fem'le	do	....
James Daniels	Deaf and dumb	45 do	do	45	Male	do	Laborer
Deborah Chapin	Insane	3 do	do	64	Fem'le	do	....
Hannah Searl	do	10 do	do	41	do	do	....
W. W. Davis	Deaf and dumb	5 do	Inflammation	6	Male	do	....
Charles W. Young	do	40 do	Not known	40	do	do	Pump mkr
Clarissa Moore	do	56 do	do	56	Fem'le	do	Tailoress
Milo S. Blair	Idiotic	22 do	Fits	32	Male	do	None
R. Rockafellow	do	14 do	do	14	Fem'le	do	do
Lucy Done	Insane	10 do	Unknown	34	do	do	do

in the county of Lake, State of Ohio, on the second Monday of May, 1856.

Birth-place.	Educated or not.	Names of Parents.	Occupation.	Birth-place.	No Children.	No. Children thus afflicted.	Relationship of Parents before Marriage
N. Jersey.	Not.....	Henry and Sally Winters......	Deceased..	N. Jersey.	3	1	None....
Ohio.....	At school.	Elisha and Polly Wood.......	Farmer...	New York.	7	1	do
do	Partially.	Ichabod and Polly Adams....	do	Massachus.	12	1	do
Penn.....	Not.....	James and Abbey Burns......	do	Pa. & N. J.	6	1	do
New York.	do	Rufus and Mahala Cole......	do	New York.	5	1	do
Ohio.....	do	John B. and Julia Hitchcock..	do	do	4	1	do
N. Hamp..	do						
New York.	do						
N. Hamp..	Common.	William and Judy Rowe......	Blacksmith	Not known	7	1	do
Ireland...	Not.....						
Massachus.	Common.	O. Turney and Deborah Phelps	Farmer...	Connectic't	9	1	do
New York.	do	H. Brown and Chloe Bunis....	do	Massachus.	13	1	do
Ohio.....	Not.....	J. Davis and Caroline Carle....	Carpenter.	Ohio.....	5	1	do
N. Hamp..	Educated	Abiather and Sally Young....	Farmer...	N. Hamp..	5	1	do
Massachus.	do	John and T. Morse...........	do	Massachus.	4	1	do
do	Not.....	A. and E. Blair..............	do	do	5	1	do
New York.	do	Wm. and Alice Rochafellow....	do	New York.	4	1	do
do	Educated	S. and A. Francis............	do	Connectic't	5	5	do

?—REP. SEC'Y. STATE.

RETURN of the number of Deaf and Dumb, Blind, Insane and Idiotic persons

Names of Persons.	Nature of Affliction.	Duration of affliction.	Cause where known.	Age.	Sex.	Color.	Occupation.
Christian Brown, jr....	Deaf and dumb	6 years..	Sickness......	7	Male..	White	None....
James Henry Lambert..	do	Not known	Unknown.....	10	"	"	" ....
Theresa Coleman.....	Idiotic........	From birth.	do	22	Female	"	" ....
Mary Mowry.........	Blind..........	18 years..	do	64	"	"	" ....
August Cook.........	do	10 do	Small Pox.....	14	Male..	"	Musician
Polly Drummond.....	Insane........	16 do	Unknown.....	37	Female	"	None....
Tabitha Joseph.......	Idiotic........	From birth.	do	22	"	"	" ....
William Joseph.......	do	do	do	12	Male..	"	" ....
James Spradling......	Blind..........	14 years..	Fever and ague	31	"	"	" ....
Jonathan Massie......	Deaf and dumb	From birth.	Unknown.....	60	"	"	Farmer..
Lavinia Massie......	Blind..........	do	do	20	Female	"	None....
Genetta Massie........	do	do	do	12	"	"	" ....
Harriet Christ.........	Idiotic........	do	do	12	"	"	" ....
Madison Ailce s r......	do	do	do	17	Male..	"	" ....
Mary Snyder.........	do	do	do	34	Female	"	" ....
James Madison Lewis..	do	11 years..	do	12	Male..	"	" ....
Robert Scotland	Insane........	20 do	Blow on head..	50	"	"	Seaman..
William Perry Scott...	Deaf and dumb	9 do	Scarlet fever...	11	"	"	None....
Margaret Bates	Idiotic........	From birth	Unknown.....	24	Female	"	" ....
Price Smith	Insane........	8 months.	Reverse fortune	50	Male..	"	Farmer..
Emerzetta Whitehead..	Deaf and dumb	From inf'cy	Whooping c'gh.	13	Female	"	None....
Clarisa Dillon	do	5 years..	Unknown......	5	"	"	" ....
James Nance..........	do	30 do	do	30	Male..	"	Farmer..
Dewit Rucker	Dumb Idiot ...	21 do	do	21	"	"	None....
Nancy Rucker........	do	30 do	do	30	Female	"	" ....
Adaline Olincatto	Idiot	14 do	do	14	"	"	" ....
John W. Dillon.......	do	6 do	do	6	Male..	"	" ....
Jacob Younkin	Blind..........	10 months.	Supposed cold.	37	"	"	Laborer..
Thomas Cozens.......	Deaf and dumb	12 years..	do	16	"	Colo'd	" ..

in the county of Lawrence, State of Ohio, on the second Monday of May, 1856.

Birthplace.	Educated or not.	Names of Parents.	Occupation.	Birthplace.	No. children	No. children thus afflicted.	Relationship of Parents before Marriage.
Ohio	Not	Christian Y. and M. J. Brown	Farmer	Ohio	10	1	None.
do	do	Richard and Cynthia Lambert	do	do	6	1	do
Germany		Unknown	None.	Germany		1	Unknown.
do	Educated	do	do	do	5	1	do
do	do	William and —— Cook	Laborer	do	5	1	do
Ohio	do	Armstrong and —— Rankin	None	Unknown	3	1	do
do	Not	Phillip and Mary Joseph	Farmer	Virginia		2	do
do	do	do do	do	do		2	do
do	do	Pleasant and Agnes Spradling	do	Unknown		1	do
Virginia	do	Robert and Mary Massie	do	Virginia	9	2	2d cousins
Ohio	do	Thomas and Abigal Massie	do	do	6	2	1st. do
do	do	do do	do	do	6	2	do
do	do	Peter W. and Maria Ghrist	do	Penn	3	1	None.
do	do	John and Mary Ailcessor	do	Eu'pe & O.	4	1	do
Virginia	do	Henry and Mary Snyder	do	Europe	4	1	do
Ohio	do	Wallace and Alvira Lewis	do	Virginia	5	1	do
Scotland	Educated	Unknown	Unknown	Scotland			Unknown.
Ohio	Not	Perry and Lucinda Scott	Machinist	Ohio	2	1	None.
do	do	Moses and Elizabeth Bates	Unknown	Unknown		1	do
Virginia	do	Augustin and Sarah Smith	Farmer	Virginia		1	do
Ohio	do	Samuel and Martha Whitehead	Blacksmith	do		1	do
do	do	J. W. and Catharine Dillon	Farmer	do	4	1	do
do	do	Elijah and Mary Nance	do	do	4	1	1st cousin.
do	do	Mordica and Susanna Rucker	do	do	6	2	None.
do	do	do do	do	do	6	2	do
Penn	do	Isaac and Leah Clincatto	do	Penn	5	1	do
Ohio	do	Seymore and Mary Dillon	do	Ohio	3	1	do
Penn	Educated	Henry and Mary Younkin	Laborer	Unknown		1	Unknown.
Ohio	Not	Henry and Susan Cozens	do	do		1	do

116

RETURN of the Number of Deaf and Dumb, Blind, Insane and Idiotic persons

Townships.	Names of Persons.	Nature of Affliction.	Duration of Affliction.	Cause where known.	Age.	Sex.	Color.
Hopewell..	Nicholas Rible.......	Blind.........	23 years..	Accident......	79	Male .	White.
"	Addison Feagans....	Deaf and dumb	34 "	Sickness......	42	"	do
"	Thomas Richardson..	Insane........	40 "	Fits..........	40	"	do
"	Benj. Richardson.....	"	38 "	....	38	"	do
"	Christal Richardson..	"	25 "	....	25	Fem'le	do
"	Mary Morrison.......	Blind.........	9 "	Unknown	73	"	do
Hanover ..	Lavina Hoyt	Idiotic.........	10 "	Fr m birth....	10	"	do
"	Joseph Francis.......	"	16 "	Kick from horse	23	Male .	do
"	Anderson Francis....	"	16 "	Unknown......	16	"	do
"	William Francis.....	"	13 "	"	13	"	do
McKean ..	Lucy E Peaslee......	Insane........	14 "	....	61	Fem'le	do
Fallsburg..	Reuben Rakestraw...	"	7 "	Unknown......	8	Male .	do
"	Franklin Martin.....	"	8 "	" "	8	"	do
"	James Thacker......	"	43 "	" "	43	"	do
"	Jackson John........	"		Fits..........	56	"	do
Eden......	Cynthia Priest.......	Deaf and dumb	22 "	Not known....	24	Fem'le	do
"	J. Wesley Priest.....	Idiotic........	13 "	Sickness......	16	Male .	do
"	Samuel Lyons	Deaf and dumb,	24 "	Measles	27	"	do
Mary Ann.	Joseph H. Smith.....	Deaf and dumb,	30 "	By a fall	33	"	do
"	David Debewise	Dumb	From birth,	Not known....	10	"	do
"	Jane Glover	Insane........	6 years..	"	67	Fem'le	do
"	David Moore	Deaf and dumb,	From birth,	"	12	Male	do
"	Joseph Wilkin......	Dumb	"	Rickets	24	Male .	do
"	John Dornan........	Idiotic........		....	42	"	do
Franklin ..	Joshua Wolf........	Dumb	21 years..	Sore mouth....	23	Fem'le	do
"	Mary Lacy	Insane........	7 "	....	30	Fem'le	do
"	Elizabeth Parr.......	Idiotic........	32 "	....	32	Male .	do
Burlington,	John Wheeler........	Blind.........	6 "	Inflammation..	30	Ma.e..	do
"	Homer Houck........	Deaf.........	14 "	....	22	Male..	do
"	Wm. Haines........	Idiotic........	From birth,	....	36	Male .	do
"	Mary Chapman	Blind.........	30 years..	From a hurt...	81	Fem'le	do
Newark...	Julius C. Pier........	Deaf and dumb,	21 "	Measles	22	Male..	do
"	Henry Scott........	"	28 "	....	28	do ..	Black
"	Thomas J. Christian..	Idiotic........	From birth,	....	12	do	White.
Granville .	Joseph Rodgers......	do	"	....	37	do	do
"	Ann M. Starr	Deaf and dumb,	43 years..	....	45	Fem'le	do
"	Albert B. Showman,	Idiotic........	From birth,	....	9	Male .	do
"	Wm. M. Gaver......	Deaf	2 years..	....	23	do	do
"	John Ridenow.......	do	1 "	....	74	do	do
"	Elizabeth A. Simpkins	do	30 "	....	69	Fem'le	do
"	Adam Stonebraker...	do	From birth,	Scarlet Fever..	55	Male..	do
"	Henry Batthias	do	25 years..	....	41	Male..	do
"	Elizabeth Cable.....	Blind	8 "	....	68	Fem'le	do
Harrison ..	Obadiah Scott, jr.....	Insane........	28 "	Sickness......	50	Male .	do
"	Thomas Tunison.....	Idiotic........	22 "	....	22	do	do
St. Albans,	Lorenzo Harrison	Deaf and dumb,	23 "	....	23	do	do
"	William Mason......	Idiotic........	20 "	Fits	40	do	do
Liberty....	Geo. Stockbarger.....	Deaf and dumb,	From birth,	....	40	"	do
Monroe ...	Isaac Moore........	Blind.........	3 years..	Inflammation..	70	Male..	do
"	Sarah Ridgeway.....	Insane........	5 months,	Spiritualism...	70	Fem'le	do
"	Alfred Phillbrook....	do	35 years..	Hereditary ...	35	Male..	do
Lima	Olivea Whitehead....	do	10 "	Fits	27	Fem'le	do
Etna......	John Paterson.......	Idiotic........	18 "	....	18	Male..	do
"	Samuel Parkison.....	Blind	40 "	Blasting rocks.	62	Male..	do
"	Samuel Warner......	Idiotic........	18 "	....	43	do ..	do
Newton ...	Theodore Vauatta....	do	35 "	....	35	do ..	do
"	Cecelia Allbaugh....	do	10 "	Erysipelas	16	Fem'le	do
"	Martha Davis	Blind	17 "	....	17	Fem'le	do

in the county of Licking, State of Ohio, on the second Monday of May, 1856.

Occupation.	Birthplace.	Educated or not.	Names of Parents.	Occupation.	Birthplace.	No. children.	No. children thus afflicted.	Relationship of Parents before Marriage
Bl'cksmth	Penn	Not	Geo. & Catharine Rible.	Farmer ..	....	..	1	Not kn'n
Farmer ..	Virginia..	do....	Jas. & Nancy Feagans..	do	Va	12	1	Cousins.
Laborer..	do	do....	W. & Rachael Richards.	do	N. Jersey)			
" ..	do	do....	" " "	do	do	11	3	Not kn'n
" ..	do	do....	" " "	do	do			
" ..	Penn	do....	David & Ester Jamison..	....	Penn	..	1	None
None	Ohio	do....	Leonard & Maria Hoyt..	Laborer ..	Ohio	5	1	....
"	do	do....	Betsy Ann Francis.....	None	Ohio)			
"	do	do....	" "	do	do	10	3	....
"	do	do....	" "	.... do ...	do			
H'se work	Vermont.	Educated	Isaac and Lucy Bigelow,	Farmer ..	N. S. & Vt.	8	1	....
None	Ohio	Not.....	John and F. Rakestraw.	do	Ohio	8	1	None.
"	do	do....	Benj. & Anna Rakestraw	do	"	3	1	do
Laborer..	do	do....	D. H. & Sarah Thacker,	Mechanic,	....	7	1	do
None	Virginia .	Educated	....	....	....	..	1	....
H'se work	Ohio	"	Milford and Ann Priest.	Farmer ..	Virginia)			
None	do	Not.....	do do do	do	"	8	2	None.
Farmer ..	do	Educated	Jas. & Mary Ann Lyons,	do	Ireland....	8	1	do
Farmer ..	N. York.	do	A. & Phoebe Ann Smith	do	New York,	11	1	do
Farmer ..	Ohio ..	.Not.....	O. & Margaret Debewise,	do	"	10	1	do
....	Virginia.	Educated	John and Mary Finch ..	do	Virginia ..	4	1	do
Farmer ..	Ohio	Not.....	Thos. & Catharine Moore	do	" ..	11	1	do
....	do	do....	Danl. & Rebecca Wilkins	do	" ..	9	1	do
....	do	Educated	Hugh Dornan	do	Ireland ...	..	1	do
Farmer ..	do	Not.....	George & Hannah Wolf,	do	Penn	6	1	do
None	Virginia..	Educated	Stacy and Mahala Lacy,	do	Va	7	1	do
"	"	do	Amelia Parr	do	Not known	..	1	Unkno'n
Br'm m'kr	Ohio	do	James Wheeler	Minister..	Ohio ,,....	2	1	None .
Farmer ..	do	do	Danl. & Hannah Houck.	Farmer ..	Unknown.	7	1	do
None	do	Not.....	Samuel & Betsy Haines,	do	"	6	1	do
"	Unknown	do....	Unknown	Unknown	....	..	1	Unkno'n
Laborer ..	Newark..	Educated	Andelusia & Abigal Pier	Trader...	Vermont..	2	1	None .
do ..	do	Not.....	Samuel and Lucy Scott.	Laborer ..	Unknown .	1	1	....
....	do	do....	T. J. & H. E. Christian,	Grocer ...	Va	5	1	None.
None	Mass.....	do....	G. and Jerusha Rodgers,	Farmer ..	Mass......	..	1	2d cous's
H'se work	N. York,	Educated	Jarius & Margt. Mullen,	do	New York,	6	1	None.
None	Ohio	Not	J & Susanna Showman,	do	Md & Pa.	3	1	do
Farmer ..	"	Educated	John & Elizabeth Gaver,	do	Va.& Penn.	7	1	do
do ..	Maryland	do	M. & Catharine Ridenow	do	Maryland.	8	1	do
Glove mkr	Virginia .	do	Thos. & Mary Simmons,	....	Virginia...	15	1	....
Tailor ...	Penn	Not	A. & Sally Stonebraker,	Farmer ..	Penn......	3	1	....
Shoem'kr,	Virginia .	ducated	Wm. & Rebecca Batthias	do	Virginia...	11	1	....
None	Penn	do	Wm. & Mary Thompson.	Bl'ksmith	Penn	7	1	....
Farmer ..	"	do	Obad'h & Thankful Scott	Farmer ..	Conn.	12	1	None.
None	N. Jersey,	Not	Jno. M. & Dinah Tunison	do	N. Jersey,	..	1	do
Farmer ..	Ohio	Educated	G. & Minerva Harrison.	do	N Y.& Ten.	6	1	do
....	Virginia .	Not	Walter and Nancy Mason	Miller ...	Virginia ..	4	1	do
Farmer ..	Penn	do	Jno. & Mary Stockbarger	....	Pensylv'ia,	10	3	....
" ..	....	Educated	....					
....	Maryland	do	Josiah & Sarah Ridgway	Miller ...	Maryland,	3	1	None.
Farmer ..	Conn	Not	Joel & Mary Phillbrook.	Farmer ..	Conn.	8	3	Cousins.
....	N. Jersey,	Educated	A. P. & Soph. Whitehead	do	N.J.& Mass	..	1	None.
None	Ireland ..	Not	Robert Patterson	None	Ireland....	1	1	Unkno'n
do	England.	do .	John and Mrs Parkeson,	do	England. .	1	1	None.
do	Ohio	Educated	Samuel and Mrs. Worner	... .	Ohio	1	1	do
do	N. Jersey,	Not	Wm. and Mary Vanatta,	Farmer ..	N. Jersey,	10	1	do
do	Ohio	do	D. & Darrity Allbaugh.	do	Marylnnd,	12	1	do
Knitting..	Ireland ..	Educated	Matthew & Margt. Davis	do	Ireland	10	3	do

RETURN of the number of Deaf and Dumb, Blind, Insane and Idiotic

Townships.	Names of Persons.	Nature of affliction.	Duration of affliction.	Cause where known.	Age.	Sex.	Color.
Newton	Catharine Davis	Blind	15 years	Not known	15	Fem'le	White.
"	Fanny Davis	"	4 "	"	4	"	do
"	Mary A. Bowman	"	1 "	Sickness	74	"	do
Perry	Chester Smith	"	4 "	Hurt	9	Male	do
"	Loren Taylor	Deaf and dumb	37 "	Sickness	40	"	do
Bennington	Alexander Dickson	" "	65 "	Unknown	65	"	do
"	Hannah Hess	Insane	25 "	Disease	60	Fem'le	do
Hartford	Ellen Boston	Blind	29 "		29	"	do
"	Aaron Franks	Deaf and Dumb	From birth,			Male	do
"	Joseph Williams	Insane	6 years		55	"	do
"	Jacob Grandstaff	"			22	"	do
"	Zimri Webb	Blind	10 years	Poisoned	57	"	do

persons in the County of Licking, State of Ohio—Continued.

Occupation.	Birth-place.	Educated or not	Names of Parents.	Occupation	Birth-place.	No. Children	No. Children thus afflicted	Relationship of parents before Marriage
None....	New York	Not...	Matthew & Marg. Davis	Farmer...	Ireland.}	10	3	None.
"	"	" ..	" " "	"	"			"
"	Virginia.	" ..	P. & Catharine Hollen.	"	Va.......	11	1	"
....	Ohio....	" ..	Jacob & Emily Smith..	"	Ohio....	3	1	....
Shoem'kr.	Maine...	Limited.	Mr. and Mrs. Taylor..	Not known	Maine....	5	1	Unknown
Farmer..	Virginia.	Not....	Unknown............	"	....	..	....	..:.
....	"	..Educat'd	Jonathan & Mrs. Conrad	Farmer...	Unknown.	1	1	Unknown,
....	Maryland	"	Wm. and Mary Boston.	Weaver..	Maryland.	4	4	2d cousi's
Farmer..	Penn....	Not....	A. & Elizbeth Franks..	Farmer ..	Germ. & Pa	9	1	None.
"	do...	Educat'd	....	....	....	..	....	....
"	Ohio....	Not....	E. & Nancy Grandstaff,	Farmer...	....	7	1	None.
" ...	Penn....	Educat'd	Richard & Mary Webb,	"	Penn.....	9	1	"

RETURN of the number of Deaf and Dumb, Blind, Insane and Idiotis persons

TOWNSHIPS.	Names of Persons.	Nature of Affliction.	Duration of Affliction.	Cause where known.	Age.	Sex.	Color.
Washington	Abraham S. Monroe	Blind	14 years	Inflam. of head	15	Male.	Wht.
Lane	Edward Reed	Fool and devil	From birth	Not known	25	"	"
Rooks Creek	Hiram Thornton	Idiotic	"	Congenital	58	"	"
"	William Steel	"	"	"	..	"	"
"	Lemuel Steel	"	"	"	..	"	"
Harrison	William Vaughan	Insane	11 years	Not known	45	"	"
"	Michael Shaffer	"	"	Fr. infancy " "	22	"	"
"	John Judy	"	"	6 years " "	45	"	"
"	Nathaniel Smith	"	"	8 " .. " "	35	"	"
"	Clark E. Forrest	"	"	Unknown . " "	23	"	"
"	Riley Miller	"	"	Fr. infancy " "	18	"	"
"	Sarah M. Bryant	"	"	Unknown . " "	21	Fem'le	"
"	Ellen Minicum	"	"	During life " "	11	"	"
"	Eliza Jones	Idiotic	"	Fr. infancy Congenital	20	"	"
"	Mary Jane Mays	"	"	" "	15	"	"
"	Dosey Green	"	"	" "	45	"	"
"	Dorcas Tumey	"	"	" "	23	"	"
"	Rebecca Lyle	Blind	"	6 years .. Not known	45	"	"
"	Enoch Blair	D'f, d'b & blind	Unknown .	" "	35	Male.	"
"	William H. Thompson	Idiotic	"	Fr. Infancy Fits	21	"	"
"	William Spencer	"	"	Unknown . "	60	"	"
"	Ruth Laney	"	"	During life. Congenital	31	Fem'le	"
"	Elizabeth Smith	"	"	" "	20	"	"
"	Susan Fulton	"	"	" "	18	"	"
"	Elizabeth Fulton	"	"	" "	14	"	"
"	Elizabeth Longsdorf	"	"	" "	38	"	"
"	Susan Longsdorf	"	"	" "	14	"	"
"	May Jones	"	"	" "	25	"	"
"	William Jones	"	"	" "	23	Male.	"
Lake	Nancy Jane Morton	Deaf and dumb	"	" "	7	Fem'le	"
"	Margaret Robinson	Idiotic	"	" "	15	"	"
Union	Sarah E. Lockhard	Deaf and dumb	6 years	Gath'g in head	6¼	"	"
"	Cynthia Ann Brown	Idiotic	13 "	Fits	14	"	"
"	William R. West	"	14 "	Congenital	14	Male.	"
Miami	Paul Huston	Blind	7 "	Inflam. of eyes	70	"	"
"	Enos Fielder	Insane	7 months.	Unknown	24	"	"

in the county of Logan, State of Ohio, on the second Monday of May, 1856.

Occupation.	Birth-place.	Educated or not.	Names of Parents.	Occupation.	Birth-place.	No. Children.	No. children thus afflicted.	Relationship of parents before marriage.
......	Ohio	Partially	L. F. and Marg. Monroe	Teacher..	Penn'a....	..	....	None.
Loafing..	N. Jersey.	Not	Deceased	....	....	..	....	....
None	Virginia .	"	....	......	....	..	....	....
"	Ohio	"	Lemuel and Sarah Steel	Farmer ..	Delaware..	7	2	....
"	"	"	" " "	....	....	..	....	....
Clerk....	Kentucky	Educated	Unknown	Tanner ..	Unknown .	..	....	Unknwn
None	Ohio	Not	"	Unknown	"	..	....	"
Farmer ..	"	"	"	"	"	..	....	"
"	"	Educated	"	Farmer ..	"	..	....	"
Unknown	Mass	"	M. D. and Harriet Forrest	" ..	"	..	....	"
None	Ohio	Not	....	" ..	"	..	....	"
"	"	"	....	" ..	"	..	....	"
"	Unknown	"	....	Unknown	"	..	....	"
Laborer..	Ohio	"	Thomas and Deb. Jones	Farmer ..	Ohio......	7	3	2d cous.
None	"	"	James and Rebecca Mays	" ..	"	..	....	Unknwn
"	"	"	Unknown............	" ..	"	..	....	"
"	"	"	"	" ..	"	..	....	"
"	New York	"	Elijah and Epsy Moore	" ..	Unknovn	..	....	1st cous.
"	Ohio	"	Unknown	" ..	"	..	....	"
"	"	Educated	"	" ..	"	..	....	"
"	Virginia.	Not	"	Unknown	"	..	....	"
"	Penn	"	Sampson and Mary Lany	Farmer ..	Ireland ...	5	1	None.
"	Ohio	"	M. and Elizabeth Smith	"	Penn'a....	8	1	"
"	"	"	Unknown	"	"	..	1	"
"	"	"	"	"	"	..	1	"
Hou ewrk	Penn	"	"	"	Unknown.	..	1	"
None	Ohio	"	"	"	"	..	1	Fr. & Dr.
Housewrk	"	"	Thomas and Deb. Jones	"	"	..	....	2d cous.
Laborer..	"	"	" "	"	"	..	....	"
None	"	"	Joseph and Jane Montz	Laborer ..	Pa. and Md	3	1	None.
" ...	Ireland ..	"	J. and Mary A. Robinson	"	Ireland ...	1	1	"
......	Ohio	"	Th. and A. E. Lockhard	Farmer ..	Virginia ..	3	1	"
......	"	"	R. V. and Eliz. Brown	"	Va. & N.J.	8	1	"
......	"	"	Joseph and Sarah West	"	Virginia ..	11	1	"
Farmer ..	Penn	Educated	....	....	....	..	....	....
"	Ohio	"	....	....	....	..	....	....

RETURN of the number of Deaf and Dumb, Blind, Insane and Idiotic persons

Townships.	Names of persons.	Nature of Affliction.	Duration of Affliction	Cause where known.	Age.	Sex.	Color.
Pittsfield	J. Stella Williams	Deaf	7 years	Gathering in head	8	Fem'le	White
Elyria	Albert Matson	Idiotic	From birth	....	5	Male	do
"	Betsy A. Broughn	Deaf and dumb	"	....	18	Fem'le	do
"	Sally Robinson	Insane	10 years	Supposed heredi'y	37	"	do
"	Joseph Bacon	Blind	10 "	Hard labor	69	Male	do
Grafton	Mary Pangborn	Deaf and dumb	33 "	Sound of drum	33	Fem'le	do
"	Simon Mirkul	Blind	20 "	Medical operations	37	Male	do
Amherst	J. G. Tyler	Insane	4 "	Fits	25	"	do
"	Lydia Reddington	Deaf and dumb		....	11	Fem'le	do
"	Elbart Reddingt'n	Deaf and dumb		....	8	Male	do
"	Isaac Whelpley	Deaf and dumb		Unknown	46	"	do
Rochester	Elvira Lane	Deaf and dumb	36 years	Unknown	36	Fem'le	do
"	Rebecca Minus	Deaf	30 "	Harsh treatment	45	"	do
"	Patia Babcock	Insane	5 "	Hereditary	78	"	do
"	Asa Hayden	Insane	4 "	Hereditary	58	Male	do
Huntington	Bickford Lang	Insane	5 "	Unknown	81	"	do
"	Cynthia Cook	Insane	6 "	Injury of spine	48	Fem'le	do
Brownhelm	F. M. Graham	Idiotic	16 "	Epilepsy	30	"	do
"	Fordom Sneider	Blind	18 "	Cataract	40	Male	do
"	Daniel Sturtevant	Idiotic	12 "	Weakness	14	"	do
"	Jacob Minster	Blind	2 "	Hard drinking	56	"	do
Russia	Datus O. Waters	Deaf and dumb	From inf'cy	Not known	9	"	do
"	Sylvia A. Newton	Deaf and dumb	From birth	Not known	11	Fem'le	do
Wellington	John Nichles	Blind & insane	11 years	Varioloid	73	Male	do
"	Wm. S. Hamilton	Deaf	28 "	Dropsy in head	33	Male	do
"	Julia A. Reed	Lunatic	29 "	Took henbane	50	Fem'le	do
"	William Bradley	Blind	12 "	Inflammation	60	Male	do
Ridgeville	Harriet Percival	Insane		....	47	Fem'le	do
"	Joseph Robinson	Insane	19 "	....	48	Male	do
"	Jane Bainbridge	Insane	16 "	....	46	Fem'le	do
Henrietta	Alice Ann Banks	Insane	13 "	Fever	33	Fem'le	do
"	Elizabeth Banks	Insane	25 "	Fever	25	Fem'le	do

in the county of Lorain, State of Ohio, on the second Monday of May, 1856.

Occupation.	Birthplace.	Educated or not.	Names of Parents.	Occupation.	Birthplace.	No. children.	No. children thus afflicted.	Relationship of parents before marriage.
.....	Wisconsin	Not	B. & Naomi W. Williams..	Farmer .	N. Y, & Vt	2	1	None
.....	Ohio	....	Sylvester Matson	Printer..	....	2	1	None
Dressm.	Ohio	Educated	Harmon & Maria Broughn.	Farming	Conn., N. Y	5	1	Cousins
Farmer	New York	Educated	John & Charity Thornton..	Mason ..	Not known	8	2	
Farm'g	Mass.....	Educated	Joseph & Abbey J. Bacon.	Mech'ic.	Mass......	3	1	
Housew	Mass.....	Educated	N. & Sarah Pangborn.....	Shoem'r	....	4	2	
None ..	Baden ...	....	J. Mirkle & Thckle Snider.	Farming	Germany	3	1	
Farm'g	Ohio	Educated	D. M. Tyler & Polly Tyler.	Farming	Conn.	5	1	None
......	Amherst .	Not	Ranson N. Reddington...	Farming	Mass.....	..	2	None
......	....	....	Malissa E. Reddington ...	....	....	..	..	
Carp'er	Vermont .	....	Jos. & Lucinda Whelpley .	....	....	..	..	
Housek	New York	Educated	Luther & Priscilla Phillips	Shoem'r	Mass.....	13	4	None
"	England .	Educated	Archabod Saunders.......	Machin't	Scotland ..	12	2	None
"	Mass	Educated	Smith Marcy	P. officer	R. Island .	9	1	None
None ..	Mass	Educated	Joel Hayden	Farmer .	Conn.....	5	2	None
Farmer	N. H.....	Educated	B. Lang & Martha Lock...	Farmer .	Greenland.	8	1	None
......	Canada ..	Educated	Friend Gibbs & Lucy Archer	Farming	Conn.....	12	3	None
......	Ohio	Educated	Benj. & Ann W. Bacon....	....	Ohio......	..	1	None
Farmer	Germany.	Educated	....	....	....	..	..	
......	Ohio	....	David & Sally Sturtevant..	....	Ohio......	5	1	None
Farmer	Germany..	Educated	....	....	Germany...	..	1	None
......	....	Not	David & Louisa Waters...	Carpen'r	....	4	1	None
......	Ohio	Not	Eber & Anna Newton ...	Farmer .	Conn.....	..	1	None
Farmer	Mass.....	Educated	Saml. & Jane Nichles.....	Farmer .	Mass.....	12	1	None
Wheelr.	New York	Educated	A. Hamilton & L. Dealand	Carpen'r	Mass. & Vt	6	1	None
Farmer	Conn.....	Educated	B. Reed & Prodenoe Smith.	Farmer .	Conn.....	5	1	None
Tanner	Mass	Educated	....	....	....	..	..	
......	Mass.....	Educated	Elisha Percival	Farmer .	Mass.....	5	1	None
Farmer	England .	Educated	Not known...............	....	....	..	..	
......	England .	Educated	William Wakden	Farmer .	England ..	3	1	
Milliner	England .	Educated	William Banks	Farmer .	England ..	6	2	None
Housew	England .	Educated	Ann Banks...............	....	....	..	..	

RETURN of the number of Deaf and Dumb, Blind, Insane and Idiotic persons

Names of Persons.	Nature of Affliction.	Duration of Affliction.	Cause where known.	Age.	Sex.	Color.
Charlot Goucher	Idiot	From birth		24	Female	White.
Matilda	Idiot	From birth		14	"	White.
Margaret Auth	Idiot	From birth		23	"	White.
Fero Winnemaker	Blind	1 year		22	"	White.
John O'Neil	Insane	3 years		23	Male	White.
George Closson	Idiotic	2 years	Congestion brain.	10	"	White.
Milton M. Morris	Insane	20 years	Worldly business.	58	"	White.
Harlow Hollister	Idiotic	33 years	Worldly business.	33	"	White.
Joseph Supp	Deaf and dumb	Always	Don't know	5	"	White.

in Lucas County, State of Ohio, on the second Monday of May, 1856.

Occupation.	Birth-place.	Educated or not	Names of Parents.	Occupation.	Birth-place.	No. chil'ren.	No. children thus afflicted.	Relationship of parents before marriage.
....	Germany..	Not....	Unknown............	....	....	....	....	....
....	Germany..	"	Unknown............	....	....	....	....	....
....	Germany..	"	Uuknown............	....	....	....	....	....
....	Germany..	Educated	Unknown............	....	....	....	....	....
....	Maumee, O.	"	James O'Neill......	Farmer...	Ireland...	2	1	None.
....	....	Not	D. F. Closson.......	Cooper....	Kentucty.	7	1	None.
Farming.	Rh. Island.	Educated	Marvin Morris......	Stne mason	Rh. Island.	5	1	None.
Farming.	New York.	Not	James Hollister.....	Farmer...	Connectic't	5	1	None.
Nothing.	Germany..	"	Jacob Supp.........	Laborer...	Germany..	3	1	Unknown.

RETURN of the number of Deaf and Dumb, Blind, Insane and Idiotic persons

Townships.	Names of Persons.	Nature of Affliction.	Duration of Affliction.	Cause where known.	Age.	Sex.	Color.
Stokes	Andrew Wilson	Blind	1½ years	Sore Eyes	41	Male	White.
Range	Hellen Rebecca Mills	"	2 years	Fever	18	Fem'le	"
do	Wilson T. Gerrard	"	4 "	Solution of silv'r	26	Male	"
do	Elizabeth Counts	Idiot	From birth		18	Fem'le	"
Pleasant							"
Union							"
Deer Creek	Clinton McMurry	Insane	From birth		5	Male	"
do	Joseph Cox	"	4 years	Masturbation	25	"	"
Jefferson	John Hann	Idiot	From birth		14	"	"
Monroe							"
Canaan	Fanny Perkins	Insane	8 years		55	Fem'le	"
do	Hester A. Brettenham	"	13 "	Sickness	14	"	"
do	William Beebe	"	From birth		26	Male	"
Pike							"
Darby							"
Fairfield	Thomas Jackson	Insane	8 years		50	Male	"
do	S. D. Chenowoth		From birth		31	"	"
Somerford	Samuel Markle	Deaf and dumb	18 years	Scarlet Fever	23	"	"
do	Daniel Rafferty	Idiot	From birth		38	"	"
do	John Wesley Rafferty	"	"		18	Fem'le	"
do	Ruth Rafferty	"	"		26	"	"
do	Milton Rafferty	Deaf and dumb	"		17	Male	"
do	Mary Ann Lewis	"	"		42	Fem'le	"
Paint	Thursa Peterson	"	4 years		7	"	"
Oak Run	Solomon Lewis	Insane	From birth		55	Male	"

in the county of Madison, State of Ohio, on the second Monday of May, 1856.

Occupation.	Birthplace.	Educated or not.	Names of Parents.	Occupation.	Birthplace.	No. children.	No. children thus Afflicted	Relationship of Parents before Marriage
Laborer...	Ireland.	Not.....	....	....	....	..	..	....
....	Ohio ...	Educated	T. and Elizabeth Mills.	Miller ..	Pa. & Va.	9	1	None.
Broom m'kr	do	Not.....	N. & Dr'thy D. Gerrard	Farmer .	Pa. & Ohio	8	1	"
....	do	....	D. and E. Counts......	"	Va. & Ohio	12	1	"
....	....	....	....	....	....	..	..	....
....	Ohio. ..	Not.....	John and — McMurry.	Farmer .	Penn.	9	1	None.
....	Penn....	Educated	....	....	....	..	..	....
....	Ohio ...	....	M. and Lucretia Hann..	Farmer .	Ohio	10	1	....
....	....	....	....	....	....	..	..	....
....	N. H. ..	Educated	....	Farmer .	N. H......	..	1	None.
....	Ohio	Not.....	J. H. & — Brettenham	....	Ohio.	4	1	"
....	do	"	Saml. and — Beebe....	Farmer..	New York.	4	1	"
....	....	....	....	....	....	..	..	....
Farmer...	N. Jersey	Not.....	J. and Nancy Jackson.	Farmer..	N. Jersey .	..	1	None.
....	Ohio ...	....	J. F. & M. Chenowoth.	....	....	..	..	....
....	do	....	Jona. & Mary Markle..	"	Maryland..	..	1	None.
....	Ky.....	....	J. and Rebecca Rafferty	"	Virginia ..	12	4	Cousins.
....	"	....	" "	"	"	..	..	....
....	"	....	" "	"	"	..	..	....
....	"	Educated	" "	"	"	..	..	....
....	....	Not.....	Gardner and Martha ..	"	New York.	3	1	....
....	Ohio ...	"	A. and Martitia Peters.	"	Ohio	3	1	2d cousins.
....	"	....	H. and Catherine Lewis	....	....	..	..	....

RETURN of the number of Deaf and Dumb, Blind, Insane and Idiotic persons

TOWNSHIPS.	Names of Persons.	Nature of Affliction.	Duration of Affliction.	Cause, Where Known.	Age.	Sex.	Color.
Springfield	Elizabeth Seidmer	Insane	Life	Unknown	35	Fem'le	Wh.te.
do	Catharine Cover	Deaf and dumb	"	"	30	"	"
do	Nancy Shafer	Insane	"	"	45	"	"
Beaver	Frederick Duterer	Idiotic & Dumb	"	Palsy of parent,	56	Male	"
do	Susanna Kleckner	Insane	1 year	Sickness	26	Fem'le	"
do	Elizabeth Culp	"	4 "	"	41	"	"
do	Jacob Knouft	Blind	7 "		69	Male	"
do	Melinda Wonderling	Insane	3 "	Sickness	5	"	"
Greene	Mary Walker	Deaf and dumb	41 "		41	Fem'le	"
do	Margaret ———	" "	50 "	By a fall	52	"	"
do	Hiram Cool	Insane	5½ "	Sickness	19	Male	"
do	Margaret Menakly	Blind	7 "		72	Fem'le	"
Smith	Gideon Hoadley	"	3 "	Old age	97	Male	"
do	Mary Davis	"	5 "	"	76	Fem'le	"
do	John Dingy	Idiotic	Life	Unknown	27	Male	"
do	Sarah Hayhurst	"	"	"	25	Fem'le	"
do	Adelia "	"	"	Incest	6	"	"
do	Elizabeth Reed	Blind	3 years	Old age	94	"	"
do	John W. Roberts	Idiotic	Life	Unknown	30	Male	"
Berlin	Sarah Middleton	Deaf and dumb	"		40	Fem'le	"
do	Evan Cessnee	Blind	20 years	Exposure to heat	68	Male	"
Ellsworth	Keziah Courtney	Deaf and dumb	20 "		34	Fem'le	"
do	John Reed	" "	Life		30	Male	"
do	Charles Reed	" "	"		19	"	"
Canfiel	Edward Hughs	Insane	Unknown		35	"	"
do	Ashbel Dran	"	"	Disapp'ted love	60	"	"
do	Michael Mahoney	"	"		33	"	"
do	Harriet Chiddester	"	"		40	Fem'le	"
do	Jacob Pfitzmyer	Idiotic	Life		33	Male	"
do	Jane Clark	do	"		18	Fem'le	"
do	Jane Cox	Insane	12 years		50	"	"
do	James Dummer	Deaf and dumb	Life		34	Male	"
Boardman	Belinda Mosser	Idiotic	5 years		5	Fem'le	"
Coitsville	Jane Maxwell	Blind	9 "	Unknown	38	"	"
do	Amos McFarland	Dumb	Life	"	40	Male	"
do	*Michael Keysecker						
Youngst'n	Samuel Gibson	Deaf and dumb	Life	Inherited	67	Male	"
do	William Smith	" "	"	"	17	"	"
do	Almira K. Walter	" "	"	Unknown	19	Feml'e	"
Austintw'n	Jane Grove	Blind	12 years	"	81	"	"
do	Reuben Buck	Idiotic	38 "	"	38	Male	"
do	John Randolph	Blind	7 "	Cataract	82	"	"
Jackson	Jonathan Freyman	Deaf and dumb	Life	Relationship of parents supposed to be the cause.	46	"	"
do	Sarah "	" "	"		36	Fem'le	"
do	Elias "	" "	"		48	"	"
do	Susanna "	" "	"		42	Feml'e	"
do	Andrew Stall	Idiotic	"		35	Male	"
do	Isaac Calhoun	"	"		47	"	"
do	Margaret Ewing	Blind	6 years	Cataract	70	Fem'le	"
Mettone	John Simpson	Idiotic	Life	Convulsions	26	Male	"
do	Mary A Kemala	Insane	4 years	Milk sickness	46	Fem'le	"
do	John Purshall	Deaf and dumb	30 "	Convulsions	30	"	"
do	Catharine Rose	Insane	4 "	Unknown	73	"	"
do	" Williams	Insane	4 "	"	72	"	"
do	" Russell	Insane	7 years	"	45	"	"
do	Jane Crays	Insane	25 "	"	42	"	"
do	Susan Glass	Idiotic	Life	"	20	"	"

*Michael Keysecker's family of children in this Township, consisting of 5 or 6, are deformed and partially doltic. The parents are blood cousins.

in the county of Mahoning, State of Ohio, on the second Monday of May, 1856.

Occupation.	Birth-place.	Educated or Not.	Names of Parents.	Occupation.	Birth-place.	No. Children	No. Children thus afflicted.	Relationship of parents before marriage.
None	Ohio	Not	John Seidner	Farmer			1	No report
"	Ohio	Not	J. Cover	"			1	"
"	Ohio	Not	J. Shafer	"			1	"
"	Penn	"	M. & Eliz. Knouff	"	Penn	10	1	"
"	Ohio	Educat'd	Jacob & Cath. Hulda	"			1	Unknown
"		"		"	Germany		1	"
Farmer	Penn	"	Jacob Knouff		Penn		1	"
	Ohio	Not	Fred. & C. Wonderling	Farmer	Germany		1	"
H'se keepr	Penn	"	A. & Mary Walker		Penn	8	1	"
"	Penn	"	J. & Hannah Beard	Farmer	Germany	17	1	"
Farmer	Ohio	Educat'd	Jacob & Susan Cool	"		4	1	"
H'se keepr	Germany	"	Not known	"			1	"
Bl'ksmith	Conn	"	G & M. Hoadley	Merchant	Conn	2	1	None.
	Wales	"		Farmer	Wales	9	1	"
	Ohio	Not	Chas. & Mary Garrett	Mechanic	Penn	9	1	"
	Ohio	"	Wm. & Jane Hayhurst		"	10	1	"
	Ohio	"	Sarah Hayhurst		Ohio	1	1	Bro. & sis.
	Maryland	Educat'd						
	Ohio	Not	D. Roberts & E. Wilson	Mechanic	Ohio	8	1	None.
	Ohio	"	N. & D. Middleton	Farmer	N. J. & Va.	10	1	Bl'd cous.
Bl'ksmith	Penn	"						
	Ohio		N. & Nancy Courtney	Farmer	Virginia	9	1	Bl'd cous.
Shoem'ker	Ohio	Educat'd	Stephen & Betsy Reed	"	Penn			"
	Ohio	"	" "	"	"			"
Miner	Ireland							
Mechanic	Conn	Educat'd						Paupers in County Infirmary and little known of them.
Miner	Ireland							
	Ohio	Educat'd						
	Penn	Not						
	Ohio	"	Illegitimate					
	Ireland	Not						
	Ohio	"		Laborer			1	None.
Roving	Ohio	Educat'd	John Maxwell	Farmer	Ireland	4	1	
		"	Wm. & E. McFarland	"	"	12	1	
Farmer	Penn	Not	J. & Harriet Smith					
"	Ohio	Educat'd		Farmer	Ohio			None.
	Penn	"	J. & Cath. Walter	Miller	Penn			Unknown
None	Penn	Partially	And. & Cath. Coon					
"	Penn	Not	David Buck					
Shoem'ker	Penn	"						
Weaver	Penn	Educat'd	Geo. & Marg't Freyman	} Weaver	Penn	12	5	Bl'd cous.
	Penn	Not	" "					
Shoem'ker	Penn	"	" "					
	Penn	"	" "					
	Ohio	"	And. & Susan Stall	Carpenter	Penn			
Farmer	Ohio	"	And. & Eliz. Calhoun	Farmer				None.
None	Penn	Educat'd		"				No report
	N. Jersey	Not	J. & S. Simpson	"	New Jersey	13	1	"
Housewife		Educat'd		Weaver				"
	Ohio	Not		Farmer				"
Housewife				"				"
				"				"
Housewife		Educat'd		"				"
	Ohio	"		"				"
	Ohio	Not	John & S. Glass	"		5	1	"

9—SEC. OF STATE.

RETURN of the number of Deaf and Dumb, Blind, Insane and Idiotic persons

Township	Names of Persons.	Nature of affliction	Duration of Affliction	Cause where known	Age.	Sex.	Color.
Gr'n Camp	Mary Walker	Blind	7 years		56	Fem'le	White
Montgom'y	Emily Penrose	Idiotic	10 "		11	"	"
"	Elenor Coats	Deaf and dumb	28 "	Unknown	28	"	"
"	Franklin Carter	Idiotic	24 "		24	Male	"
"	Susan Anderson	Idiotic	44 "	Unknown	44	Fem'le	"
Prospect	Wm. Patten	Dumb & Idiotic	18 "	Fits	18	Male	"
"	Sidney Ann Grigsby	Deaf and Dumb	18 "		18	Fem'le	"
"	Wm. H. H. Grigsby	" "	16 "		16	Male	"
"	Daniel Grigsby	" "	20 "		20	"	"
Waldo	Hiva Wilcox	Blind	1 "	Cold	75	"	"
"	Margaret Ditterick	"	17 "	Cold	71	Fem'le	"
"	Abagail Snow	"	24 "	Unknown	24	"	"
"	Harriet Swartz	Idiotic	.. "	By fright	35	"	"

in the county of Marion, State of Ohio, on the second Monday of May, 1856.

Occupation.	Birthplace.	Educated or not.	Names of Parents.	Occupation.	Birthplace.	No. Children.	No. Children thus afflicted.	Relationship of Parents before marriage.
....	Maryland	Educat'd	James and E. Sullivan....	Farmer.	Maryland	5	1	....
None ..	Ohio	Not	Elisha and Susan Penrose	Farmer.	Ohio	4	1	None.
" ..	Ohio	Educat'd	Not known................	....	....	..	..	Not kno'n.
" ..	Ohio	Not	James and C. Carter......	Farmer.	Penn	9	1	None.
" ..	"	"	Wm. and Rachel Anderson	"	Va. & Del.	13	1	"
....	"	"	Thomas and M. Patton...	"	Ohio	4	1	"
None ..	"	Educat'd	John and Mrs. Grigsby...	"	"	11	3	"
" ..	"	Limited.	" " ..	"	"	11	3	"
" ..	"	Not	" " ..	"	"	11	3	"
Farmer.	Conn....	Educat'd	Jehiel and Azube Wilcox.	"	Conn	9	2	"
"	Europe ..	Educat'd	Peter & Margaret Ditterick	"	Europe ..	9	1	"
....	N. York.	....	Samuel and S. Alsworth..	St'em'an	Maine ...	14	1	"
....	N. York.	....	Wm. and Mary Swartz...	Cooper.	N. York.	8	1	"

RETURN of the number of Deaf and Dumb, Blind, Insane and Idiotic persons

TOWNSHIPS	Names of Persons.	Nature of affliction.	Duration of affliction.	Cause where known.	Age.	Sex.	Color.
Sharon....	—— Bissell	Deaf and dumb	25 years	Unknown	25	Female	White
Hinckley..	Leonard Hodgman ..	do	23 do	Fever	25	Male..	"
Guilford ..	Caroline L Conkey...	do	....'.......	Whoop'g cough	4	Female	"
do	Susan Houts.........	do	....	Measles	3	do	"
do	Luther Scranton	Insane.......	...../.....	....	..	......	"
Vl.of S'vlle	Melissa Harris.......	Idiotic........	26 years	Fits	27	Female	"
Vl.of M'dna	Cornelia Munyer	do	22 do	do...........	25	do	"
Brunswick.	Sylvester Carpenter ..	do	13 do	Sickness	14	Male..	"
do	Abigail Page	Deaf and dumb	42 do	do	43	Female	"
do	James Holden	do	66 do	do	66	Male..	"
do	Thomas Holden......	do	56 do	do	56	do	"
do	John Gould	do	5 do	do	6	do	"
Westfield..	Nancy Gridley	Idiotic........	57 do	....	57	Female	"
York	Harriet Welber	do	22 do	....	22	do	"
do	Abraham Gildersleve	Deaf and dumb	22 do	....	22	Male..	"
do	Alva Wilson	do	8 do	Measles	9	do	"
Liverpool .	Rachel Bikel	do	20 do	....	21	Female	"
do	Philip Dunderman....	Idiotic........	20 do	....	20	Male..	"
do	John Dimeling	do	40 do	....	40	do	"
do	Lewis Nolinburg	do	19 do	....	19	do	"
do	Christopher Hitzelberg	do	15 do	....	15	do	"
Litchfield.	Alexander McKengel .	Deaf and blind	15 do	Inflammation..	71	do	"
Homer	Benjamin Bulhand ...	do	3 do	....	84	do	"
Spencer ...	James Clark.........	Idiotic........	23 do	....	23	do	"
do	Elizabeth Clark......	do	5 do	....	5	Female	"
do	Martly Stutler.......	Deaf and dumb	5 do	....	5	do	"
do	Chauncey Hastings :	Blind	18 do	....	40	Male..	"

in the county of Medina, State of Ohio, on the second Monday of May, 1856.

Occupation	Birthplace.	Educated or not.	Names of Parents.	Occupation.	Birth-place.	No. Children.	No. children thus afflicted
....	Ohio.....	Educat'd..	Erastus Bissell...............	Farmer....	....	..	1
Farmer...	New York	Not......	William and Mary Hodgman	do	Vermont..	9	1
....	Guilford..	....	Ezekiel Conkey............	do	....	..	....
....	do	....	George Houts...............	do	....	..	....
....	Seville....	Not......	Samuel Harris.............	Farmer...	Connecticut	6	1
....	New York	do	P. E. Munger...............	Physician.	New York	1	1
....	Hinckley..	do	Rufus and Alsena Carpenter	Farmer...	do	8	1
....	Canada...	do	Aaron and Lydia Page......	do	do	7	1
Farmer...	England.	do	Ralph and Mary Holden....	do	England..	12	1
do	do	do	do do	do	do	12	1
....	Ohio......	do	John and Sylvia Gould.....	do	N. Y. & O.	4	1
....	New York	....	David O. and Mary Gridley..	do	Connectic't	10	1
....	do	....	Jeremiah and Rachel Welber	do	New York	1	1
....	do	Educat'd..	Obadiah and Jane Gildersleve	do	....	6	1
....	Ohio......	Not......	Alva and Anise Wilson.....	do	New York	11	1
....	do	do	John and Elizabeth Bikel...	do	Germany.	1	1
....	do	do	Philip and Mary Dunderman	do	do	4	1
....	Germany..	do	Geo. and Catharine Dimeling	do	do	2	1
....	Ohio.....	do	Lewis and Bena Nolenburg..	do	do	3	1
....	do	do	Wm. and Dorothy Hitzelberg	do	do	4	1
....	....	Educat'd..	John and Mary McKengel..	do	do	..	..
....	England..	do	John and Mary Bulhand....	Brick-layer	Unknown.	14	1
....	Ohio.....	Not......	James and Elizabeth Clark..	Farmer...	New Jersey	2	2
....	do	do	do do	do	do	2	2
....	do	do	John and Nancy Stutler....	do	Germany..	3	1
....	New York	Educat'd..	Jonathan and Dolly Hastings	Shoemaker.	Massach'ts	1	1

134

RETURN of the Number of Deaf and Dumb, Blind, Insane, and Idiotic Persons

Townships.	Names of persons.	Nature of Affliction.	Duration of Affliction.	Cause where known.	Age.	Sex.	Color.
Bedford	Deborah Sloan	Insane	9 years	Unknown	56	Fem'le	White
"	Benjamin Palmer	Idiotic	15 "	Fits	36	Male	do
"	Charles Duncan	Blind	8 "	Cataract	74	Male	do
"	Susan Stancart	Deaf and dumb	10 "		10	Fem'le	do
"	Steven Riddle	Idiotic	2 "		18		do
"	Ruth Donnard	Idiotic	18 "	Sickness	30	Fem'le	do
Rutland	Luana Hott	Deaf	10 "	Fever	14	Fem'le	do
"	John Bellows	Deaf and dumb	47 "	Cold	49	Male	do
"	Maria Bellows	Idiotic	47 "	Unknown	47	Fem'le	do
"	Geo. W. Chase	Deaf and dumb	3 "	Fever	17	Male	do
Salem	James Halliday	Insane	54 "	Unknown	54	Male	do
"	Wm. Lynch	Idiotic	37 "	"	37	Male	do
"	Mary Montgomery	Insane	10 "	"	10	Fem'le	do
"	Joshua Folden	Idiotic	7 "	"	7	Male	do
"	C. Vonschritts	Insane	42 "	"	42	Fem'le	do
"	Noah McLaughlin	Idiotic	38 "	"	38	Male	do
"	Mary Stewart	Idiotic	15 "	"	15	Fem'le	do
Salisbury	Arch'd Armitage	Insane	3 "	Spiritual rapping	55	Male	do
"	Betsy Everton	Deaf and dumb	39 "		39	Fem'le	do
"	John Davis	Blind	4 "	Burned by powder	33	Male	do
"	Enos Gilmore	Idiotic	27 "	Fits	37	Male	do
Olive	John Congrow						do
"	Barbara Congrow	Idiotic	15 years	Unknown	15	Fem'le	do
"	Martha Saunders	Rickets	7 "	Unknown	7	Fem'le	do
Letart	Jerusha Haymarn	Blind	3 "	Chronic	55	Fem'le	do
"	Alfred Sagre	Deaf and dumb	28 "		28		do
"	Wesley Hayman	Insane	5 "	Unknown	30	Male	do
Lebanon	S. Torrence	Insane	27 "	Sickness	27	Fem'le	do
"	Hiram Perry	Idiotic	17 "		17	Male	do
Columbia	Mahala Awmiller	Idiotic & dumb	15 "		15	Fem'le	do
"	Wm. Connor	Insane	8 "	Fits	21	Male	do
Chester	Mary Kaff	Deaf and dumb	14 "	Hooping cough	18	Fem'le	do
"	Elizab'h Kendal	Idiotic	5 "	Unknown	30	Fem'le	do
"	Alexander Adams	Idiotic			30	Male	do
"	Elizab'h Guilgurt	Idiotic			60	Fem'le	do
Scipio	Rufus Douglass	Dumb	34 "		34	Male	do
"	Mary Kirkendoll	Insane	18 "	Hardship	58	Fem'le	do
Sutton	M. M. Hayman	Deaf and dumb	9 "		9	Male	do
"	Martha Cullen	Blind	7 "	Small pox	73	Fem'le	do
"	Rachael Carnahan	Idiotic	10 "	Fever	11	Fem'le	do
"	Geo. Webster	Deaf and dumb	13 "	Fever	16	Male	do
"	Wm. Webster	Blind	3 months	Sickness	1	Male	do
"	Geo. Fallance	Deaf and dumb	17 years	Scarlet fever	18	Male	do

in the county of Meigs, State of Ohio, on the second Monday of May, 1856.

Occupation.	Birthplace.	Educated or not.	Names of parents.	Occupation.	Birthplace.	No. of child'n	No. of child'n thus afflicted.	Relationship of parents before marriage.
Farm'g	Canada	....	Frederick & Sarah Tubs	Farmer	Unknown	4	1	Unknown
......	Ohio	Not	J. & Mary M. Palmer	Farmer	Ohio	13	1	"
Potter	Virginia	Educated	Chas. & Susana Duncan	Potter	Va	10	2	"
......	Ohio	Not	Gab. & Elizab'h Stancart	Farmer	Ohio	6	1	"
......	Ohio	....	Daniel & Mrs. Donnard	....	Unknown	8	1	
Sewing	"	Educated	Chas. M. & Maria E. Hott	Hotelk'r	Ohio	2	1	None
Farm'g	"	Not	Benj. & Elizabeth Bellows	Farmer	N. J. & Pa.	10	1	"
None	"	Not	....	....	....	...	...	....
Farmer	"	Educated	Francis & Louisa Chase	Farmer	Maine	3	1	None
None	Scotland	Not	Alex. & Jane Halliday	Weaver	Scotland	7	1	2d cousins
"	Penn	Can read	James & Elizabeth Lynch	Farmer	Penn	6	1	Cousins
"	Ohio	Not	Wm. & Laura Montgomery	"	Ohio	1	1	None
"	"	"	Robert & Mary Folden	"	Va	4	1	Cousins
"	"	"	A. & Elizab'h Vonschrittz	"	Unknown	11	1	None
"	"	"	McLaughlin	Unkno'n	Unknown	1	1	Bro. & Sis.
"	"	"	Jos. & Elizab'h Stewart	Farmer	Penn	12	1	None
Farmer	Penn	Educated	John & Nancy Armitage	"	....	8	1	"
ieams's	....	Not	David & Betsy Romine	"	....	...	...	
Coaldig	Wales	Educated	Richard & Catharine Davis	"	Wales	8	1	
one	Ohio	Not	Saml. & Elizab'h Gilmore	Cooper	....	..	...	None
......	......	....	....	....	....	...	...	....
one	Ohio	Not	John & Mary Congrow	Farmer	Ohio	6	1	None
"	"	Not	David & Judy Saunders	Laborer	Ohio	2	1	"
......	"	Educated	Ezra & Elizabeth Chapman	....	Conn	5	1	"
aborer	"	"	D. B. & Phebe Sagre	Mason	Va	6	1	"
Engin'r	Virginia	"	Josiah & Nancy Hayman	Farmer	Maryland	10	1	"
......	Ohio	Not	Aaron & Lucy Torrence	Farmer	Conn	5	1	"
......	"	"	John & Hannah Perry	Laborer	Unknown	8	2	"
None	"	"	D. & Catharine Awmiller	Farmer	Va	7	1	"
None	"	"	David & Delilah Connor	Farmer	Ohio	7	1	"
None	Germany	"	Peter & Elizabeth Kaff	Farmer	Germany	8	1	"
None	Unknown	Educated	Owen & Sophia Kendal	Farming	Ohio	12	2	"
......	Ohio	Not	Polly Adams	....	Ohio	5	...	
None	N. Jersey	"	Daniel & Mary Guilgurt	Farmer	N. Jersey	7	1	
......	Ohio	"	John & Ellenor Douglass	Farmer	....	9	1	None
......	....	Educated	....	Farmer	....	7	1	"
......	Ohio	Not	Spencer H. Hayman, jr	Miner	Ohio	5	1	"
......	N. Jersey	"	Israel Brooks	Weaver	N. Jersey	12	1	"
......	Virginia	"	Stephen Carnahan	Broom'r	Ohio	4	1	Cousins
......	Ohio	"	John Webster	Boatman	Va	9	1	None
......	"	"	John Webster	Farmer	Va	9	...	"
......	"	"	Sallance	"	Ohio	8	1	"

RETURN of the number of Deaf and Dumb, Blind, Insane and Idiotic persons

Townships.	Names of persons.	Nature of affliction.	Duration of affliction.	Cause where known.	Age.	Sex.	Color.
Gibson	Henry Hedrick	Deaf and dumb		Unknown	48	Male	
Marion	Mary Chubb	Blind	5 years	Unknown	50	Fem'le	Col'd.
do	R. H. Kalphoff	Deaf and dumb	47 years	Unknown	47	Male	White
do	Elizabeth Rushaw	Insane	Unknown	Unknown	46	Fem'le	"
do	Catharine Bergman	Insane	Unknown	Unknown	35	"	"
Washington	Mary Ann B. Sells	Idiotic	2 months	Ague	22	"	"
do	August Rabe	Idiotic	1 year	Typhoid fever	24	Male	"
Butler	Edward Keith	Blind	7 years	Sickness	75	"	Black
Dublin	Sarah Eline	Insane	18 years	Fits	18	Fem'le	White
do	Nancy Kauffman	Idiotic	26 years		26	"	"
Jefferson	Seymour Craig	Insane	3 weeks	Unknown	60	Male	"
do	Mary E. Pierson	Insane	1 year	Unknown	30	Fem'le	"
do	Ann Hunter	Insane	9 years	Ir. menstruation	35	"	"
Centre	Sarah Erline	Insane	18 years	Fits	18	"	"
do	Nancy Kaufman	Idiotic	26 years		26	"	"

in the county of Mercer, State of Ohio, on the second Monday of May, 1856.

Occupation.	Birth-place.	Educated or not.	Names of Parents.	Occupation.	Birth-place.	No. Children.	No. children thus afflicted.	Relationship of parents before marriage.
Farmer..	Ohio....	Not....	H.Hedrick & H.Braden	Shoem'ker	Va.&Eng'd	8	2	....
....	N. Carol'a	Educ'ted	....	....	....	..	..	....
Shoemakr	Germany.	Educ'ted	....	....	....	..	..	....
....	Germany.	Educ'ted	....	....	....	..	..	....
....	Germany.	Not....	A. & Mrs. Bergmau..	Farmer..	Germany..	5	1	None.
....	Germany.	Educ'ted	....	....	....	3	1	None.
Farmer..	Germany.	Educ'ted	John & Mariah Rabe..	....	....	..	..	....
Farmer..	Virginia.	Not....	....	....	....	..	..	....
....	Penn....	Not....	David & Rachel Eline.	Farmer..	....	7	1	None.
None...,.	Penn....	Not....	C. & Nancy Kauffman.	Farmer..	Penn.....	5	1	2d Cousins.
Farmer..	Kentucky.	Educ'ted	J. & Elizabeth Craig..	Farmer..	Virginia..	10	1	....
....	Ohio....	....	S. and Sarah Craig...	Farmer..	Kentucky.	15	1	None.
Teacher..	Penn....	Educ'ted	Thomas & Ann Hunter	Baker...	Ireland...	5	1	....
....	Penn....	Not....	David & Rachel Erline	Farmer..	Penn.....	7	1	None.
None....	Penn....	Not....	C. & Nancy Kauffman.	Farmer..	Penn.....	5	1	2d Cousins.

RETURN of the number of Deaf and Dumb, Blind, Insane and Idiotic persons

Township.	Names of Persons	Nature of affliction	Duration of affliction.	Cause, where known.	Age.	Sex.	Color.
Spring cr'k	James G. Hilliard	Blind	5 years	Blasting Rock.	28	Male	White.
"	Samuel Minnear	do	15 do	Injuries to head	80	do	do
"	Jacob Zigler	Idiotic	47 do	Unknown	48	do	do
"	Josiah M'Kinney	do	16 do	Chill and fever.	16	do	do
"	Rebecca Ann Mott	do	16 do	Typhoyd fever.	14	Fem'le	do
Union	Henry Zook	do	Since birth	Hereditary	30	Male	do
"	Michael Zook	do		do	27	do	do
"	Abraham Zook	do		do	25	do	do
"	Polly Zook	do		do	23	Fem'le	do
"	Elizabeth Zook	do		do	21	do	do
"	Nancy Zook	do		do	19	do	do
"	Lydia Zook	do		do	18	do	do
"	Joseph O. Coate	do	47 years	Injury of head.	52	Male	do
"	Henry Pearson	Insane	5 do	Unknown	30	do	do
"	Henry Shearer	Deaf and dumb	27 do	Sickness	29	do	do
"	J. Shearer (h.s wife)	do do	25 do	do	25	Fem'le	do
"	Sarah A. Underwood	Idiotic	17 do	Unknown	17	do	do
"	Jacob Snyder	do	15 do	do	40	Male	do
"	George Evans	Deaf and Dumb	3 do	Sickness	3	do	do
Bethel	Mary Ann Mong	Idiotic	From birth	Unknown	43	Feml'e	de
"	George M. Mong	do	do	do	25	Male	do
Foster cre'k	Mary Long	do	30 years	Whoop'g cough	49	Fem'le	do
"	Serinus A. Brag	Insane	24 do	Unknown	24	Male	do
"	David Turner	do	3 do	do	67	do	do
"	Abgail Turner	do	12 do	Fits	42	Fem'le	do
Brown	Benjamin Bowersock	Blind	3 months.	Unknown	76	Male	do
Elizabeth	John S. Mott	Deaf and Dumb	8 years	Scarlet fever	10	do	do
"	Jacob Ullery	do	42 do	Unknown	42	do	do
Washingt'n	Christopher Kloffier	do	From birth.	do	40	do	do
"	O. Hadley (his wife)	do	do	do	37	Fem'le	do
"	John Roland	Insane		do		Male	do
Stannton	Mary Wagoner	do	4 years	Dysmenorrhœa.	25	Fem'le	do
"	Isabella Dye	Idiotic	20 do	Unknown	20	do	do
"	David T. Sayre	Insane	26 do	do	37	Male	do
"	A. H. Covault	Blind	2 do	Measles	12	do	do

139

in the county of Miami, State of Ohio, on the second Monday of May, 1856.

Occupation.	Birthplace.	Educated or not.	Names of Parents.	Occupation.	Birth-place.	No. Children	No. Children thus afflicted.	Relationship of parents before marriage.
Farmer	Ohio.....	Educat'd	Joseph Hilliard..........	Farmer	N. Jersey	7	1	None.
do	Penn......	do	Jno. and Mary Minnear...	Bl'ksmth	do	9	1	do
None...	do	do	Jno. and Mary Zigler.....	Farmer	Penn....	6	1	do
do	Ohio.....	Not	A. and Almira McKinney .	do	do	5	1	do
do	do	do	Jno. and Susan Mott.....	do	Ger. & O.	10	1	do
Farmer	do	do	Nancy Zook.............	Farmer	Unkno'n	7	7	do
do	do	do	do	do	do	..	1	....
do	do	do	do	do	do	..	....	....
do	do	do	do	do	do	..	....	....
do	do	do	do	do	do	..	....	....
do	do	do	do	do	do	..	....	....
do	do	do	do	do	do	..	....	....
do	S. Carolina	do	Samuel Coate............	Farmer	S. C'rlna	8	1	3d cousins.
do	Ohio	Educat'd	Robert Pearson	do	do	10	1	None.
do	do	do	Eli Shearer..............	do	Ohio....	8	1	do
do	do	do	Not known..............	....	....	..	....	....
do	Penn......	Not	Thos. Underwood........	Farmer	Penn....	7	1	None.
do	Ohio	do	Henry Snyder	Mechanic	Unkno'n	2	1	do
None...	do	do	Wm. Evans	....	do	2	1	do
do	do	do	Jac. and Margaret Mong..	Farmer	Md.&Irl.	..	2	do
do	do	do	do do	....	....	..	....	....
Farmer	Virginia..	Partly ..	Jas. and Sarah Long......	Farmer	Ireland	12	1	do
do	N. Jersey..	Not	Isaac and Elizabeth Brag .	do	N. Jersey	9	1	do
do	Penn.....	Educat'd	Abm. and Elizabeth......	do	America.	4	1	do
None...	do	do	David and Elizabeth......	do	England	6	1	do
Bl'ksmth	do	do	George Bowersock........	do	Germany	12	1	do
Farmer	Ohio......	Not	Mary A. and Josiah Mott..	do	Ohio....	10	1	do
do	Kentuckey.	do	Jacob and Catherine Ullery	do	Ky.	13	1	do
Plasterer	Germany	do	....	....	....	..	....	....
....	England ..	Educat'd	James Hadley...........	Shoem'kr	England.	3	1	do
None...	Ohio......	Educat d	John and Cath. Wagoner..	Farmer ..	O. & Va	5	1	do
do	do	Not	Benj. and Elizabeth Dye ..	do	O. & Ky.	2	1	do
do	do	Educat'd	Jno. and Matilda Sayre ..	Carpent'r	O. & N J.	8	1	do
do	do	Not	W. W. and Harriet Covault	Farmer..	O. & Pa.	6	1	do

RETURN of the Number of Deaf and Dumb, Blind, Insane and Idiotic persons

Township.	Names of Persons.	Nature of Affliction.	Duration of Affliction.	Cause Where Known.	Age.	Sex.	Color.
Adams	John Miller	Deaf and dumb	28 years	Natural	28	Male	White
do	David Palmer	Blind	10 do	do	70	"	"
Benton	Abigal Dye	Idiotic	36 do	do	36	Fem'le	"
do	Sarah Judge	Blind	2 do	Pain in head	70	"	"
do	Susannah Walker	Insane	14 months	Cold	34	"	"
do	Mary E. Wenmoth	do	17 years	Not known	20	"	"
do	John Hill	Idiotic	9 do	do	12	Male	"
Bethel	Benjamin McVey	Insane	13 do	do	26	"	"
do	Joseph Wise	Idiotic	22 do	do	22	"	"
Franklin	James Dailey	Deaf			30	"	"
do	Thomas Dailey	do			10	"	"
Green	John Wittche	Deaf and dumb	29 years	Scarlet Fever	34	"	"
do	Barbara Wittche	do	29 do	do	32	Fem'le	"
do	Ann Wittche	do	29 do	do	29	"	"
do	Nicholas Wittche	do	28 do	do	28	Male	"
do	Frederick Wittche	do	25 do	From birth	25	"	"
Jackson	Mary Lucretia Melott	Blind	2 do	Scarlet fever	8	Fem'le	"
Ohio	Peter Anshutz	do	1 do	Disease	58	Male	"
do	Elizabeth Lishee	Idiotic	fr'm inf'ncy	Unknown	36	Fem'le	"
do	John Bachman	do	do	do	37	Male	"
do	Mary Tomb	do	do	do	21	Fem'le	"
do	Thomas Longwell	Deaf and dumb	do	do	47	Male	"
do	Magdalena Sutter	Idiotic	do	do	36	Fem'le	"
do	John F. Miller	Insane	20 years	do	50	Male	"
Perry	James L. Paris	Idiotic	from birth		23	"	"
Salem	Nicholas Fanhouser	Deaf and dumb	do		30	"	"
do	Mary Smith	Idiotic	do		24	Fem'le	"
do	Catharine Rongher	do	do		64	"	"
do	James Forest	do	3 years	Epilepsy	5	Male	"
do	James Notts	Insane	1 do	Unknown	30	"	"
do	John Yoho	Idiotic	From birth	Epilepsy	19	"	"
Sunsbury	Daniel Stuckey	Deaf and dumb	Since birth	Unknown	48	"	"
do	John Stuckey	do	do	do	42	"	"
do	Elizabeth Pittman	Insane	10 years	Exposure	36	Fem'le	"
Switzerland	Salathiel Smith	Idiotic	From birth	From birth	37	Male	"
do	Josephus Smith	do	do	do	27	"	"
do	Seecrisa Smith	do	do	do	18	"	"
do	Ann Crabb	Insane	do	do	33	Fem'le	"
do	Cercillia Trehappat	do	15 years	Scarlet fever	18	"	"
Wayne	Martha Moore	Idiotic	11 do	Convulsions	12	"	"
do	Margaret Bates	do	2 do	do	3	"	"
do	Enoch Craig	Insane	11 do	Not known	50	Male	"
do	Margaret Cronin	Idiotic	From birth	do	38	Fem'le	"

141

in the County of Monroe, State of Ohio, on the second Monday of May, 1856.

Occupation.	Birth-place.	Educated or not.	Names of Persons.	Occupation.	Birth-place.	No. children.	No. children thus afflicted.	Relationship of Parents before marriage.
Farmer ..	Switzerl'nd	Not	John and Eliz. Miller	Farmer ..	Switzerla'd	6	1	None ....
do	Penn.....	Limited .	John Palmer	"	....	..	..	....
....	Ohio	Not	James and Eliz. Dye	"	Virginia ..	..	1	Unknown
....	Nova Sco'a	Limited .	....	..	....	..	..	....
....	Penn......	Educated	Aaron Walker	Farmer ..	Pennsylva.	10	1	....
....	do	Not	John Wenmoth	"	England ..	1	1	....
....	Ohio	do	Edward Hill	"	New York	1	1	....
....	do	do	Isaac and M. McVey	"	Virginia ..	5	1	None ....
....	do	do	Jos. and Eliz. Wise..	"	Penn.....	14	1	"
Farmer ..	do	Educated	Vincent and M. Dailey	"	Ohio	8	2	"
do	do	Not	do do do	"	do	8	2	"
Cabin't mr	Switzerl'nd	Educated	Jacob and M. Wittche	"	Switzerl'nd	10	5	"
....	do	Not	do do do	"	do	10	5	"
....	do	do	do do do	"	do	10	5	"
....	do	Limited .	do do do	"	do	10	5	"
....	do	do	do do do	"	do	10	5	"
....	Ohio	Not	John P. and M. Melott	"	Ohio	7	1	"
Farmer ..	Europe ...	Educated	N. and Marg. Anshutz	Joiner ...	Europe ...	7	1	Unknown
....	U. States..	Not	Jacob and C. Fisher..	Farmer ..	do	12	1	"
None	Europe ...	do	Chris. and C. Bachman	"	do	4	1	"
do	do	Educated	Jacob and May Tani .	"	do	6	1	"
Boatman .	U. States..	Not	John and R. Longwell	"	U. States..	9	2	"
....	Europe ...	do	John and Ann Suter..	"	Europe ..	6	1	"
Preacher .	do	Educated	Unknown	Unknown.	Unknown .	..	..	....
None	Ohio	Not	Peter and M. A. Paris	"	France....	12	1	None ....
Farmer ..	Switzerl'nd	do	Samuel Fanhouser....	"	Switzerl'nd	2	1	"
....	Ohio. ...	do	John and M Smith...	"	Ohio	7	1	"
None	Pennsylva.	do	....	..	....	..	..	....
do	Ohio	do	H. and Martha Forest	Farmer ..	Ohio	5	1	None ....
Farmer ..	Pennsylva.	do	L. and Elizabeth Motts	"	Penn	5	1	"
do	Ohio.....	do	John and Sarah Yohe	"	Ohio	4	1	"
do	New Jersey	Educated	Joseph and R Stuckey	"	New Jersey	4	2	"
do	do	do	do do do	"	do	4	2	"
....	Ohio	Not	David and S. Vannert	"	do	8	1	"
None	do	do	Zachary and E. Smith	"	Pennsylv'a	6	3	"
do	do	do	do do do	"	do	..	....	"
do	do	do	do do do	"	do	..	....	"
do	Germany..	do	Benedict Crabb	"	Germany..	2	1	"
do	Ohio	do	Jac. and S. Tschappat	"	Switzerla'd	10	1	"
do	do	do	Jos. and Sarah Moore	"	Maryland .	8	1	"
do	do	do	David and J. Bates ..	"	Virginia ..	4	1	1st cous.
Farmer ..	....	Educated	Daniel and B. Craig..	"	Europe .	..	..	....
....	Ohio	Not	M. and P. Cronin	"	Virginia ..	12	1	None ....

RETURN of the number of Deaf and Dumb, Blind, Insane and Idiotic persons in

Names of Persons.	Nature of affliction.	Duration of affliction.	Cause where known.	Age.	Sex.	Color.	Occupation.
Margaret Runk	Deaf	From birth	Not known	46	Fem'le	White	House w'k
Louisa McClain	Blind	1 year	"	35	"	White	
Mary Jane McCord	Deaf	From birth	"	20	"	White	Hous w'k
Daniel Unger	Blind	12 years	"	70	Male	White	Farming
Elizabeth Unger	Insane	20 "	"	55	Fem'le	White	"
Samuel Aughry	"	F'm infan'y	"	60	Male	White	
George Homer	"		Intemperance	50	"	"	
Daniel Davidson	Deaf and dumb	4 years	Bilious fever	11	"	"	
Eli Hoover	Blind	31 "	Born	31	"	"	Br'm makr
James Elliott Hoover	"	21 "	"	21	"	"	"
William Hoover	"	19 "	"	19	"	"	"
Charles Hoover	"	10 "	"	10	"	"	
Samuel Martin	Deaf	25 "	"	25	"	"	Farming
Precilla Rose	Blind	46 "	"	46	Fem'le	"	
Henry S. Beck	Deaf and dumb	46 "	Unknown	46	Male	"	Shoemak'r
Mary Ann Beck	" "	24 "	Fever	26	Fem'le	"	
Harriet Beck	" "	9 "	Unknown	9	"	"	
Lydia Jane Coffey	Insane	9 "		9	"	"	
Catharine Fontz	Blind	69 "	Born	69	"	"	Flax spinn
Hannah Fontz	"	67 "	"	67	"	"	"
Hannah Hoover	"	33 "	"	33	"	"	Knitting
Nancy Andrews	Idiot	From birth	Unknown	20	"	"	
Gabriel Andrews	Idiot	"	"	10	Male	"	
Isaac Brukett	Deaf and dumb	"	"	53	"	"	Farming
Elenor Honning	" "	26 years	"	28	"	"	"
Jeremiah Campbell	Insane	50 "	Fits	54	"	"	
Jacob Tussel	"	15 "	Unknown	25	"	"	
Nancy Swartzel	Idiot	F'm 6m. old	Spasms	38	Fem'le	"	
Elizabeth Swartzel	Insane	6 years	Unknown	50	"	"	Farming
Alfred Schenck	Idiot	From birth	"	32	Male	"	None
David Brumbaugh	Deaf and dumb	"	"	19	"	"	Farmer
John Aunnon	Blind	Infancy	"	44	"	"	None
Addison Nicholas	Idiotic	From birth	"	19	"	"	None
John Stiver	Deaf and dumb	"		28	"	"	Farming
Susan Bateman	Idiot	6 years	Measels	9	Fem'le	"	None
Joseph P. Steele	"	F'm infan'y	Unknown	33	Male	"	"
Sallie Perine	"	"	Injury of Spine	15	Fem'le	"	"
Hary Diple	Blind	2 years	Unknown	56	Male	"	Laborer
Susanna Helbrade	"	4 years	Sickness	42	Fem'le	"	
Margaret Galiam	"	2 "	Inflammation	70	"	"	
Sarah Staley	"	1 "		65	"	"	
Catharine Hand	Idiotic	11 "		22	"	"	
Charles Laglor	"	8 "		9	Male	"	
Mary Ann M. Shado	"	7 "	Fits	14	Fem'le	"	
Cherib Eberz	Blind	2 "	Sickness	36	Fem'le	"	
Ernstina Weckel	Blind	30 "	Yellow Fever	30	"	"	
Jordan A. Clifton	Idiotic	20 "	Fits	36	Male	"	

the County of Montgomery, State of Ohio, on the second Monday of May, 1866.

Birth-place	Educat'd or not.	Names of Parents.	Occupation.	Birth-place	No. Children	No. Children thus Afflicted	Relationship of parents before marriage.
Germany..	Not....	John Runk................	Laborer..	Germany..	3	1	None.
Ohio.....	Educat'd	John and Elizabeth Vail....	Farmer..	Penn......	10	1	"
Ohio. ...	"	Enoch and Sarah McCord....	Carpenter.	Penn......	4	1	"
N. Carolina	"	....	Farming ..	N. Carolina	3	1	"
Ohio	Not	Bouzer....................	"	Virginia...	..	..	....
Penn......	"	....	"	Penn......	7	1	None.
Ohio	"	Francis and Jane R. Davidson	Farmer ...	Ross co...	6	1	None.
"	Educat'd	Daniel and Susan Hoover......	"	O.&N.Car	10	5	2d cousins.
"	"	" "	"	" "	10	5	"
"	"	" "	"	" "	10	5	"
"	....	" "	"	" "	10	5	"
"	Educat'd	Joseph and Susan Martin......	"	Pa. & Ohio	14	2	....
Kentucky .	....	William and Elizabeth Rose...	Brick makr	Eng.&N.O	5	1	....
Maryland .	Educat'd	....	....	....	..	..	....
Ohio	....	Jacob and Margaret Beck......	Farming ..	Md. & Ohio	8	2	....
"	....	" "	"	"	8	2	....
"	....	Jacob E. and Mary Coffy	Blacksmith	Ohio & Pa.	5	1	....
N. Carolina	....	David and Elizabeth Fontz...	Farming ..	Maryland .	9	6	First cous.
"	....	" "	"	"	9	6	"
Ohio	Educat'd	Daniel and Susan Hoover.....	"	O. & N. O.	10	5	2d cousins.
Ohio	Not	John and Elizabeth Andrews..	"	....	2	2	None.
Ohio	Not	" "	"	....	2	2	"
Ohio	Not	Henry and Elizabeth Brukett .	"	....	2	4	"
Penn......	Educat'd	Wm. F. and Hannah Houning	"	Penn......	9	1	"
Ohio	Not	Not known...............	Dead	New Jersey	4	1	"
"	Not	David and Hannah Tussel....	Fatherdead	Ohio	6	1	"
"	Not	Philip and Eve Swartzel......	Farming ..	Penn......	11	1	"
Maryland .	Educat'd	Henry and Christine Christ....	"	Maryland .	6	1	"
Ohio	Not	Peter and Patience Schenck....	Carpenter..	Penn'a....	3	1	"
"	Not	David & Elizabeth Brumbaugh	Farming ..	"	10	1	"
Penn	Not	George and Mary Aunnon.....	"	"	2	1	"
Ohio......	Not	Bemjamin and Abby Nicholas.	Laborer ...	"	8	1	"
"	Not	Catherine & Casper Stiver....	Farming ..	"	6	1	"
"	Not	John and Ellen Bateman......	....	Ireland ...	3	1	"
Dayton ...	Not	James and Phebe Steele	Merchant .	Va. & Rd. I	2	1	"
"	Not	Jane and —— Perrine........	"	N.J.& O..	5	1	"
Germany..	Not	....	....	....	..	..	....
Penn'a....	Not	Henry Oaks...............	Farming ..	Penn'a....	4	....	None.
Ireland ...	Educat'd	Martin Munk..............	Laborer ..	Ireland ...	5	1	"
Maryland .	....	....	....	....	..	..	....
Germany..	....	John and Lena Hand	Shoemaker	Germany..	4	1	None.
Dayton O.	....	Christena Laglor............	....	Germany..	9	1	"
"	....	George and Rebecca Shado....	....	Ohio	3	1	"
Germany..	Educat'd	Tynoly and Elizabeth Eberz..	Shoemaker	Germany..	..	..	....
....	"	John G. & Maria R. Weckel...	"	....	8	1	None.
Ohio	"	Henry and Rhoda Clifton.....	Laborer..	Virginia ..	9	1	None.

RETURN of the number of Deaf and Dumb, Blind, Insane and Idiotic persons

Names of Persons.	Nature of affliction.	Duration of affliction.	Cause where known.	Age.	Sex.	Color.	Occupation.
BLOOM TOWNSHIP.							
Jedediah Lehew	Deaf and dumb	F'm inf'ncy	Scarlet fever	24	Female	White.	None.
Edith Border	" "	12 years	Lung fever	15	do	do	do
Andrew Fouts	" "	18 "	Unnkown	21	Male	do	At scho'l
CENTRE TOWNSHIP.							
Jane Paxton	Idiotic	F'm infa'cy	Fits	31	Female	do	
William Paxton	"	"	"	38	Male	do	
Sally Paxton	"	"	"	2	Female	do	
John Paxton	"	"	"	28	Male	do	
Joseph Newton	"	"	Unknown	10	do	do	
Mary A. Stevenson	"	"	"	14	Female	do	
Jacob Phillis	"	"	"	17	Male	do	
David Donaldson	"	"	Fits	16	do	do	
MARION TOWNZHIP.							
Charles Kirk	Insane	3 years	Spiritualism	25	Male	do	Dentist
William Crew	Idiotic	F'm infa'cy	Unknown	3	do	do	
Eliza Wood	"	"	"	8	Female	do	
Elmer Strahl	Blind	45 years	"	50	Male	do	
Hannah Stevens	Insane	15 "	"	65	Female	do	
MALTA TOWNSHIP.							
James McGunegal	Blind	23 years	Inflammation	52	Male	do	Farmer
James L. Newman	"	F'm inf'ncy		13	do	do	
MEIGSVILLE TOWNSHIP							
William Neely	Idiotic	45 years	Fright	50	Male	do	
Robert Neely	Blind	12 "	Opera'n for cat't	51	do	do	Farmer
John Little	Deaf and dumb	From birth,		26	do	do	Farmer
James Murray	" "	"		9	do	do	Farmer
UNION TOWNSHIP.							
George Vanhorn	Deaf & Insane,	20 years	Scarlet Fever	30	Male	do	
WINDSOR TOWNSHIP.							
James White	Blind	8 years	Inflam. f'm cold	53	Male	do	Farmer

in the County of Morgan, State of Ohio, on the second Monday of May, 1856.

Birth-place.	Educated or not.	Names of Parents.	Occupation.	Birth-place.	No. children	No. children thus afflicted.	Relationship of parents before marriage.
Ohio	Educated	Wm. and Sarah Lehew	Farmer ...	Ohio	12	1	None.
"	.. Not	George and Eliza Border	do	do	9	1	do
"	.. At asyl'm	Jacob and Marg. Fouts	do	Penn	10	1	do
Ohio	Not	Samuel and Ellen Paxton	Farmer ...	Maryla'd			
do	do	do do do	do	do			
do	do	do do do	do	do	11	4	1st cousi's
do	do	do do do	do	do			
do	do	Alex. & Izabell Newton	do	Virginia ..	4	1	None.
do	do	Thomas and Ann Stevenson ...	Peddler ...	Ireland ...	5	1	1st cousi's
do	do	Joseph and Elizabeth Phillis ..	Farmer ...	Penn	7	1	None.
Penn	do	Wm. and Rebecca Donaldson ..	do	do	4	1	do
Ohio	Educated	Aguilla and Sarah Kirk	Farmer ...	Maryland .	7	1	None.
do	Not	Henry and Edith Crew	do	Ohio	8	1	do
do	do	Samuel and Orpha Wood	do	Penn	3	1	do
Penn	....	John and ——— Strahl	do	do	..	1	do
do	Not	....	....	....	..	1	....
Conn	Educated	Dan and Amy McGunegal	Farmer ...	Conn	..	1	None.
Ohio	Not	Wm. and Jane Newman	do	Ohio	..	1	do
Ireland ...	Limited ..	John and Elizabeth Neely	Farmer ...	Ireland .	10	2	None.
do	Common .	do do do	do	do ..			
do	Not	John and Margaret Little	do	do	6	1	do
Ohio	do	James and Harriet Murray	do	Ohio	5	1	do
Virginia ..	Not	Thomas and Ann Vanhorn	Farmer ...	Va	10	1	None.
Ohio	Common .	....	....	....	..	1	....

10—REP, SEC'Y. STATE.

RETURN of the number of Deaf and Dumb, Blind, Insane and Idiotic persons in

Township.	Names of Persons.	Nature of Affliction.	Duration of Affliction.	Cause where known.	Age.	Sex.	Color.
Bennington	Mary O. McDonald	Deaf and dumb	3 years	Sickness	4½	Fem'l	White
Lincoln	Emeri Shoup	Deaf	14 "	Fever	19	Male	do
Cardington	John P. Volly	Insane	5 "	Unknown	72	Male	do
"	Sidney White	Idiotic	29 "	Congenital	29	Male	do
"	Allen White	Idiotic	24 "	"	24	Male	do
"	Zebulon White	Idiotic	17 "	"	17	Male	do
"	Summerlot	Insane	11 months	Unknown	35	Male	do
Westfield	Abigail Aldrich	Blind	3 years	Unknown	56	Male	do
"	Catharine Jenkins	Blind	9 "	Cataract	77	Male	do
"	Jacob Sultz	Idiotic	Congenital		14	Male	do
"	Emily Springer	Idiotic	"		16	Fem'l	do
Canaan	Lydia Weber	Idiotic	12 years	Medicine	13	Fem'l	do
"	Samuel Christy	Blind	39 "	Accident	40	Male	do
"	Elmira Knight	Blind	14 "	Hooping cough	2½	Fem'le	do
Congress	John Stott	Deaf and dumb	6 months	Fever	42	Male	do
"	Asonatto Stott	Deaf and dumb	Congenital	Congenital		Fem'l	do
"	Lydia Snell	Deaf and dumb	"	"		Fem'l	do
"	Alex. Maine	Deaf and dumb	"	"	16	Male	do
S. Bloomfi'd	Amand. Allington	Deaf and dumb	30 years	Sickness	40	Fem'le	do
"	Mary Lyon	Blind	8 "	Cataract	70	Fem'l	do
"	Emeline French	Insane	4 "	Sickness & trouble	28	Fem'le	do
Chester	Pemberton Carey	Idiotic	18 "	Unknown	18	Male	do
"	Joshua Emelon	Idiotic	12 "	Scarlatina	13	Male	do
"	Mary Evans	Insane	2 "	Unknown	40	Fem'le	do
"	Columbus Hunt	Idiotic	14 "	"	14	Male	do
"	Susan Mozier	Idiotic	8 "	"	30	F. m'l	do
"	Joseph Stilley	Idiotic	18 "	"	18	Male	do
Harmony	Isaac Brown	Insane	Nearly life		60	Male	do
"	Elizabeth Brown	Insane	"		50	Fem'l	do
Troy	Mary Ettinger	Insane & dumb	14 years	Fits	36	Fem'le	do
Franklin	Sylv'r Montaney	Deaf	40 "	White swelling	45	Male	do
Peru	Dorcas Benedict	Idiotic	13 "	Fits	15	Fem'le	do
"	Martha Vanduzor	Blind	2 "	Unknown	80	Fem'l	do

the county of Morrow, State of Ohio, on the second Monday of May, 1856.

Occupation.	Birth-place.	Educated or not.	Names of Parents.	Occupation.	Birth-place.	No. children	No. children thus afflicted	Relationship of parents before marriage.
....	Penn.....	Not	Mat. A. & O. R. McDonald	Farming	Penn.....	6	1	None
Asylum.	Ohio	Educated	Geo. & Mary Shoup	Farming	Maryland..	11	1	None
Shoema'r	Holland .	Not	Unknown	....	....	..	..	....
....	Ohio	Not	Noau & Fanny White....	Farmer .	Vermont ..	7	3	None
....	Ohio	Not	"	Farmer .	....	..	....	
....	Ohio	Not	"	Farmer .	....	..	....	
Farmer .	....	Educated	Johial & Zubah	Farming	Conn	10	2	None
Farmer	Va	Not	Rich. & Rebecca Ashwell.	Farming	Eng. & Fra	9	1	None
....	Indiana..	Not	....	....	....	..	..	
....	Ohio	Not	Pete Springer...........	Loafing	....	..	..	
....	Canaan .	Not	Jno & Nancy Weber	Fa mer .	Ger & Ohio	3	1	None
Brooma'r	Ohio	Not	D. & Martha Christy	"	Pa. & Ohio	16	1	None
Servant .	Ohio	Not	Thos & Sarah Knight...	"	Ohio	2	1	1st cous's
Farmer .	Penn....	Educated	John & Sarah Stott	"	Germany..	3	3	
Farmer .	Ohio	Not	"	"	....	..	..	
....	....	Not	D. & Mary Snell	"	New Eng.	12	4	
Farmer .	Ohio	Not	Charles Maine	"	Penn......	7	1	
Spinning	Penn.....	Partially	Geo. Allington..........	"	....	..	1	None
None ...	N. J.....	Partially	....	....	....	..	..	
"	Ohio	Educated	Lucius French	Farmer .	Unknown .	2	1	None
"	Oh o	Not	Jno. & Margaret Carey...	"	N. J......	8	1	"
"	Penn. ...	Not	Josh & Susan Emelon....	"	Penn......	4	1	"
"	Wales ...	Educated	....	"	Wales	6	1	"
"	Ouio	Not	L. & Phebe Hunt........	"	N. J......	5	1	"
"	O io	Educated	M & Laura Mozier	"	N. J.. ...	6	1	"
"	Ohio	Not	John Stilley	"	Penn......	8	..	"
Farmer .	....	Partially	....	....	....	..	..	
....	Penn.....	Partially	Jno. & Mary Ettinger....	Farmer .	Penn......	4	1	None
Farmer .	N. J.....	Not	....	....	....	..	..	
....	Penn.....	Not	D. & Grace Benedi t.....	Farmer .	N. Y. & O.	6	1	None
....	Conn	Educated	Samuel Griswold	Blksmith	Unknown .	3	1	Unknow

148

RETURN of the Number of Deaf and Dumb, Blind, Insane and Idiotic persons

Township.	Names of Persons.	Nature of affliction.	Duration of affliction	Cause where known.	Age.	Sex.	Color.
Zanesville,	Belinda McGinnis	Deaf and Dumb	21 years	[grains in ears Putting coffee	23	Fem'le	White.
"	David B. Hersh	Idiotic	16 "		16	Male	do
"	Mrs. Sam. Richardson	Blind	3 "	Intermit. Fever	45	Fem'le	do
"	David Caldwell	do	1 "	Cataract	64	Male	do
"	Ann Moore	Deaf and Dumb	9 "	Unknown	9	Fem'le	do
Madison	John Stoner	Blind	29 "	Sickness	68	Male	do
Blue Rock	Wm. H Hawarth	Deaf and Dumb	29 "	Cold	30	"	do
"	Hannah H White	Blind	11 "	Inflama in head	12	Fem'le	do
"	Mary A. McClane	do	13 "		13	"	do
Cass	Ruth Hopper	do	2 "	Influenza	70	"	do
Falls		Idiot				Male	do
Highland	Hannah Ramsay	Deaf and Dumb	44 years	Sickness	49	Fem'le	do
"	Israel Smith	Idiot	48 "		48	Male	do
"	Jane Jamison	Deaf and Dumb	9 "	Unknown	9	Fem'le	do
"	Andrew L. Bowman	Idiotic	18 "	do	18	Male	do
Hopewell	Nancy Taylor	Insane	18 "	do	55	Fem'le	do
"	Julia A Settles	Deaf and Dumb	6 "	do	6	"	do
"	Lucinda Bell	Dumb	16 "	do	16	"	do
"	Jesse France	Blind	8 "	do	8	Male	do
"	Alfred W. German	Idiotic	24 "	do	24	"	do
"	Resson Calvin	Idiotic & Blind	52 "	do	52	"	do
"	Elizabeth Allen	Insane	29 "	do	46	Fem'le	do
"	Ezekiel Prior	Dumb & Cripple	23 "	do	23	Male	do
"	Cyrus Weekly	Dumb	11 "	do	11	"	do
"	Eliza Perr'ne	Insane	10 "	Trouble	44	Fem'le	do
"	Ben. F. Harlan	Blind	2½ "	Cataract	3	Male	do
"	W. B. Eaton	Idiotic	13 "	Unknown	16	"	do
Jackson	Wyerd W. Whyde	do	20 "		20	"	do
Jefferson	Harriet Holt	Deaf and Dumb	30 "	Unknown	32	Fem'le	do
"	Rebecca Mills	Blind	2 "	Fever	19	"	do
Union	Wm. Vandivort	Idiotic	32 "	Unknown	32	Male	do
Licking	James Norris	do	27 "		27	"	do
"	Berick Stump	do		Malpractice	19	"	do
Monroe	David Eeson	Insane	9 "		35	"	do
Perry	Mahala Bowers	Deaf and Dumb	25 "	Cold	27	Fem'le	do
"	Philomela Bowers	do do	20 "	do	22	"	do
Newton	A. R. Keyes	Idiotic	12 "	Fits	12	Male	do
"	Sarah Morrow	Deaf and Dumb	26 "	Unknown	26	Fem'le	do
"	Amelia W. Moore	do do	22 "	do	22	"	do
"	Mr. Bash	Dumb & insane	8 "	Sickness	10		do
"	James C. Moore	Blind	2 "	do	36	Male	do
Washington	John Wesley Stotts	Idiotic	13 "	Unknown	13	"	do
"	Jeremiah Jones	"	9 "	do	9	"	do
"	Lydia Rhodes	Insane	3 "	Smoking & snuff	48	Fem'le	do
"	Elisha Fox	"	6 "	Epiletic Fits	35	Male	do
"	John Hunter	Deaf and dumb	24 "	Unknown	24	"	do
Rich Hill	Zeambra Warne	Insane	½ "		21	"	do
"	Wm. Robinson	Idiotic	From Child	Caught in storm	67	"	do
"	Eva Alice Dickson	Deaf and dumb	"		2	Fem'le	do
"	Darcus Howell	do do	"		30	"	do
Salem	John Taylor	Insane	3 years	Intemperance	60	Male	do
Salt Creek	Z. R. Chandler	Blind	6 "	Erysipelas	78	"	do
Fobs	John Spaulding	"	3 "	Cold	31	"	do
"	Martin French	Idiotic	32 "	Fever	34	"	do
"	Fanny Starrett	Insane	16 "		66	Fem'le	do
"	Fan. y Monroe	Idiotic			55	Fem'le	do
"	Francis Smith	Insane	7 years		30	Male	do
"	Abraham Lane	Deaf and dumb	28 "	Congenital	28	"	do

149

in the County of Muskingum, State of Ohio, on the second Monday of May, 1856.

Occupation.	Birthplace.	Educated or not	Names of Parents.	Occupation.	Birth place.	No. of child'n	No. of child'n thus afflicted.	Relationship of parents before marriage.
None...	Ohio....	Educa'ed	David and Susan M'Ginnis	Druggist	Penn...	1	1	None...
"	....	Not....	John and Nancy Hersh...	Clerk...	......	..	1	do
H keeper	....	Educa'ed	....	....	......	..	1	do
....	....	"	....	....	......	..	1	do
None...	Ohio....	Not....	Smith and B. Moore......	Drayman	Pa. & Md	11	1	do
Farmer.	Pennsylva	Educa'ed	John and Catharine Stoner	Farmer.	Penn...	8	1	do
None...	"	"	Warner & Orpha Haworth.	"	"	6	1	do
....	Ohio....	"	James and Sarah White..	"	Ire & Md	12	1	do
None...	"	"	John and Rebecca M'Clane	Laborer.	Unkn'wn	7	1	Unkn'wn
....	Maryland	"	Bayel Ricket............	Farmer.	Maryla'd	3	1	None...
Laborer.	Ohio.....	Not....	Quartus & Frances French.	Forgem'n	....	2	1	do
Wife...	Pennsylva	"	James and Jane Ross......	Farm er	Penn...	..	1	do
....	Virginia.	"	Thomas & Elizabeth Smith	"	Va & Pa.	15	1	do
....	Ohio....	"	John and Sarah Jamison ..	"	Penn...	4	1	do
....	"	"	Daniel & Margaret Bowman	"	Pa & Va.	10	1	do
None...	Unknown	Educa'ed	....	.....	......	..	....	....
"	Ohio....	....	Perry and Jula S. Settles.	Potter..	Ohio...	4	1	None...
"	"	Not....	David and Mrs. Bell.......	Farmer.	Penn...	6	1	"
"	"	....	William and Susan France	Laborer.	Virginia	8	3	Cousins.
"	"	Not....	Jesse and Mrs. German...	Carpen'r	Maryla'd	8	1	None...
"	Pennsylva	"	George and Hannah Colvin	None...	Penn...	..	1	"
"	N. Jersey	Educa'ed	Noah and Mrs. Allen.....	Farmer.	N. Jersey	7	1	"
"	Ohio....	....	John and Patience Prior..	"	Penn...	12	1	2d Cous
"	"	Not....	Nathan & Margaret Weekly	"	Virginia	6	1	None...
"	Pennsylva	Educa'ed	Archibald & Mrs. Perine..	"	Ireland.	9	1	"
....	Ohio....	....	Wm. and Mary J. Harlan.	"	Delaware	3	1	"
None...	"	Not....	Leven and Hannan Eaton.	"	Unkn'wn	1	1	"
Farmer.	"	"	Thomas and Mary Whyde.	....	Penn...	2	1	"
None...	England.	Educa'ed	Henry and Anna Holt....	Black'th	England	6	1	1st Cous.
"	Ohio....	"	Thomas & Elizabeth Mills	Miller..	Virginia	9	1	None...
....	"	Not....	Barnet & Eliza. Vandiwort	Farmer.	N Y & Pa	11	1	"
None...	"	"	Isaac and Anna Norris...	"	Unkn'wn	1	1	"
"	"	"	James and Cinthia Stump.	"	"	4	1	"
....	"	....	James and Lydia Eleson..	....	......	2	1	"
....	"	Educa'ed	Peter Bowers............	Farmer.	Penn...	10	2	"
....	"	"	Philomela Johnson.......	"	Conn...	..	....	....
....	"	Not....	A. R. and Sarah Keyes..	Black 'th	Virginia	9	1	None...
Seamst's	Unknown	Limited.	....	Farmer.	......	..	....	....
"	Ohio....	Educa'ed	Elija and Frances Moore..	"	Virginia	8	3	Cousins.
None...	"	Not....	Martin Bash............	"	Ohio...	7	1	None...
Tailor..	Pennsylva	Educa'ed	....	....	......	..	....	....
None...	Ohio....	Not....	Abraham & Eliza Stotts.	Farmer.	Penn...	16	1	None...
"	"	"	America & Rebecca Jones.	Laborer.	Ohio...	6	1	"
House'rk	Virginia.	Educa'ed	....	....	......	6	1	"
Farmer.	"	"	James and Mary Fox.....	Cooper..	Virginia	9	1	"
"	Ohio....	"	Samuel M. & Ann Hunter.	Farmer.	"	9	1	Cousins.
"	"	"	Jesse and Mercy Warne...	"	Penn...	6	1	None...
"	Pennsylva	"	Wm & Elizabeth Robinson	"	Ireland.	4	1	"
....	Ohio....	"	W. Dickson & E. Finney.	"	Ohio...	3	1	"
....	"	Educa'ed	James and Hetty Howell..	"	Penn...	6	1	"
Farmer.	Maryland	"	....	....	......	..	....	....
"	Vermont.	"	John and Mary Chandler..	....	Vermont	8	1	None...
Carpen'r	Ireland..	"	P. & Elizabeth Spaulding.	Farmer.	Ireland.	8	1	"
Laborer.	Ohio...	Not....	Quartus French..........	Forgem'n	N. York	3	1	"
Seamst's	Maryland	"	Francis French..........	....	"	..	....	....
....	Ohio	....	....	....	......	..	....	....
Soldier..	Ireland..	Educa'ed	....	....	......	..	....	....
....	Ohio....	Not	....	....	......	..	....	....

RETURN of the number of Deaf and Dumb, Blind, Insane and Idiotic

Names of Persons.	Nature of affliction.	Duration of affliction.	Cause where known.	Age.	Sex.	Color.	Occupation.
Anna E. Furby	Idiot			12	Fem'le	White	
Ann Lane	Insane			60	"	do	
Ann Carrigan	Insane		Epileptic fits	22	"	do	
Cassius Wine	Insane			26	Male	do	
Casander Carns	Idiot			28	Fem'le	do	
Conrad Zunkle	Insane			40	Male	do	
Christian Furnace	Insane			55	Fem'le	do	
Elizabeth Robinet	Idiot			46	"	do	
Elizabeth Starrett	Insane			64	"	do	
El zabeth Evergreen	Idiot			38	"	do	
Elizabeth Scofield	Insane	8 years	Disapp'd love	30	"	do	
Emaretta Selover	Insane			28	"	do	
Elizabeth Worthington	Insane			35	"	do	
Edward H. Rix	Insane	8 years	Loss of property	52	Male	do	Miller
Ellis Hart	Insane			40	"	do	
Geo. A. Downer	Insane	15 years		30	"	do	Clerk
Hiram Burshare	Idiot	5 "	Fever	56	"	do	
Hannah Brown	Insane			60	Fem'le	do	
Jesse Joseph	Idiot			28	"	do	
John Ayers	Idiot			50	"	do	
Jacob Harricut	Insane				"	do	
John Cristi	Insane	8 years		43	"	do	
Isabela Hoyt	Insane			35	Fem'le	do	
James M. Fulton	Insane	20 years		60	Male	do	Teacher
Lavina Welch	Idiot			19	Fem'le	do	
John Hughs	Idiot			18	Male	do	
Lucinda Cossibone	Idiot			22	Fem'le	do	
Lydia A. Smalley	Idiot			12	"	do	
Mary Shrigley	Idiot			27	"	do	
Mary A. Dickenson	Idiot	8 years		28	"	do	
Julia Reynolds	Insane			28	"	do	
Mary Clementine	Idiot			9	"	do	
Mila A. Kelts	Insane		Epileptic fits	11	"	do	
Motlene Burkey	Idiot		Epileptic fits	41	"	do	
Ma garet Winder	Insane			50	"	do	
Nancy Cordery	Insane	7 years		49	"	do	
Milton Thompson	Insane	5 "	Hard labor	25	Male	do	Farmer
Nancy Anderson	Insane	10 "		53	Fem'le	do	
Rachel Brookover	Insane		Epileptic fits	25	"	do	
Robert Meredith	Idiot			12	Male	do	
Temperance A. Vance	Insane				"	do	
Thomas Delemeter	Idiot			53	"	do	
Washington Woodruff	Insane			25	"	do	
Rob't B. Wallace	Insane				"	do	Clerk
Wm. Mack	Insane			70	"	do	Farmer
Wm. Davis	Insane	12 years		65	"	do	Farmer
Wm. Goff	Insane	15 "	Contusion head	60	"	do	Mason
Washington Stotts	Idio'			35	"	Black	

NOTE —All the above named persons are in County Infirmary.

persons in Muskingum County, Ohio—Continued.

Birthplace.	Educated or not.	Names of Parents	Occupation.	Birthplace.	No. of child'n	No. thus Afflicted.	Relationship of parents before marriage.
Ohio							
	Educated						
Ohio							
"							
Germany							
Ohio							
Ohio							
"							
"							
England							
Ohio	Educated	Appleton & Juliet Downer					
Ohio							
	Educated						
Ohio							
Penn							
N. J.							
Vt.							
Va.	Educated						
Ohio							
"							
"							
"							
"							
Ohio							
Germany							
Pa.							
Ohio							
Pa.							
Ohio							
Ohio							
N. Y.							
Ohio	Educated						
Ireland	Educated						
England	Educated						

RETURN of the number of Deaf and Dumb, Blind, Insane and Idiotic persons

Townships.	Names of persons.	Nature of Affliction.	Duration of Affliction.	Cause where known.	Age.	Sex.	Color.
Wayne...	John Parry...........	Insane........	2½ years	..Sickness......	34	Male.	White
do	John Kelsey........	Idiot..........	48 "	..Disease of head	50	Male.	do
Sharon...	Lucinda Scott......	Insane........	6 "	....	26	Fem'le	do
Seneca....	Catharine Musser....	Insane........	20 "	..Fits..........	29	"	do
Olive.....	Hannah Shepherd....	D'f, d'mb & bl'd	14 "	..Scarlet fever...	17	"	do
Noble....	Elizabeth McKee.....	Idiot..........	6 "	..Not known....	26	"	do
Marion...	William M. Haskell..	Idiot..........	11 "	..Epileptic fits..	20	Male.	do
do	James Crawford....	Idiot..........	16 "	..Unknown.....	16	"	do
do	Osborn Crawford....	Idiot..........	14 "	..Not known....	14	"	do
do	David Crawford......	Want of speech.	12 "	..Not known....	12	"	do
do	Amy Ann Hare......	Deaf and dumb	10 "	..Fever.........	12	Fem'le	do
do	Ruth E. Hare........	" "	4 "	....	4	"	do
do	Catharine Snider.....	Insane........	4 "	..Unknown.....	63	"	do
do	George Ray..........	Idiot..........	8 "	..Not known....	8	Male.	do
Enoch....	Zephaline Sanford....	Deaf and dumb	13 "	..Scarlet fever...	15	Fem'le	do
do	William Blazier......	Idiot..........	14 "	..Not known....	14	Male.	do
do	Nancy Armstrong....	Deaf and dumb	13 "	..Scarlet fever...	23	Fem'le	do
do	Lucy H. Ransom.....	Deaf and dumb	13 "	..Scarlet fever...	15	"	do
do	Henry T. Harris.....	Idiot.........	1 "	....	1	Male.	do
Center....	Reed McGeary......	Deaf and Dumb	25 "	..Not known....	31	"	do
Buffalo..	Mortimore B. Marcks..	Idiotic........	14 "	..Unknown.....	27	"	do
Beaver....	William H. Fickenson.	Idiotic........	23 "	..Fits..........	24	"	do
do	Margaret Moore......	Idiotic........	19 "	..Scalded.......	22	Fem'le	do
do	Thomas Carpenter...	Deaf and dumb	57 "	....	57	Male.	do
do	Thomas Carpenter....	Deaf and dumb	10 "	....	10	"	do
do	Weadow George......	Deaf and dumb	49 "	..Not known.	49	"	do
do	Lewis George........	Deaf and dumb	56 "	..Unknown.....	56	"	do
do	Sarah George........	Deaf and dumb	67 "	..Unknown.....	67	Fem'le	do
do	James Falls.........	Deaf and dumb	35 "	..Sickness......	40	Male.	do
do	John Brotton........	Insane........	14 "	..Sickness......	50	"	do
do	Sarah Hipsley......	Idiot	32 "	..Unknown.....	32	Fem'le	do
do	Jacob Jordan........	Insane........	24 "	..By cut on knee.	32	Male.	do
do	Linus Bacon........	Insane........	10 "	..Kick from horse	64	"	do
Elk......	Elizabeth Harper....	Idiotic........	12 "	..Unknown.....	12	Fem'le	do
do	John Stuart.........	Idiotic........	24 "	..Unknown.....	24	Male.	do
do	Philip Nihart........	Idiotic........	8 "	..Unknown.....	8	"	do
do	John Masters.......	Insane........	6 "	..Religion......	39	"	do
do	Gideon Mason......	Idiotic........	15 "	..Unknown......	15	"	do
do	Eliza G. Davidson....	Deaf and Dumb	14 "	..Unknown.....	14	Fem'le	do
do	Caroline Graver.....	Insane........	14 months.	....	31	"	do

153

in the County of Noble, State of Ohio, on the second Monday of May, 1856.

Occupation.	Birthplace.	Educated or not.	Names of Parents.	Occupation	Birth-place.	No. Children.	No. children thus afflicted.	Relationship of parents before marriage.
Farmer ..	Ohio	Educated	John & Rachel Parry...	Farmer ..	Penn	10	1	None.
"	Penn	Not	Smuel & Mary Kelsey..	Shoemakr	"	7	1	do
....	Ohio	Educated	James & Johanna Scott.	Farmer ..	"	9	1	do
None ...	Penn	Not.....	Henry and Sarah Musser	"	"	7	1	do
"	Ohio	"	Michael Shepherd......	"	Maryland.	17	1	do
Farmer ..	Ohio	"	William & Sarah Murray	....	New York.	..	....	Unknwn.
"	Ohio	"	Samuel & Catharine	Farmer ..	Ireland ...	7	1	None.
"	Ohio ..⎫							
"	Ohio ..⎬	"	...Leonidas and Lydia....	Farmer ..	Va. & Del.	5	3	Cousins.
"	Ohio ..⎭							
....	Ohio	"	Charles and Sarah Hare.	Merchant.	England ..	6	2	None.
Farmer ..	Ohio	"	" "	"	"	6	2	
Farming .	Maryland	"	C. & Rosanna Cowgill..	Cooper...	Maryland .	8	1	do
....	Ohio	"	Andrew and Sarah Ray.	Carpenter.	Virginia ..	5	1	do
....	Ohio	Educated	D. & Lucretia Sanford .	....	Maine	13	1	do
None	Ohio	Not	P. & Margaret Blazier...	Farmer ..	Ohio	5	1	do
....	Ohio	"	J. and Jane Armstrong..	"	....	9	1	do
None	Ohio	Educated	T. and Eliz. Ransom...	"	Ohio	5	1	do
....	Ohio	Not	Francis Meranda Harris.	....	"	4	1	do
Farming .	Ohio	Educated	John and Jane McGeary.	Farmer ..	Ireland ...	..	....	Unknwn.
None	Ohio	Not	M. and Hannah Marcks.	"	Virginia ..	10	1	1st cous.
"	Virginia .	"	Alexander Fickenson ...	"	Ohio	13	1	None.
"	Ohio	"	A. and Mary Moore	None	"	6	1	Unknwn.
"	Ohio	"	J. and Sarah Carpenter..	"	"	11	1	Unknwn.
"	Ohio	"	T. and Lavina Carpenter	"	"	5	1	Cousins.
Farmer ..	Virginia .	Educated	....	..	....	..	....	None.
"	Virginia .	Not	....	...	....	..	....	do
"	Virginia .	"	....	...	....	..	....	do
Shoemakr	Penn	Educated	....	...	....	..	....	
Farmer ..	N. Hamp.	"	....	...	....	..	....	
....	Ohio	Not	....	...	....	..	....	
....	Ohio	Educated	....	...	....	..	....	
Farmer ..	Mass	"	....	...	....	..	....	
....	Ohio	Not	J. G. and Jane Harper..	Bl'ksmith	Ohio	4	1	None.
None	Ohio	"	T. and Martha Stuart....	Farmer ..	Penn	1	1	do
"	Ohio	"	H. and Cath'e Nihart...	"	Germany..	1	1	do
Farmer ..	Ohio	Educated	....	...	....	..	....	
None	Ohio	Not	Gideon and Heater Mason	Farmer ..	....	..	1	None.
"	Ohio	"	L. and Asena Davidson..	"	Delaware .	..	1	do
"	Germany .	Educated	....	...	....	..	....	

RETURN of the number of Deaf and Dumb, Blind, Insane and Idiotic persons

Names of Persons.	Nature of Affliction.	Duration of Affliction.	Cause where known.	Age.	Sex.	Color.	Occupation.
Simon Grill	Dumb & idiot	6 years	Fits	6	Male	White	None
Samuel H. Davis	Dumb	26 "	Borne so	26	Male	do	None
Nelson Gertarl	Idiot	8 "	Not known	40	Male	Black	Farmer
Ashibald Beardsley	Insane	8 "	Not known	48	Male	White	Farmer
Susan Maria Porter	Deaf and dumb	Born so	Unknown	10	Fem'le	do	None
Catharine Eliza Ulthoff	Idiot	8 years	Fits	8	Fem'le	do	
Christina Braton	Blind	10 "	Unknown	56	Fem'le	do	
Ruth Ficox	Insane	40 "	By fever	55	Fem'le	do	
Louisa Reed	Insane	18 "	Sickness	19	Fem'le	do	None
Hannah Felton	Insane	8 "	Sickness	4	Fem'le	do	None

RETURN of the number of Deaf and Dumb, Blind, Insane and Idiotic persons

TOWNSHIPS.	Names of Persons.	Nature of Affliction.	Duration of Affliction.	Cause Where Known.	Age.	Sex.	Color.
Paulding	Lydia Haney	Idiotic		Fits	13	Fem'le	White
Jackson	William Stillwell	Deaf and dumb		Scarlet Fever	35	Male	White

in the county of Ottawa, State of Ohio, on the second Monday of May, 1856.

Birth-place	Educated or not.	Names of Parents.	Occupation.	Birth-place	No Children.	No. Children thus Afflicted	Relationship of parents before marriage.
New York.	Not	Adam & Margaret Grill	Shoemaker	Germany	4	1	None
New York.	Not	J. P. & Polly Davis	Farmer	New York.	19	1	None
Virginia	Not						
New York	Educated						
Ohio	Not	Truman & S. Porter	Farmer		7	1	None
Germany	Not	Henry & Mary Ann Ulthoff	Farmer	Germany	5	1	None
New Jersey	Educated				3	1	
New York.	Educated						
Ohio	Not	John & Susanna Reed	Farmer	Penn.	12	1	None
Ohio	Not	Martin & Lydia Felton	Farmer	Ohio	8	1	None

in the County of Paulding, State of Ohio, on the second Monday of May, 1856.

Occupation.	Birth-place.	Educated or not.	Names of Parents.	Occupation.	Birth-place.	No. Children	No. Children thus afflicted	Relationship of parents before marriage.
	Ohio	Not	W Haney and M. A. Tower	Farmer	Penn	4	1	None
Farmer	Ohio	Educat'd	Nich and Eliz. Stillwell	Farmer	Virginia	4	1	None

RETURN of the number of Deaf and Dumb, Blind, Insane and Idiotic Persons

Township	Names of Persons	Nature of affliction	Duration of Affliction	Cause where known	Age	Sex	Color
Reading	Sarah L. Barbee	Insane	14 years	Sickness	15	Female	White.
do	Eliza Jane Goble	do	19 do	Not known	19	do	do
do	Christian Ridenhour	Deaf	20 do	Sickness	40	Male	do
do	Alsinda Henderson	Insane	30 do	Not k-·wn	30	Female	do
do	Franklin Thomas	do	15 do	By a fall	17	Male	do
do	Mary Fredenhour	Blind	3 do	Fits	4	Female	do
do	George Beckwith	Idiotic	6 do	Not known	6	Male	do
Thorn	James R. Smutz	do	7 do	Nervous Spasm	10	do	do
do	Lucy Jane Stiner	Deaf and dumb	16 do	Cold in head	17	Female	do
do	Reuben Diltz	Insane	6 do	Worms	10	Male	do
do	Solomon Foster	do	15 do	Cold in head	17	do	do
do	David Starkey	Insane & Idiotic	30 do	Not known	30	do	do
do	Samuel Hite	Insane	10 do	Fever	24	do	do
do	Manda Garloch	do	14 do	Cold in head	16	Female	do
Jackson	John D. Middagh	do	14 do	Fits	24	Mule	do
do	Michael Fitzgerald	Idiotic	6 do	Medicine	7	do	do
do	Rachel Poling	Blind	16 do	Natural	16	Female	do
do	Isaac E Tavener	Deaf and dumb	24 do	do	24	Male	do
Pike	Sarah McGohon	do	38 do	Sickness	29	Female	do
do	Thomas Hutches	do	49 do	do	51	Male	do
do	Margaret Vickroy	do	36 do	do	38	Female	do
Clayton	John L. Gardner	Blind	3 do	Hurt	7	Male	do
do	Samuel H. Kochler	Idiotic	12 do	Not known	12	do	do
do	Henry Curl	do	25 do	do	25	do	do
Madison	Ferdinand Brown	Deaf and dumb	From birth	do	42	do	do
do	Moses Brown	do	do	do	38	do	do
do	George Diltz	Insane	3 years	do¯	84	do	do
Hopewell	Elizabeth Patterson	do	5 do	Erysipelas	45	Female	do
do	Abraham Bowser	Blind	14 do	Blasting rocks	44	male	do
do	Mary Gall	Deaf and dumb	28 do	Not known	28	Female	do
Harrison	Hannah Wiley	Insane	25 do	do	59	do	do
do	Stephen H. Ellis	Idiotic	35 do	do	39	Male	do
do	Rebecca Morrow	Insane	24 do	Measles	40	Female	do
Bearfield	Misal Deever	Deaf and dumb	39 do	Fever	42	Male	do
do	Elickum Robinett	Idiotic	28 do	Fits	42	do	do
do	Levi Robinett	do	1 do	do	34	do	do
do	Delilah Robinett	do	1 do	do	30	Female	do
Monday creek	Thomas D. Fox	Idiot	50 do	Not known	50	Male	do
do	William Hillery	Blind	1 do	Medicine	25	do	do
do	Lucinda Larimer	Idiot	11 do	Not known	13	Female	do
do	John F. Dodd	do	29 do	do	29	Male	do
Saltlick	Newman Jones	Deaf	14 do	Sickness	18	do	Col'rd.
do	Ezekiel Davison	Dumb	15 do	Fits	15	do	White.
do	Sarah Harbaugh	Insane	From birth	do	49	Female	do
do	Benjamin Wiles	Idiot	31 years	Sickness	33	Male	do
Monroe	Daniel Drake	Deaf and dumb	32 do	do	33	do	do
do	Richard Dawson	Blind	30 do	Not known	43	do	do
do	Susan Post	Idiotic	16 do	do	16	Female	do
Pleasant	Not any						

in the County of Perry, State of Ohio, on the second Monday of May, 1856.

Occupation.	Birthplace.	Educated or not.	Names of Parents.	Occupation.	Birthplace.	No. children	No. children thus afflicted.	Relationship of Parents before Marriage.
None.....	Ohio.....	Not	Samuel and E Barbee	Farmer...	Virginia...	5	1	2d cous.
do	do	do	Reuben Goble........	do	New Jersey	4	1	None.
Farmer...	Penn.....	Educated	Lewis Ridenhour	do	Penn.	8	1	do
None. ...	Ohio.....	Not j....	James Henderson	Carpenter .	do	9	1	do
do	do	do	Jesse and Eliz Thomas	Farmer...	Virginia...	11	1	do
do	do	do	....	Brewer....	Germany..	1	1	do
do	do	do	Benoni & M. Beckwith	Tanner ...	Ohio.	4	1	do
do	do	do	Jos. and Mary Smutz	Carpenter .	Maryland .	4	1	do
At school..	do	Educated	Fred. and Lydia Stiner	Saddler ..	Ohio	5	1	do
None	do	Ger. edu.	Wm. and Chris. Diltz	Farmer...	Can. & Eur	3	1	do
do	do	Not	Benj. and Mary Foster	do	Ohio	9	1	do
do	do	do	Jesse and C. Starkev .	do	do	8	2	do
Farmer...	do	Partially.	Samuel and Anna Hite	do	Penn.	7	1	1st cous
Sewing ...	Penn......	Not	Peter and C. Garloch .	do	do	1	1	None.
None	Ohio	Partially.	Thos. and M. Middagh	do	Ohio	9	1	do
do	do	Not	Morris & R. Fitzgerald	do	Irel'd & Pa.	8	1	do
do	do	do	Martin and N. Poling	do	....	9	1	1st cous
Laborer ...	Virginia ..	Educated	L. and Chris. Tavener	Carpenter	Virginia...	1	1	None.
House work	Ohio	do	Jas. and F. McGohon.	Farmer...	Irel'd & Pa.	9	1	do
Carpenter..	New York	Not	N. and Mary Hutches	do	New York	5	1	do
Milliner ..	Virginia ..	. do	S. and Eliz. Vickroy .	do	Virginia ..	3	1	do
None	Ohio	do	L. D. and E. Gardner.	do	Ohio	7	1	Unk'wn
do	do	do	Jacob and M. Kochler	do	Maryland .	13	1	do
do	do	do	Henry and Eliz. Curl	Shingle mr	Penn.	5	1	2d cous.
Farmer...	Maryland .	do	Samuel and M. Brown	Farmer ...	Germany..	6	2	None.
do	do	do	do do do	do	do	6	2	do
do	New Jersey	Educated	Peter and Marg. Diltz	do	England ..	8	1	do
None	Ohio......	do	Elizabeth Patterson ..	Sch teacher	Ireland....	4	1	do
Farmer...	do	Not..'...	John and M. Bowser	Farmer ...	Penn.	6	1	do
None	Virginia ..	Educated	Jacob and Anna Gall	do	Germany..	4	1	do
do	Penn'a....	do	Benj. and C. McZane	do	Scotland ..	6	1	Cousins.
do	Virginia ..	Not	Henry and Jane Ellis	Shoe maker	Virginia ..	6	1	None.
do	Maryland..	Educated	John and E. Morrow..	Farmer ...	Maryland .	6	1	do
Farmer...	Ohio......	Not	James and S. Deeyer	do	do	13	1	do
None.....	Maryland .	do	Jos. and Eliz Robinett	Gardener	do	3	3	do
do	do	do	do do do					
do	do	do	do do do					
do	Virginia ..	do	Caleb and Eliz. Fox..	Cooper....	Virginia ..	7	1	None.
Carpenter .	do	Educated	Elisha and E. Hillery	Farmer ...	do	10	1	do
None	Ohio......	Not	Jas. and Em. Larimer	do	Ohio	11	1	do
do	do	do	Sol. W. and R. Dodd .	do	Delaware .	7	1	do
Farmer...	do	do	Emeline Jones.......	Washing..	Virginia ..	1	1	Unk'wn
do	do	do	William Davison	Farmer...	New Jersey	5	1	None
None	Penn'a....	do	John Harbaugh......	Carpenter.	New York	12	1	do
do	Ohio......	do	John Wiles..........	Laborer...	Ohio.	3	1	do
Carpenter .	New Jersey	do	Ralph and C. Drake..	Carpenter.	New Jersey	13	1	do
Peddler ...	....	....	....	....	....	..	..	....
....	Ohio	Not	W. and Rebecca Post .	Farmer ...	Ohio	8		None

RETURN of the number of Deaf and Dumb, Blind, Insane and Idiotic persons

Township	Names of persons.	Nature of Affliction	Duration of Affliction.	Cause where known	Age.	Sex.	Color.
Saltcreek..	Alex. Montgomery..	Blind	33 years..	Exposure....	84	Male.	White
Pickaway..	Cerepta Brand......	Idiot	7 "	Unknown....	7	Fem'le	do
"	Russel Towers......	"	31 "	"	31	Male.	do
"	Mary Towers........	"	27 "	"	27	Fem'le	do
Washington	Enoch Vanvickel....	Insane	Unknown.	"	60	Male.	do
"	Joseph Robinson.....	Idiot	From birth	"	35	do	do
"	Lovina Walker......	Idiot	"	"	30	Fem'le	do
Walnut....	James McCoy........	Blind	9 years..	Fever........	74	Male.	do
Madison..	None..............						
Harrison...	None..............						
Circleville.	Edson Hammel......	Dumb	8 years..	From birth....	8	Male.	White
"	Lucinda M. Shaw....	Blind	25 "	Inflammation..	25	Fem' e	do
"	Guy W. Doan.......	Blind	11 "	Amaurosis....	68	Male.	do
Wayne....	None.............						
Jackson...	John Caldwell......	Deaf and dumb	7 years..	Fever........	15	Male.	White
Scioto.....	Benjamin Walston....	Insane	30 "	Fall........	55	do	do
"	Joseph Everts.......	"	31 "	Fever........	35	do	do
"	Sarah Hickey........	"	20 "	"	45	Fem'le	do
"	John Gulick........	"		"	50	Male.	do
"	Sophia E. Sellers....	Blind	4 years..	Cold........	61	Fem'le	do
Monroe....	Ann Simmons.......	Insane	26 "	....	26	do	do
Darby.....	Margaret Philips.....	"	18 "	Rickets......	23	do	do
Darby.....	Lewis Taylor.......	Idiot	From birth	....	24	Male.	do
Muhlenberg	Isaiah Rock........	Blind	17 years..	Measels......	34	do	do
"	Charlotte ——	"	14 "	Fever........	70	Fem'le	do
Perry......	Zadoc Lewis........	"	From birth	....	47	Male.	do
"	Margaret Lewis......	"	"	....	53	Fem'le	do
Deercreek..	Edward Louper......	"	15 years..	Exposure.....	69	Male.	do
"	Anna Hansucker.....	Insane	36 "	Fits........	38	Fem'le	do
"	John N. Downing....	Idiot	10 "	....	22	Male.	do
"	Norris Harris.......	Insane	7 "	....	70	do	do
"	Isaac Hynes........	Deaf and dumb	From birth	....	64	do	do

in the county of Pickaway, State of Ohio, on the second Monday of May, 1856.

Occupation	Birthplace	Educated or not.	Names of Parents	Occupation	Birthplace	No children	No. children thus afflicted	Relationship of Parents before Marriage
Tailor	Penn	Educated	Wm. Montgomery	M'ufact'er	Ireland	14	1	None.
....	Ohio	Not	Israel Brand	Bl'ksmith	Ohio	4	1	do
....	"	do	John Towers	Farmer	Maryland	6	3	do
....	"	do	"	do	Marylnnd	..	..	do
....	"	do	Not known	....	....	..	..	....
....	"	do	"	....	....	..	..	....
....	Kentucky	do	"	....	....	..	..	....
Farmer	Virginia	Educated	John McCoy	Farmer	Va	11	1	None.
....	....	....	....	....	....	..	..	....
....	Ohio	Not	Isaiah Hammel	Carpenter	Ohio	7	1	None.
Music te'h	Ohio	Educated	Hugh Shaw	Farmer	Penn	5	1	do
Lawyer	Conn	do	William Doan	do	Conn	3	1	do
....	....	....	....	....	....	..	..	....
Farmer	Ohio	Not	Henry Caldwell	Farmer	Ohio	6	1	None.
Farmer	do	do	Charles Walston	....	....	..	1	do
....	do	do	Henry Eve.ts	....	....	..	1	do
....	do	do	James Hickey	Br'mmakr	Virginia	3	1	do
....	Virginia	do	John Gulick	Farmer	....	..	1	do
....	Germany	do	....	....	....	..	1	do
....	Ohio	do	Abijah Simmons	Farmer	Maryland	4	1	1st cous.
....	do	do	Curtis Philips	do	Virginia	4	1	None.
....	do	do	Warner Taylor	do	"	12	1	do
B'sk'tm'kr	Virginia	Educated	Henry Rock	....	"	4	1	do
....	Maryland	Not	Levi ———	....	Maryland	5	1	do
Merchant	Ohio	do	Zadoc Lewis	Farmer	do	11	2	Cousins.
....	Maryland	do	"	do	do	11	2	do
Farmer	N Jersey	Educated	I. Louper	do	N. Jersey	5	1	None.
....	Ohio	Not	Jacob Hansueker	....	Virginia	10	1	do
Farmer	do	Not	John Downing	Farmer	Delaware	5	1	do
Farmer	Kentucky	Educated	....	....	....	5	1	do
Farmer	Virginia	Not	Henry Hynes	Farmer	....	..	1	do

RETURN of the number of Deaf and Dumb, Blind, Insane and Idiotic persons

Townships.	Names of Persons.	Nature of Affliction.	Duration of Affliction.	Cause where known.	Age.	Sex.	Color.
Sunfish	Elizabeth Chesnut	Insane	27 years	Fits	28	Fem'le	White
"	Nancy Copas	Idiotic	6 "	Unknown	6	Fem'le	do
Mifflin	Henry Kisling	Deaf and dumb	16 "	Cold	24	Male	do
Pellel	John Hayns	Insane	13 "	Not known	13	Male	do
"	Martha Harris	Blind & insane	16 "	Not known	16	Male	Black
Perry	Mary J. McBride	Deaf	5 "	Mumps	10	Fem'le	White

in the County of Pike, State of Ohio, on the second Monday of May, 1856.

Occupation.	Birth-place.	Educated or not.	Names of Parents.	Occupation.	Birth-place.	No. Children.	No. Children thus Afflicted	Relationship of parents before marriage.
None	Ohio	Not	Elisha & Eliz. Chesnut	Farming	Penn	11	1	None
None	Ohio	Not	Josiah & Elizabeth Copas	Farmer	Ohio	2	1	Unknown
Mecha'c	Virginia	Educated	Peter & Elizabeth Kisling	Farmer	Virginia	5	1	None
None	Ohio	Not	Peter & Eliza Hayns	Farmer	Virginia	5	1	None
None	Virginia	Not	Charles Ada Harris	Farmer	Ohio	11	1	3d cous's
None	Ohio	Not	James & Eliza McBride	Farmer	Ohio	6	1	None

11—SEC. OF STATE.

RETURN of the number of Deaf and Dumb, Blind, Insane and Idiotis persons

TOWNSHIPS.	Names of Persons.	Nature of Affliction.	Duration of Affliction.		Cause where known.	Age.	Sex.	Color.
	George Fields	Insane	25	years	Unknown	35	Male	White
	Ira H. Day	Insane at times	35	"	Hereditary	50	"	"
	Edgar Day	"	1	"	Hard Study	20	"	"
	Henrietta A. Likens	Deaf and Dumb	10	"	Unknown	10	Fem'le	"
	Florence Hunt	Idiotic	8	"	Fits	12	"	"
	Caroline Curtis	Insane	1	month	Sleep. dis. per			"
	Caroline C. Hanners	Blind	13	years	Scarlet fever	18	Fem'le	"
	Rodolphus Bancroft	"	9	"	Int'pce and heat	74	Male	"
	Arvilla Ferguson	Idiotic	44	"		44	Fem'le	"
Freedom	Amanda Hurlburt	Insane	26	"	Taking Iodine	76	"	"
"	Isaac H. Loveland	"	22	"	Hereditary	38	Male	"
Shalersville	Mary Ann Nyman	"	16	"			Fem'le	"
"	Margaret Hall	"				56	"	"
"	Rachel Coosard	"				47	"	"
"	Jane Prentiss	"				38	"	"
"	Almira Gronger	"			Disap. in Love	49	"	"
"	Louisa Gloid	"				60	"	"
"	Louisa Gloid	"				40	"	"
"	Clarinda Richards	"				39	"	"
"	Lewis Woolcut	Idiotic				39	Male	"
Windham	John Streator	"	38	years	Unknown	40		"
Brimfield	Christiana Geistevite	Insane	22	"	Turn of Life	74	Fem'le	"
"	Devain Furry	Deaf and Dumb	5	"		5	Male	"
"	Charley Furry	"	2	"		2	"	"
Deerfield	John Taylor	Idiotic	60	"	Unknown	60	"	"
"	George Taylor	"	57	"	"	57	"	"
"	Leander Taylor	"	54	"	"	54	"	"
"	Martin Hartzell	Scrofula	6	"	"	6	"	"
"	Matilda Whittle	Insane	17	"	Reading	34	Fem'le	"
"	William Mell	Blind	4	"		84	Male	"
Charlestown	William Rood, Jr.	Partially Insane	Some years			50	"	"
"	Harmon Rood	" Idiotic	50 years			50	"	"
Streetsboro'	S. M. Jenkins	Blind	2	"	Amorosis	34	Fem'le	"
"	Barbara Branker	"	8	"	Inflammation	81	"	"
Suffield	John Ryts	Deaf and Dumb	37	"	Fits	40	Male	"
Randolph	Stephen Schultz	Idiotic	15	"	"	15	"	"
"	Reuben Buckman	"	10	"		60	"	"
"	Olive A. Buckman	Deaf	2	"	Tonsils	6	Fem'le	"
"	Silby C. Koontz	Idiot	2	"		2	"	"
"	Mordecai Sebril	Insane	38	"	Fits	38	Male	"
"	Catharine Stoll	Idiotic	23	"	Rickets	25	Fem'le	"
"	John Wise	Blind	61	"	Small pox	61	Male	"

163

in the county of Portage, State of Ohio, on the second Monday of May, 1856.

Occupation	Birthplace	Educated or not.	Names of Parents	Occupation	Birthplace	No. children	No. children thus Afflicted	Relationship of Parents before Marriage
None	Kentuc'y	Educated	Unknown	Minister	Unknown	4	1	None.
Farmer	N. York	"	"	Merchant	"	5	2	"
Teaching	Ohio	"	Ira R. and Har't Fields	Farmer	N. Y. & Ky	5	1	"
None	"	Not	Lewis and H. P. Likens	"	Poland	4	1	"
	"	"	Richard and Jul. Hunt	"	N. Y. & O.	2	1	"
Student	Ohio	Educated	John and Olar. Hanners	Farmer	Mass. & Ct.	4	1	None.
Farmer	Mass	"	John and Grace Bancroft	"	"	7	1	"
	"	Not	John and L. Ferguson	"	"	5	1	"
Housework	Conn	Educated	S. and Nancy Hurlbert	"	Connnect'ct	6	1	"
Laborer	Mass	"	Colby and L. Loveland	"	Massach'ts	8	1	"
		"						
	Mass	Educated						
		"						
		Educated						
	Mass	"						
None	Ohio	Not	John and Mrs. Streator	Farmer	Massach'ts	4	1	1st cousins.
Housekp'r	Penn	Educated	Jacob Stchob	"	Unknown			
	Ohio	Not	Joseph and Mrs. Furry	Farmer	New York	5	2	None.
	"	"						
None	Virginia	"						
"	Ohio	"	Geo. and Eliz. Taylor	Farmer	Pennsylv'a	7	3	None.
"	"	"						
"		"	Fred. and Mary Hartzell					
"	England	Educated	D. and Eliz'h Whittle	Farmer	England	7	1	None.
Farmer	Penn	"	A. and Barbara Mell		Penn			"
"								
	N. York	Educated	D. and E. Leonard	Farmer	Mass	11	1	None.
Housekp'r	Penn	Not	J. and E Poorman	Phys'ian	Germany	3	1	"
Farmer	"	"	Mr. and Elizabeth Ryts	Farmer	Penn	5	1	"
	Ohio		S. and Cath Schultz		Ohio	6	1	"
Farmer	Mass	Not	M. and A. Buckman	Farmer	Ohio	2	1	None.
	Ohio							
	"		William and C. Koontz	Mason				None.
			Benjamin and S. Sebril	Farmer				"
	Ohio		James and O. Stoll	"				

RETURN of the number of Deaf and Dumb, Blind, Insane and Idiotic persons

Names of Persons.	Nature of Affliction.	Duration of Affliction.	Cause where known.	Age.	Sex.	Color.	Occupation.
Edward W. Swain	Idiotic	From inf'cy	Not known	6	Male	White	None
Mercy Runnion	Idiotic	"	Not known	62	Fem'le	do	do
Elizabeth Runnion	Idiotic	"	Not known	60	Fem'le	do	do
Sophronia Runnion	Partially idiotic	"	Mother idiotic	33	Fem'le	do	do
William Thompson	Idiotic	Unknown	Fits	30	Male	do	do
Elizabeth Wright	Idiotic	From inf'cy	Unknown	23	Fem'le	do	do
Frank Wright	Dumb & idiotic	"	Unknown	8	Male	do	do
Stephen Parker	Idiotic	Unknown	Blow on head		Male	do	do
Eliza Smith	Idiotic	"	Disapp'd love		Fem'le	do	do
Catharine Kate	Insane	"	"		Fem'le	do	do
Samuel Crumbaker	Insane	5 or 6 years	Intense study		Male	do	Farming
Frank Griffis	Insane	3 years	Unknown	23	Male	do	Farming
Samuel Eller	Idiotic					do	
Lydia Show	Partially insane	20 years	Use of tobacco.	42	Fem'le	do	Housew'k
Preston Collins	Insane	6 "	Unknown	25	Male	do	Farming
Mary B. Woolman	Blind	10 "		64	Fem'le	do	Farming
Thomas M. Conger	Insane	18 months	Fall from horse.	26	Male	do	Farming
Jennet M'Dill	Insane	3 years	Neuralagy	61	Fem'le	do	None
Sarah Marshall	Insane	25 "	Unknown	45	Fem'le	do	do
Elizabeth Garver	Insane	25 "	"	68	Fem'le	do	do
John Moore	Insane	6 "	"	40	Male	do	Merchant
Rebecca Whiteman	Insane	18 "	Fits	25	Fem'le	do	None
Elizabeth Peters	Idiotic	From inf'cy	Unknown	24	Fem'le	do	do
James W. Phillips	Idiotic & deaf.	16 years	Fever	20	Male	do	do
Sophia Hammon	Blind	15 "	Unknown	51	Fem'le	do	do
Jacob Brower	Insane & dumb	From inf'cy	Fits	40	Male	do	do
Daniel Eller	Idiotic					do	
James M'Grew	Blind	30 years	Weakness	67	Male	do	Farming
Francis M. Emmons	Blind	2 "	Measles	7	Male	do	None
Hannah Oblinger	Deaf & dumb	12 "	Scarlet fever	16	Fem'le	do	do
James Johnson	Blind	From inf'cy	Unknown	26	Male	do	do
Elisha Worden	Idiotic	"	"	28	Male	do	do
Harriet Worden	Idiotic	"	"	30	Fem'le	do	do
James Moore	Blind	5 years	"	21	Male	do	do
David Brower	Partially idiotic	29 "	Fits	37	Male	do	Farming
Margaret M'Whinney	Deaf and dumb	19 "	Disease of head	19	Fem'le	do	Housew'k
Alexander M'Whinney	Insane	5 months	Derange't liver.	24	Male	do	Farming
John M. Lanear	Idiotic	From inf'cy	Unknown	15	Male	do	None
Nathaniel Smith	Idiotic	6 years	Fits	43	Male	do	Farming
Elizabeth Snyder	Idiotic	From inf'cy	Sickness	28	Fem'le	do	None
William H. Rice	Idiotic	"	Spinal disease.	17	Male	do	do
Samuel Maddock	Insane	25 years	Unknown	47	Male	do	Farming
—— M'Veigh	Blind	8 "	Hurt	51	Male	do	Shoema'r
Hannah Miller	Insane	8 "	Unknown	45	Fem'le	do	None
Ann C. Scheying	Idiotic	16 "	Convulsions	17	Fem'le	do	do
Conrad Scheying	Insane	40 "	Unknown	65	Male	do	do
Catharine Wykle	Idiotic	21 "	"	21	Fem'le	do	do
John Snyder	Idiotic	From inf'cy	"	19	Male	do	do
Lavina Snyder	Idiotic	14 years	Convulsions	15	Fem'le	do	do

165

in the county of Preble, State of Ohio, on the second Monday of May, 1856.

Birth-place.	Educated or not.	Names of Parents.	Occupation.	Birth-place.	No Children	No. Children thus Afflicted	Relationship of parents before marriage
Ohio	Not	James & Elizabeth Swain	Unknown	Unknown	4	1	Unknown
Kentucky	"	John & Mary Runnion	Farming	Kentucky	10	9	1st cous's
"	"	John & Mary Runnion	Farming	"			1st cous's
Ohio	"	Peggy Runnion	None	"	6	1	None
Virginia	"				5	1	Unknown
Ohio	"	John & Mary Wright	Com. labor	Unknown		2	"
Ohio	"	John & Mary Wright	"	"			"
Unknown	Partially	Unknown	Unknown	"		1	"
Ohio	Not	Unknown	"	"		1	"
Ireland	Unknown	Unknown	"	Ireland		1	"
Virginia	Educated	Jonas & —— Crumbaker	Farming	Virginia		1	"
Ohio	"	John & Catharine Griffis	Farming	Wales	10	1	None
Ohio	Not	John & Nancy Show	Butcher	Maryland	11	1	None
Ohio	Educated	John & Anna Collins	Farmer	Penn	10	1	"
N. Jersey	"	Joseph & Susannah Brown	Farming	N. Jersey	8	1	"
Ohio	"	Aaron R. & Ruth Conger	"	Tennessee	5	1	"
S. Carolina	"	Wm. & Mary Caldwell	"	Ireland	9	1	"
Georgia	"	Robert & Sarah Marshall	"	"	7	1	"
Penn	Not	Unknown	Unknown	Unknown		1	Unknown
Ireland	Educated	Thos. & Elizabeth Moore	Farming	Ireland	4	2	None
Ohio	"	James & Rebecca Whiteman	"	Virginia	9	1	"
Ohio	Not	John & Elizabeth Peters	"	Virginia	9	1	"
Ohio	"	Hezekiah & Sophia Phillips	"	Ohio	9	1	"
Georgia	"	Isaac & Margaret Hammon	"	Penn. & Va	11	1	"
Virginia	"	Daniel & Sarah Brower	"	Penn. & Va	11	1	"
Penn	Pducated	John & Jane M'Grew	Farming	Penn	6	1	"
Ohio	Not	Jeremiah & Alice Emmons	"	N. Jersey	6	1	"
"	Educated	David & Catharine Oblinger	Carpenter	Penn	12	1	"
"	"	Moses and Mary Johnson	Carpenter	N. Jersey	3	1	"
"	Not	D. & Mary Worden	Unknown	Unknown		1	Unknown
"	"	D. & Mary Worden	"	"			"
"	"	James & Agnes Moore	"	"			"
"	Can read	Abram & Sarah Brower	Farming	Va. & Penn	6	1	None
"	Can read	Thos. J. & Nancy M'Whinney	"	N. C.&Ten.	9	1	"
"	Educated	Thos. J. & Nancy M'Whinney	"	"		1	"
"	Not	Sampson & Nancy Lanear	"	Ken. & O.	8	1	"
New York	"	Joseph B. & Mary Smith	"	N. Y., Scot.	11	1	"
Ohio	"	John & Sarah Snyder	"	Pa. & Va.	8	1	"
"	"	John & Eleanor Rice	"	Kentucky	6	1	"
"	Educated	Francis & Phœbe Maddock	"	Ga. & S. C.	8	1	"
Penn	"	—— M'Veigh	Distiller	Ireland	3	1	2d cous's
Maryland	"	M. Earnest	Farming	Germany	8	2	Unknown
Ohio	Not	Barnhart Scheying	Farmer	Germany	7	1	"
Germany	Educated	Jacob Scheying	"	Germany	3	1	"
Ohio	Not	George Wykle	"	Maryland	10	1	"
"	"	Henry Snyder	"	Virginia	11	2	"
"	"	Henry Snyder	"	Virginia	11	2	"

RETURN of the number of Deaf and Dumb, Blind, Insane and Idiotic persons

Names of Persons.	Nature of Affliction.	Duration of Affliction.	Cause, Where Known.	Age.	Sex.	Color.
William F. Long............	Idiotic........	11 years..	From medicine	13	Male ..	White.
Elizabeth Wattner..........	do	18 " ..	Unknown.....	43	Fem'.e	"1
Doty Belbey...............	Deaf and dumb	18 " ..	Sickness......	30	"	"
Sebastian Nahir............	Blind	Born.....	....	22	Male..	"
Maria Anna Gaking.........	Deaf.........	12 years..	Nervous disease	25	Fem'le	"
Rosanna Fairchilds..........	Idiotic........	25 " ..	Unknown	25	"	"
Martha J. Hoskinson........	Deaf and dumb	From infan	"	12	"	"
Almira "	" "	"	"	8	"	"
Elisha Mervine............	Deaf and dumb	23 years ..	Scarlet Fever..	24	Male .	"
....	Idiotic........	5 "	....	5	"	"

in the county of Putnam, State of Ohio, on the second Monday of May, 1856.

Occupation.	Birth-place.	Educated or not.	Names of Parents.	Occupation.	Birth-place.	No. Children.	No. children thus afflicted.	Relationship of parents before marriage.
....	Ohio	Not	Samuel & Elizabeth Long	Carpenter	Penn'a....	3	1	1st cous.
....	Penn	Educated	Jacob and Sarah Wattner	....	Germany..	8	1	Unknwn
....	Germany.	Not	John Belbey.......... ..	Farmer ..	"	1	1	"
....	"	"	Adam & Hannah Nahir	Carpenter	"	8	1	"
Housewrk	"	Educated	Arnold & Agnes Gaking	Farmer ..	"	6	1	None.
....	Ohio	....	John & Eliza. Fairchild	"	Penn a....	7	1	"
....	"	....	S. & Mary Hoskinson ..	"	Ohio......	3	2	Unknwn
....	"	....	Do. do.	"	"	3	2	"
Cabin'tmr	"	Educat'd	William Mervine........	....	....	..	..	...
....	"	....	D. and Mary Nicewarner	....	....	..	..	.....

RETURN of the number of Deaf and Dumb, Blind, Insane and Idiotic persons

Townships	Names of Persons	Nature of affliction.	Duration of affliction.	Cause where known.	Age.	Sex.	Color.
Franklin..	Catharine Tooker....	Idiotic........	21 years..	Unknown.....	21	Fem'le	White.
Perry.....	Addison Gibson......	do	46 do	do	46	Male.	do
do	Henry Baker.........	do	34 do	Fits..........	34	do	do
do	Eli Baker............	do	11 do	do	21	do	do
do	Wm. Algire.........	do	14 do	Unknown.....	14	do	do
do	Sarah Coon..:.......	do	16 do	Fits..........	22	Fem'le	do
do	Margaret Coon	do	20 do	Unknown.....	20	do	do
do	Sophia Coon	do	18 do	do	18	do	do
W'rthingtn	Hezekiah Vaughn....	D'mb, bl'd idiot	37 do	do	37	Male.	do
do	James Norris.........	Idiotic........	27 do	do	27	do	do
Mifflin....	Nancy J. Walters	do	21 do	do	21	Fem'le	do
Monroe ...	Sarah Yeslay........	Deaf and dumb	19 do	Sickness......	20	do	do
do	Daniel Beason.......	Insane........	35 do	Unknown.....	58	Male.	do
Jackson...	Christiana Schenk...	Deaf and dumb	37 do	Sickness......	39	Fem'le	do
do	Mary Sterick	Deaf..........	10 do	Cold	73	do	do
do	John Buhee.........	Idiotic........	12 do	Unknown.....	47	Male.	do
Sandusky.	Snyder McJunkin....	do	41 do	Natural	41	do	do
do	Mary Catharine Shultz	do	6 do	....	6	Fem'le	do
do	Eli Jacoby..........	Deaf..........	4 do	White swelling.	17	Male.	do
Weller	Catharine Cofenbery..	Insane........	Unknown.	....	..	Fem'le	do
do	David Morehead.....	do	do	....	17	Male.	do
do	John Tucker	do	do	....	29	do	do
do	Jacob Stouffer	do	do	....	49	do	do
do	Susan Palmer	do	do	....	33	Fem'le	do
do	Ann Lapslay.........	do	do	....	40	do	do
do	John Faraw	do	do	....	23	Male.	do
do	Mary Palmer........	do	do	....	..	Fem'le	do

169

in the County of Richland, State of Ohio, on the second Monday of May, 1856.

Occupation	Birth-place	Educated or not	Names of Parents	Occupation	Birth-place	No. children	No. children abus afflicted	Relationship of parents before marriage
None	Ohio	Not	Wm. and Catharine Tooker	Farmer	N. J. & Pa.	11	1	None
Farmer	Virginia	do	Sol. and Rebecca Gibson	do	....	10	1	do
do	Ohio	do	Christian and Anna Baker	do	Maryland	10	2	do
do	do	do	do do	do	do	..	..	do
do	do	do	John and Rebecca Algire	do	Penn	6	1	do
....	do	do	Jacob and Mary Coon	do	do	9	3	do
....	do	do	do do	do	do	..	..	do
....	do	do	do do	do	do	..	..	do
None	do	do	John and Rachel Vaughn	do	do	6	1	do
do	Penn	do	Jonathan and Jane Norris	do	Ireland	4	2	do
do	Ohio	do	Sol. and Mary Walters	do	U. States	1	1	do
do	do	Educated	Henry & Christina Yealay	None	None	2	1	do
Farmer	Penn	do	David and Barbara Beason	....	....	12	1	....
Housewrk	Germany	do	Henry & Eliz. Schneck	Farmer	Germany	5	1	None
....	Maryl'nd	do	Mr. and Mrs. Shank	do	....	..	..	....
None	Penn	do	John and Ellis Blank	do	Penn	..	..	....
....	do	Not	John and Mrs. McJunkin	do	do	8	1	None
....	Ohio	do	Jacob and Mrs. Shultz	Carpenter	do	7	1	do
....	Penn	do	John Jacoby	Farmer	do	6	1	do
....	Unkno'n	....	....	....	....	..	..	....
....	do	....	....	....	....	..	..	....
....	do	....	....	....	....	..	..	....
....	do	....	....	....	....	..	..	....
....	do	....	....	....	....	..	..	....
....	Ireland	....	....	....	....	..	..	....
....	Unkno'n	....	....	....	....	..	..	....
....	do	....	....	....	....	..	..	....

RETURN of the number of Deaf and Dumb, Blind, Insane and Idiotic persons

Names of Persons.	Nature of Affliction.	Duration of Affliction.	Cause where known.	Age.	Sex.	Color.
Peter Noble	Idiotic	27 years	From birth	27	Male	White.
Nancy Waters	Blind	7 "	Old age	100	Fem'le	"
George Nauman	Insane	6 "	Disease	26	Male	"
Caroline Vincent	Idiotic	27 "	Natural	27	Fem'le	"
Caira Moomaw	"	40 "	Unknown	40	Male	"
Ada Snyder	"	26 "	Epilepsy	29	Fem'le	"
Matthew B. Pricer	"	23 "	"	25	Male	"
Renegar M. Zinnerman	Deaf and dumb	36 "	Ear-ache & fever	40	"	"
James Purgit	Idiotic	24 "	Measles & Fits	25	"	"
Mary Shotts	Blind	8 "	Old age	89	Fem'le	"
Elizabeth Brown	Idiotic	3 "	Epilepsy	4	"	"
Susan Snyder	Blind	19 "	Unknown	22	"	"
Elizabeth A. Rinehart	Idiotic	16 "	Epilepsy	21	"	"
Lorons Marr	"	29 "	Burn	32	Male	"
Avarilla Moots	"	17 "	From birth	17	Fem'le	"
Sarah Gibson	Blind	12 "	Unknown	75	"	"
Lydia Cames	"	4 "	From childbed	28	"	"
George Jordan	Idiotic	16 "	From birth	16	Male	"
Sarah Jordan	"	18 "	"	18	Fem'le	"
Samuel Jones	Deaf and dumb	14 "	"	14	Male	"
Susanna Jones	Dumb	7 "	"	7	Fem'le	"
Susanna Moss	Deaf and dumb	8 "	"	8	"	"
Edward Moss	" "	4 "	"	4	Male	"
Franklin Moss	Blind	1 "	"	1	"	"
Jesse Moss	Deaf and dumb	30 "	"	30	"	"
Nancy Boggs	Blind	5 "	Fever & cataract	54	Fem'le	"
Peter Zimerman	Idiotic	25 "	Spasms	25	Male	"
Lydia Barnhart	Insane	16 "	Unknown	40	Fem'le	"
Alexander Shoults	Deaf and dumb	14 "	Bronchitis	14	Male	"
Elizabeth Routt	Idiotic	23 "	Unknown	24	Fem'le	"
William Martin	"	40 "	"	40	Male	"
Anson Perry Thomas	"	22 "	"	22	"	"
Thomas Jones	Insane	14 "	"	36	"	"

in the county of Ross, State of Ohio, on the second Monday of May, 1856.

Occupation.	Birthplace.	Educated or not.	Names of Parents.	Occupation.	Birthplace.	No. children	No afflicted	Relationship of Parents before Marriage.
None...	Ohio.....	Not	Wm. and Ann Noble ..	Farmer ...	Ohio	14	1	No rela.
"	Virginia ..	do	Phillip & Polly Waters .	Weaver...	Unknown ...	..	1	do
Farmer .	Penn	Educated	C. & Margaret Nauman	Farmer ...	Penn	9	1	do
None...	Ohio	Not	W. & Caroline Vincent .	do	Delaware .	7	1	do
"	do	do	J. and Sophia Moomaw	Carpenter	Penn	9	1	do
"	do	do	P. and Mary Snyder....	Farmer ...	do	9	1	do
"	do	do	David and Grace Pricer.	do	do	8	1	do
Shoema'r	Penn	Educated	G. & Cathar. Zinnerman	Hatter	do	11	1	do
None...	Ohio	Not	F. and ——— Purgit	Farmer ...	Virginia ..	6	1	do
"	Penn	Educated	P. & Catharine Wagoner	do	Germany..	15	1	do
"	Ohio.....	Not	J. and Sarah Brown....	do	Virginia ..	9	1	do
"	Germany..	do	P. and Susan Snyder ...	do	Penn.....	9	1	do
"	Penn	Educated	B. and Rebecca Rinehart	do	do	9	1	do
" .	New York.	Not	F. and Catharine Marr..	Brewer ...	Germany..	5	1	do
"	Ohio	do	A. and Sarah Moots	Cooper...	Ohio	8	1	do
Weaver .	New Jersey	Educated	J. and Martha Cooper ..	Farmer ...	New Jersey	13	1	do
Laborer.	Ohio	do	J. and Nancy Young ...	do	Kentucky.	8	1	1st cous.
"	do	Not	J. and Mary Jordan	Laborer...	Virginia ..	9	2	do
"	do	do	Same.............	do	do	9	2	do
....	do	do	P. and Catharine Jones .	Farmer..	Ohio	7	2	do
....	do	do	S. and Bethany Jones...	do	do	6	1	do
....	do	do	} Wm & Elizabeth Moss	Farmer ...	Ohio	5	3	1st cous.
....	do	do						
....	do	do						
Farmer .	do	do	John and Mary Moss ...	Farmer ...	Penn.....	5	1	1st cous.
H keeper	Virginia ..	Educated	S. and ——— Stillwell...	Shoema'kr	New Jersey	3	1	No rela.
Wood s'r	Ohio	Not	J. and Eliza. Zinnermon	Cabinet mr	....	5	4	None.
Farmer .	do	Educated	C. and Catharine Betzer	Farmer ...	Penn.....	11	4	"
Farmer .	do	Not	J. and Martha Shoults..	do	Unknown .	10	1	"
....	do	do	T. and Mary Routt	do	do	7	1	"
None ...	do	do	J. and Nancy Martin ..	do	Virginia .	9	1	"
"	do	do	H. and Elizab'th Thomas	do	do	8	1	"
Farmer .	do	Educated	J. and Hannah Jones...	do	New Jersey	3	1	"

RETURN of the number of Deaf and Dumb, Blind, Insane and Idiotic persons

Township.	Names of persons.	Nature of Affliction.	Duration of Affliction.	Cause where known.	Age.	Sex.	Color.
Washington	Jacob Witner	Dumb	20 years	Unknown	20	Male	White
Sandusky	Louis Moss	Idiotic	10 "	Unknown	10	"	do
"	John Orton	do	4 "	Unknown	4	"	do
"	Allen Smith	do	10 "	Sickness	10	"	do
"	Charley Day	do	28 "	Hurt	40	"	do
Ballville	Geo Bemsburgh	Blind	2 "	Sickness	35	"	do
Woodsville	Gibson Fenner	Deaf and dumb	23 "		23	"	do
"	Betsy Rood	Blind	10 "	Inflammation	50	Fem'le	do
Townsend	Robert Tew	Blind	48 "	Burned	48	Male	do
"	Emily C. Keefer	Blind	10 "	Sickness	10	Fem'le	do
"	Jane Bu-h	Idiotic	7 "	Not known	7	"	do
Green Creek	Sophia McMiller	Insane	31 "		56	"	do
Jackson	Christ'na Andrew	Insane		Disease	13	"	do
"	Catharine Tefler	Insane			18	"	do
York	Mary J. Billman	Deaf	1 year	Scarlet fever	9	Fem'le	do

173

in the County of Sandusky, State of Ohio, on the second Monday of May, 1856.

Occupation.	Birth-place.	Educated or not.	Names of Parents.	Occupation.	Birth-place.	No. children.	No. children thus afflicted.	Relationship of parents before marriage.
Farmer ..	Switzerl'd	Not	John and Eliz. Witner	Carpenter .	Switzerl'nd	1	1	None.
None	Ohio	Educated	J. T. and E. Moss....	Merchant .	Ohio	1	1	Cousins.
"	"	Not	C. J. Orton..........	Editor	New York.	5	1	None.
"	"	do	J. M. and S. Smith...	None	do	3	1	do
Farmer ..	New York	do	S. C. aud Mary Day..	Farmer ..	do	2	2	do
"	Maryland	Educated	Not known..........	....	....	..	....	...
Laborer..	Ohio	do	....	....	....	..	....	....
Housekpr.	New York	Not	....	....	....	..	....	....
None	"	do	William Tew........	Farmer ..	Massach'tts	7	1	None.
"	Ohio	do	John Keefer.........	do	Ohio	3	1	do
"	"	do	Zopher Bush	do	do	6	1	do
....	Ireland ..	do	Edward Beaucamp...	....	....	5	1	....
None	Ohio	do	William Andrew.....	Farmer ...	Unknown .	13	1	None.
"	"	do	John and Mrs. Tefler.	do	do	10	1	do
....	"	Limited .	G. & Hannah Billman.	Fence makr	Penna	9	1	do

RETURN of the Number of Deaf and Dumb, Blind, Insane and Idiotic persons

Names of Persons.	Nature of Affliction.	Duration of Affliction.		Cause where known.	Age.	Sex.	Color.	Occupation.
Nathaniel Tucker	Idiotic	26	years	Unknown	56	Male	White.	Farmer
Beuajah Odell	"	15	"	"	38	"	do	"
Mary Henry	Deaf and Dumb	5	"	Winter fever	8	Fem'le	do	None
Rachel Slack	"	12	"	Sickness	12	"	do	Housework
Wesley Thompson	"	12	"	"	13	Male	do	Farmer
Milton O. Wright	D'f. d'b. & ins.	9	"	Medicine	9	"	do	
Emazilla Carmine	Insane	7	"	Fear and alarm	52	Fem'le	do	Farmer
George W. Thornton	Blind	26		Dropsy in head	26	Male	do	Musician
Joseph Reineger	Deaf and dumb	8	"	Scarlet fever	10	"	do	None
Mary Paul	Idiotic	Unkn'wn		Unknown	49	Fem'le	do	"
Mary Kessler	Insane	"		"	28	"	do	"
Mathias Hilbert						Male	do	
Thomas Braut	Dumb	32	years		32	"	do	
David Crull	Idiotic	45	"	Fits	47	"	do	None
Charles Cox	Insane	2	"		50	"	do	Farmer
George Smith	Blind	25	"		55	"	do	Teaming
Chee Randall	"	1½	"		39	"	do	Farmer
Mary Castor	Idiotic	31	"	Fits	32	Fem'le	do	
Sarah Pile	"	22	"	"	23	"	do	

175

in the County of Scioto, State of Ohio, on the second Monday of May, 1856.

Birth-place.	Educated or not	Names of Parents.	Occupation	Birth-place.	No. Children	No. Children thus afflicted.	Relationship of parents before Marriage
Ohio.....	Limited.	John and Sarah Tucker.......	Farmer...	Unknown.	9	1	None.
"	Not....	Ransom and Lydia Odell.....	"	Eas. States	8	2	"
"	"	Joseph and Martha Henry....	Blacksmith	Delaware.	3	1	"
Missouri..	"	George W. and Catharine Slack	Farmer...	England..	8	1	"
Ohio.....	"	Thomas and Martha Thompson	"	Ohio.....	4	1	"
"	"	William and Mary Ann Wright	Wag.mak'r	"	4	1	"
Virginia..	Limited.	James and Mary Lomison....	Blacksmith	England..	8	1	"
Ohio.....	Educat'd	John H. and Sally Thornton...	Shoemaker	Conn.....	6	1	"
"	Not....	Charles F. and Barbary Rineger	Farmer...	Germany..	11	1	"
Vermont..	"	Unknown..................	Unknown.	Unknown.			Unknown.
Germany..	"	"	"	Germany.			"
"							
Ohio.....	"	Christian and Elizabeth Brant	Millwright	Penn.....	7	1	None.
"	"	David and Mary Crull.......	Farmer...	Virginia..	5	1	"
Penn.....	Educat'd	Josiah Cox..................	"	Unknown.			"
....		....					
Ohio.....	Not....	Hezet and Susannah Castor.	Farmer...	Md and Pa.	13	1	None.
Virginia..	"	Elizabeth Pile.............	"	Virginia.	9	1	"

RETURN of the number of Deaf and Dumb, Blind, Insane and Idiotic persons

Names of Persons.	Nature of Affliction.	Duration of Affliction.	Cause where known.	Age.	Sex.	Color.
John Weiker	Insane	7 years	Unknown	21	Male	White
Benjamin F. Coup	Deaf	6 months	Fits	4	"	"
Eugenia Ernst	Insane	5 years	Fits	65	Female	"
Barbara Seitz	Deaf and dumb	Life	Unknown	20	"	"
Hannah Seitz	"	"	"	18	"	"
Lewis Seitz	"	"	"	13	Male	"
Lorenzo Seitz	"	"	"	10	Fem'le	"
Abraham Seitz	Idiotic	"	"	16	Male	"
Mary Newman	Insane	"	"	59	Fem'le	"
Barbara Morio	Deaf and dumb	13 years	Sickness	16	"	"
Anna Morio	"	13 "	"	22	"	"
Sarah Ann Stinebaugh	Idiotic	29 "	Fits	30	"	"
Elizabeth Raull	Insane	7 "	Fright	57	"	"
George W. Reynolds	Deaf and dumb	9 months	Not known	8	Male	"
Daniel Thomas Todd	Idiotic	Life	"	19	"	"
Roxey Shaw	"	33 years	Whooping Cough	33	Female	"
John Cain	"	6 "	Not known	6	Male	"
Mary Jane Powell	Dumb	20 "	"	21	Female	"
Mary Hoffer	Idiotic	27 "	Fits	32	"	"
Andrew J. Mocks	Blind	22 "	Cold	22	Male	"
George Long	Idiotic	37 "	Fits	37	"	"
John Lynch	Blind	15 "	Palsey	56	"	"
James Welch	Blind	10 "	Unknown	45	"	"
Abraham Feble	Idiotic	Life	Fits	33	"	"
Rebecca Rinebold	"	Life	Rickets in head	8	Female	"
Isabell Sloan	Blind	6 months	Not known	76	"	"
Debolt Schwaverly	Idiotic	Life	"	31	Male	"
John Limpach	Insane	18 months	Disappointment	29	"	"
Louisa Hoffman	Idiotic	Life	Not known	20	Female	"
Elizabeth Bope	Blind	3 years	Old age	80	"	"
Margaret Cowdry	Insane	30 "	Not known	39	"	"
Esther C. Watson	Blind	12 "	Fever	12	"	"
Susan O. Tittle	Idiotic	14 "	Fever	15	"	"
Aaron A. Benham	"	18 "	Fits	18	Male	"
John Brand	"	Life	Not known	15	"	"
Lucy Wilson	Insane	Life	"		Female	"
John H. Price	Blind	Life	"	22	Male	"
Ananias Wise	Idiotic	5 years	Fits	17	"	"
Elizabeth Kuhn	Deaf and dumb	Life	Not known	29	Female	"
Mathas Rinehart	Blind	7 years	"	36	Male	"
Catharine Hoffner	Blind	4 "	Fever	75	Female	"
Arnette Bowman	Deaf and dumb	Life	Not known	26	"	"
Manam Huter	Dumb	Life	"	5	Male	"
Zadock Elliott	Deaf and dumb	Life	Sickness	12	"	"
John E. Musted	Insane	18 montns	Unknown	26	"	"
Adam J. Waggoner	Blind	59 years	Small pox	67	"	"
Charles W. McOlary	Idiotic	21 "	Unknown	21	"	"

in the county of Seneca, State of Ohio, on the second Monday of May, 1856.

Occupation	Birth-place	Educated or Not	Names of Parents	Occupation	Birth-place	No Children	No. Children thus Afflicted	Relationship of parents before marriage
Farmer	Penn	Educat'd	Jos. Weiker & N. Hawkins	Farming	Penn	11	1	None.
"	Ohio	Not	Levi and Margaret Coup	"	Maryland	8	1	"
"	Ireland	Educat'd	Not known					"
Domestic	Seneca co.	Partly	Lewis and Barbara Seitz	Farmer	Ohio	14	1	"
"	"	Educat'd	" "	"	"	14	1	"
"	"	Not	" "	"	"	14	1	"
"	"	"	" "	"	"	14	1	"
"	"	"	" "	"	"	14	1	"
"	Conn	"	Isaiah Austin	Miller	Conn	6	1	"
"	Germany	"	N. Philip Morio	Farmer	Germany	6	1	"
"	"	"	"	"	Germany	6	1	"
"	Maryland	"	Philip & C. Stinebaugh	"	Maryland	8	1	"
"	Penn	"	Samuel & Molly Swartz	"	Penn	11	2	"
"	Ohio	"	Chas. L. & N. A. Reynolds	"	Virginia		1	"
"	"	"	Lance L. & Mary Todd	"	Maryland	3	1	"
House kpr.	N. York	Partly	Robert and Sarah Shaw	"	Penn	8	1	"
Domestic	Ohio	Not	John and Mary Cain	"	Ireland	1	1	"
"	"	Not	Robert and Chloe Powell	"	Penn	9	1	Illegit.
"	"	Can read	Jacob & Elizabeth Hoffer	"	Germany	1	1	None.
"	Penn	Not	John H. and Mary Mocks	"	Penn	1	1	"
"	Ohio	"	Daniel and Margaret Long	"	Virginia	1	1	"
"	Ireland	"	No account of parents	None				
None	Virginia	"	No account of parents					None.
Farmer	Penn	"	Frederick and O. Feble	Farming	Penn	1	1	"
None	Ohio	"	Abraham & Eliza Rinebold	"	Ohio	1	1	"
"	Penn	Educat'd	Not known	None				"
"	Germany	Not	"	"				"
"	Luxamb'g	'ducat'd	"	"				"
"	Unknown	Not	'	"				"
"	Germany	Educat'd	"	"				"
"	Ohio	Not	S. and Elizabeth Cowdy	Farming	Virginia	7	1	"
"	Ohio	Partly	Wm. & Jane Watson	"	Penn	2	1	"
"	Penn	Not	Jonathan and Susan Tittle	"	"	9	1	"
"	Ohio	"	Alden and Mary Benham	Physic'n	Vermont	6	1	"
"	Ohio	"	John and Mary Brand	Farming	France	9	1	"
"	N. York	"	George and Nancy Wilson	None		10	1	"
"	Maryland	"	Benjamin and M. A. Paine	Farming	Missouri	7	1	Cousins.
"	Ohio	Educat'd	John and Elizabeth Wise	Blacks'h	Penn	7	1	None.
"	Rinehine	Not	Theobold G. Kuhn	Teacher	Rinehine	6	1	"
"	Kittshine	Educat'd	Michael & M. Rinehart	"	Kittshine	4	1	"
H'se work	Alsop	Educat'd	Joseph & Mary Hoffner	St'e cutr	Alsop	8	2	"
None	Switerla'd	Not	Henry & Elizabeth Bowman	Cooper	Switzerl'd	10	1	"
None	Ohio	"	Eli and Susan Huter	Farming	Ohio	1	1	"
None	Ohio	"	Daniel & Ruth Elliott	Farming	Maryland	6	1	"
Farmer	Maryland	Educat'd	Eli and C. Musted	Farming	Maryland	3	1	"
None	Germany	Not	Jacob & M. A. Waggoner	Landl'd	Germany	1	1	"
None	Ohio	Not	Thomas & Sarah McClary	Trader	Penn	2	1	Cousins.

12—SEC. OF STATE.

178

RETURN of the number of Deaf and Dumb, Blind, Insane and Idiotic persons

Townships	Names of Persons.	Nature of Affliction.	Duration of Affliction.	Cause where known.	Age.	Sex.	Color.
Franklin	Delinda Blue	Idiotic	10 years	Fits	11	Fem'le	White.
do	Jesse Blue	Idiotic	24 do	Fits	26	Male	do
Van Buren	Henry Shaffer	Blind	11 do	Fever	37	do	Mul'to
Jackson	Barbara Bauer	Blind	10 do	Cataract	26	Fem'le	White.
do	Robert Blakely	Idiotic	20 do	Unknown	20	Male	do
Dinsmoor	Mary Lorton	Deaf and dumb	32 do	do	32	Fem'le	do
Salem	Lydia Lefever	Deaf and dumb	23 do	Scarlet fever	23	do	do
do	John Sowers	Insane	3 do	Unknown	13	Male	do
Perry	Mary Jane Niswanger	Idiotic	9 do	Fits	18	Fem'le	do
do	Mary Jane Beeson	Idiotic	13 do	Fright of mother	13	do	do
do	John Bowersock	Deaf and dumb	50 do	Inflam'n brain.	51	Male	do
do	Wm. W. Bowersock	Deaf and dumb	13½ do	do do	16	do	do
do	Huldah G. Kiser	Idiotic	22 do	Unknown	22	Fem'le	do
Orange	Philip F. Randolph	Blind	5 do	Burn'g charcoal.	78	Male	do
do	Mary Young	Blind	9 do	Unknown	84	Fem'le	do
do	Nancy Jackson	Idiotic	40 do	do	40	do	do
do	Abraham Ferrie	Idiotic	9 do	Fits	23	Male	do
do	Daniel Shaw	Partially idiotic	40 do	Unknown	40	do	do
Cynthian	Josephine Loewinguth	Idiotic	8 do		8	Fem'le	do
do	George Loewinguth	Idiotic	6 do		6	Male	do
Loramie	Henry Stuart	Blind	2 do	Shot in the eyes	26	do	do
do	Emily Day	Idiotic	16 do	Unknown	16	Fem'le	do
do	Martha Noland	Deaf and dumb	8 do	do	8	do	do
do	George Wise	Deaf and dumb	45 do	do	45	Male	do
Washi'gton	John W. Monroe	Idiotic	11 do	do	11	do	do
do	Arthur Silver	Idiotic	26 do	Fever	28	do	do
do	Susan Horner	Idiotic	22 do	Unknown	22	Fem'le	do

179

in the county of Shelby, State of Ohio, on the second Monday of May, 1856.

Occupation	Birthplace	Educated or not	Names of Parents	Occupation	Birthplace	No. Children	No. children thus afflicted	Relationship of parents before marriage
....	Ohio	Not	Michael O. Blue	Farmer	Ohio	6	1	None.
Farmer	Ohio	do	Michael M. & Mrs. Blue	Farmer	Penn	12	1	do
Farmer	Ohio	Limited	Daniel & Rosanna Shaffer	Farmer	Virginia	3	1	do
None	Germany	....	Cornelia Bauer	Laborer	Germany	3	1	do
None	Ohio	Not	James & Barbara Blakeley	Farmer	Virginia	7	1	do
....	....	do	William Lorton	....	....	..	..	....
....	Ohio	Educat'd	David and Elacta Lefever	Farmer	Penn	9	1	None.
....	Ohio	Not	George and Eliz. Sowers	Gunsmith	Penn & O.	2	1	do
....	Ohio	Educat'd	J. and Charity Niswanger	Farmer	O.& N. J.	9	1	do
....	Ohio	Not	Wm. and Nancy Beeson	Farmer	N. C. & O.	10	1	do
Mason	Penn	do	B and C. Bowersock	Farmer	Unknown	12	1	do
Farmer	Ohio	do	John and Ellen Bowersock	Mason	Pa. & Ky.	9	1	do
....	Ohio	do	Peter and Mary Ann Kiser	Farmer	Ohio	6	1	Cousins.
Bl'ksmith	N. Jersey	Educat'd	....	....	....	..	..	....
H'sekeepr	Virginia	Not	....	....	....	..	..	....
....	Ohio	do	Edward and Mrs. Jackson	Farmer	Virginia	11	1	None.
None	Ohio	do	Joseph and Mrs. Ferrie	Farmer	Penn	7	1	do
Farmer	Ohio	do	Unknown	....	....	..	..	....
....	Ohio	do	V. and S. Lowinguth	Tailor	Germany	6	2	Cousins.
....	Ohio	do	do do	do	do	6	2	do
....	N. Bruns	do	George and Ann Stuart	Farmer	Ireland	6	1	None.
....	Ohio	do	Jonathan and Matilda Day	Farmer	Maryland	1	1	do
....	Ohio	do	Philip and Mary Noland	Cooper	Ohio	4	1	do
Farmer	Ohio	do	Unknown	....	....	..	..	....
....	Ohio	do	Hanson and Eliza Monroe	Farmer	Virginia	16	1	Cousins.
None	Ohio	do	David and Ann Silver	Teamster	Virginia	8	1	None.
do	Ohio	do	John and Nancy Horner	Cooper	....	5	1	do

RETURN of the number of Deaf and Dumb, Blind, Insane and Idiotic persons in

Townships	Names of Persons.	Nature of Affliction.	Duration of Affliction.	Cause where known.	Age.	Sex.	Color.
Paris	—— Swartz	Deaf d'b & bl'd	8 years	Teething	9	Male	White
Washing'n	John Wallace	Idiotic	13 "	Hereditary	13	Male	do
"	Margaret W. Laddee	Deaf and dumb	5 "	Sickness	9	Fem'le	do
Lexington	Edward White	Dumb	9 "	Hereditary	9	Male	do
"	Anna Karn	Deaf d'b & id'c	11 "	"	11	Fem'le	do
"	Jacob Bloch	Idiotic	18 "	"	18	Male	do
"	Eleanor Minere	Blind	7 "	Erysipelas	22	Fem'le	do
Marlboro	Pemelia Welch	Blind	1½ "	Accident	20	Fem'le	do
"	—— Snyder	Insane	2 "	Unknown	23	Fem'le	do
Nimishill'n	August Mariot	Idiotic	10 "	Hereditary	10	Male	do
"	David Spangler	Insane	40 "	"	40	Male	do
"	Daniel Holben	Deaf	8 "	Sickness	22	Male	do
Sandy	Simon Deal	Deaf and dumb	6 "	Infla'n of brain	8	Male	do
"	George Deal	Idiotic	53 "	Fever	55	Male	do
"	Ebenezer Roach	Blind	5 "	Intemperance	60	Male	do
"	Mary A. Miller	Deaf and dumb	36 "	Infla'n of brain	37	Fem'le	do
Pike	O. M. Leachley	Blind	23 "	Accident	33	Fem'le	do
"	William Rudy	Deaf and dumb	12 "	Born so	12	Male	do
"	Susan Rudy	Deaf and dumb	10 "	"	10	Fem'le	do
"	Julia A. Rudy	Deaf and dumb	6 "	"	6	Fem'le	do
"	Isaac Hownestine	Deaf and dumb	16 "	Sickness	18	Male	do
"	Solomon Cristleib	Idiotic	29 "	Teething	31	Male	do
Canton	John Rudy	Deaf and dumb	50 "	Hereditary	50	Male	do
"	Ann Affalter	Deaf and dumb	19 "	"	19	Fem'le	do
"	Frederick Affalter	Deaf and dumb	13 "	"	13	Male	do
"	Florence Getz	Deaf and dumb	46 "	Not known	49	Male	do
"	Joseph Hentzell	Deaf and dumb	2 "	Sickness	7	Male	do
"	Joseph Furnace	Deaf and dumb	29 "	Hereditary	29	Male	do
Plain	Caroline Monnier	Deaf & dumb	19 "	"	19	Fem'le	do
"	Pauline "	Deaf & dumb	13 "	"	13	Fem'le	do
"	Fra' cis "	Deaf & dumb	15 "	"	15	Male	do
"	Theodaline "	Deaf & dumb	21 "	"	21	Fem'le	do
"	Lewis Troto	Idiotic	3 "	Sickness	9	Male	do
"	Catharine Schiltz	Deaf and dumb	7 "	"	8	Fem'le	do
Lake	—— Fulmer	Idiotic	19 "	Hereditary	19	Male	do
"	—— Fulmer	Idiotic	17 "	"	17	Male	do
Perry	George Runser	Deaf and dumb	26 "	Fits	28	Male	do
"	John Laklear	Deaf & dumb	12 "	Hereditary	12	Male	do
"	Gotleip "	Deaf & dumb	10 "	"	10	Male	do
"	Ulrich "	Deaf & dumb	8 "	"	8	Male	do
Bethlehem	John Robertson	Deaf and dumb	34 "	Fall	39	Male	do
"	Isabella "	Deaf and dumb	35 "	Hereditary	35	Fem'le	do
"	Mary J. Rider	Deaf and dumb	5 "	"	5	Fem'le	do
"	Elizabeth Bauhoff	Deaf and dumb	26 "	"	26	Fem'le	do
Sug. Creek	—— Shunk	Idiotic	30 "	"	30	Male	do
"	Elizabeth Stiner	Deaf	56 "	"	56	Fem'le	do
"	Eli Trump	Idiotic	19 "	Scrofula	20	Male	do
"	Wilson Reed	Deaf and dumb	24 "	Fever	29	Male	do
"	Margaret Rife	Deaf and dumb	19 "	Unknown	19	Fem'le	do
"	Lavina Reed	Deaf and dumb	22 "	"	22	Fem'le	do
"	Mary Schlichter	Insane	25 "	Hereditary	25	Fem'le	do
"	Nathaniel Kilgore	Dumb & insane	23 "	Fever	25	Male	do
"	Margaret Shutt	Insane	40 "	Unknown	57	Fem'le	do
Tusca'was	Nancy Stump	Idiotic	32 "	Hereditary	32	Fem'le	do
"	Josephus Shilling	Idiotic	14 "	"	14	Male	do

the county of Staık, State of Ohio, on the second Monday of May, 1856.

Occupation	Birthplace	Educated or not.	Names of Parents.	Occupation	Birthplace	No. children	No. children thus afflicted	Relationship of parents before marriage
None	Germany	Not	Geo. A Swartz	Farmer	Germany	4	1	None
None	Ohio	"	Benj & Susan Wallace	Farmer	Ohio	4	1	do
None	Scotland	"	Andrew & Gracie Laddee	Dead	Scotland	2	1	do
"	Ohio	"	Israel White	Mecha'c	Unknown	3	1	do
"	Europe	"	Jacob Karn	Farmer	Europe	8	1	do
"	"	"	Harry Bloch	Farmer	"	6	1	do
"	N. Jersey	Educated	Wm. Minere	Miller	N. Jersey	13	1	do
Teacher	Ohio	"	Samuel & Margaret Welch	Farmer		6	1	do
None	Ohio	Unkno'n	Jacob Snyder	Farmer			1	Unknown
"	Ohio	Not	Geo. & Caiharine Mariot	Farmer	France	5	1	do
"	Penn	"	Joseph Spanger			4	1	do
"	Ohio	Educated	D. & C. Hulben	Farmer	Pa. & O.	10	1	do
"	Ohio	Not	John & Mary Deal	"	Penn.		1	None
Farmer	Penn	Not	Peter & Barbara Deal	"	"	5	1	do
None	Virginia	Educated	Wm. & Mary C. Roach	"	Pa. & Md.	10	1	do
Farmer	N. York	Educated	Wm. & Rachael Brownson	"	N. York	6	1	do
None	Ohio	Not	Nicholas & Susan Leachley	"	Europe	4	1	do
"	"	"	Henry & Catharine Rudy	"	Maryland	5	3	Unknown
"	"	"	" " "	"	"	5	3	do
"	"	"	" " "	"	"	5	3	do
"	"	Educated	Samuel Howenstine	"	Penn.	4	1	do
"	"	Not	John & E. Cristleib	"	"	5	1	do
"	Switzerl'd	"	John & Susan Rudy	Unkno'n	Switzerl'd	7	2	do
"	"	"	Andrew & Barbara Affalter	"	"	7	2	de
"	"	"	Andrew & Barbara Affalter	"	"	7	2	do
"	France	"	R. G. Getz	"	France	8	1	do
"	Ohio	"	Jacob Hentzell	"	France	6	1	None
"	Unknown	"	Louis Furnace	"	Unknown	9	1	do
"	Ohio	Educated						
"	"	"	Chas. & Josephine Monnier	Farmer	France	8	4	do
"	"	Not						
"	"	Educated	John & Margaret Troto	Cooper	France	3	1	do
"	"	Not	John H. Schiltz	Shoema'r	Germany	5	1	do
"	Unknown	"	Daniel Fulmer	Farmer	"	7	2	1st cous's
"	"	"	Daniel Fulmer	"	"	7	2	do
Mecha'c	France	"	John G. Runs r	"	France	8	1	None
None	Switzerl'd	"	Ulrich & Eliza'b Laklear	"	Switzerl'd	6	3	do
"	"	"	" " "	"	"	6	3	do
"	"	"	" " "	"	"	6	3	do
Mecha'c	Unknown	Educated	Denny & Ellen Robertson	"	Ireland			Unknown
None	"	"	James Chapman	"	America			do
"	Ohio	Not	Wm. & Rebecca Rider	Carpen'r	Virginia		1	None
"	Germany	Educated	Christian & E. Bauhoff	Baker	Germany	9	1	do
"	Penn	Not	John Shunk	Farmer	Penn.	10	1	do
"	Switzerl'd	"	John & E. Stiner	"	Switzerl'd	5	1	do
"	Ohio	"	John & Susan Trump	"	Ohio	8	1	do
Farmer	"	Educated	Robert & Sarah Reed	"	Penn.	5	1	do
None	"	"	Phillip & E. Rife	"	Ohio	9	2	do
"	"	"	Robert & Jane Moore	"	Ohio	3	1	do
"	Penn	Not	Geo & Sarah Schlichter	"	Penn.	2	1	do
"	"	"	David & Hannah Kilgore	"	Ohio	12	1	do
"	"	"	John Reed	Mecha'c	Germany	4	2	do
"	Ohio	"	Michael & Mary Stump	Farmer	Penn.	8	1	Cousins
"	"	"	Peter & Nancy Shilliug	"	Ohio	8	2	do

RETURN of the number of Deaf and Dumb, Blind, Insane and Idiotic

Townships.	Names of persons.	Nature of Affliction.	Duration of Affliction.	Cause where known.	Age.	Sex.	Color.
Lawrence	Wm. Langhorn	Dumb & idiotic	12 years	Hereditary	13	Male	White.
"	Mary Yockey	Idiotic	3 "	Fits	4	Fem'le	"
"	John Simmons	Idiotic	23 "	Hereditary	23	Male	"
"	George "	Idiotic	21 "	"	21	"	"
"	Catharine "	Idiotic	25 "	"	25	Fem'le	"
"	Michael "	Idiotic	17 "	"	17	Male	"
"	Wilhelm "	Idiotic	11 "	"	11	"	"
"	A Wolfsperger	Idiotic	8 "	Fits	14	"	"

persons in Stark County, Ohio—Continued.

Occupation.	Birthplace.	Educated or not.	Names of Parents.	Occupation.	Birth-place.	No. Children.	No. Children thus afflicted.	Relationship of parents before marriage
None	Stark co.	Not	John Langhorn	Laborer	England	1	1	None.
Laborer.	"	Not	Philip Yockey	"	Germany	11	1	"
"	"	Not						
"	"	Not	George & C. Simmons.	..	Germany	5	5	None.
"	"	Not	The mother idiotic.					
"	"	Not						
None	"	Not						
"	"	Not	Geo. Wolfsperger	Miller	Germany	3	1	None·

RETURN of the number of Deaf and Dumb, Blind, Insane and Idiotic persons

Names of Persons.	Nature of Affliction.	Duration of Affliction.		Cause Where Known.	Age.	Sex.	Color.
John Dissinger............	Blind.........	4	years	Old age........	80	Male	White.
Elijah Mason..............	do	4	"	Inflamation.....	60	"	"
Eliza Singletary...........	do	21	"	Scrofula........	58	Fem'le	"
George Pease.............	do	37	"	Accident........	49	Male	"
Cynthia Carpenter..........	Idiotic........	16	"	Being in water...	19	Fem'le	"
Phillip Grill...............	do	40	"	Unknown......	40	Male	"
William Fonser............	do	25	"	do	25	"	"
John Fonser..............	do	24	"	do	24	"	"
Eliza Fonser..............	do	26	"	do	6	Fem'le	"
Ann Fonser...............	do	20	"	do	20	"	"
Pomeroy Holcomb...........	do	31	"	From birth......	31	Male	"
Joseph Bennage............	do	10	"	Inflamation of eyes	28	"	"
Eliza Crist................	do	From infan		Unknown......	..	Fem'le	"
Margaret Spotts...........	Blind and Idiot	38	years	From injury rec'd	50	"	"
Lydia Ann Garrett..........	Deaf and dumb	6	"	Dropsy in head ..	8	"	"
Samuel Wise..............	do do	21	"	Unknown......	21	Male	"
Mary Ann Wise...........	do do	13	"	do	13	Fem'le	"
R. Jane Boden............	Dumb........	6	"	do	6	"	"
Rebecca Sparhawk.........	Deaf and dumb	....		....	50	.....	"
Cynthia Thompson...........	do do	26	years	Rickets in head..	29	Fem'le	"
Eva Spade................	do do	35	"	Cold...........	37	"	"
—— Myers................	do do	9	"	....	9	Male	"
Edwin Case...............	do do	28	"	....	28	"	"
George Douglass...........	do do	......		Scarlet Fever	..	"	"
Col. Smith................	do do	40	years	....	40	"	"
Margaret Allen............	Insane........	2	"	....	62	Fem'le	"
Rebecca M. McConnoughy...	Partially insane	30	"	Unknown.......	54	"	"
Abigail Haney.............	do do	5	"	do	35	"	"
Juliana Tiffany............	Insane........	16	"	Disap. and study.	38	"	"
Ephraim Tousley...........	do	15	"	....	35	Male	"
David Bennage............	do	3	months	Intemperance....	29	"	"
James Fight...............	do	32	years	Unknown.......	52	"	"
Mary Wright..............	Partially insane	8 or 10 yrs		Supposed heredi'y	36	Fem'le	"
Aaron Cox................	Demented	14	years	Fall & inj. of brain	28	Male	"
George Haaford............	do	....		Unknown.......	..	.....	"

in the county of Summit, State of Ohio, on the second Monday of May, 1856.

Occupation.	Birth-place.	Educat'd or not.	Names of Parents.	Occupation.	Birth-place.	No. children.	No. afflicted.	Relations'ip of parents before marriage.
Farmer .	Penn......	Educat'd						
	New York.	Partially	Timot! y and Anna Bi-hop			9	9	
Farmer .	Ohio	Not	Ebenezer and Polly Pease.	Farmer ...		3	1	None ..
	"	Not	A. nd Thirza Carpenter .	Carpenter .	New York	13	1	"
None...	Penn	Not	John Grill............ ...	Farmer ...	Penn	10	1	"
do	Ohio	Not	G. and Nancy Fonser	do	do	4	4	"
do	"	Not	do	do	do	4	4	"
do	"	Not	do	do	do	4	4	"
do	"	Not	do	do	do	4	4	"
	Hudson ..	Not	G. W. and —— Holcomb..	do	Connecicut	11	1	"
None ...	Ohio	Not	Jacob Bennage........	do	Penn	8	2	"
		Not						
	Penn	Not	L. and Susan Spotts......	Farmer ...	Penn	14	2	None ..
	"	Not	D. and Margaret Garrett ..	do	do	10	1	"
	Ohio	Not	J, and Christiana Wise. ..	do	do	8	2	1st Cous
	Ohio	Not	Same................	do	do	8	2	"
	Ohio	Not	D. and Eliza Boden	Mechanic .	do	2	1	"
	Vermont..		H. and Lucinda Sparhawk					None ..
	Quebec ...	Educat'd	A. and Sarah Thompson ..	Laborer ..		4	1	"
	Ohio	Not	J. and Elizabeth Spade....	Farmer. ..	Penn	10	..	"
	Ohio	Not	John and Ann Myers.....	do	do	7	1	"
Shoema'r	Vermont..	Educat'd	E. and A. Case..........	do	Vermont..	2	1	1st Cons
Farmer .	Tallmadge	Partially						
Shoema'r	Unknown .	Well Ed						
	Ireland ...							
	Maryland .	Educat'd	C. and E izabeth Nisbet ..	Farmer ...		9	2	None ..
	Mass	Educat'd	Z. and Clarissa Graham...	Shoemaker	Mass	8	1	"
	Ohio	Educat'd	B. and Rhoda Oviat:.....	Farmer ...	Connecicut	11	2	"
Farmer .	Ohio......	Educat'd	J. and Rebecca Tousley...	do	do	10	2	"
Physicin	Ohio	Educat'd	Jacob Bennage........	do	Penn	8	2	"
	Ohio	Educat'd	Unknown...............	do	Maryland .	8	..	"
	Ohio	Educat'd				2	..	"

RETURN of the Number of Deaf and Dumb, Blind, Insane and Idiotic persons

Townships.	Names of Persons.	Nature of affliction.	Duration of affliction.		Cause Where Known.	Age.	Sex.	Color.
Vernon	Adeline E. Trunkey	Deaf and dumb	14	years	Scarlet fever	15	Fem'le	White.
do	Nelson Chapman	Insane	19	"	....	33	Male	"
do	Jennet Sackett	Idiotic	13	"	Sickness	16	Fem'le	"
do	Luther Burns	"	52	"	....	52	Male	"
do	Pagna Burns	"	37	"	....	37	Fem'le	"
Liberty	Lydia Herring	"	27	"	Sickness	27	"	"
do	Benjamin Booth	Deaf	31	"	Severe cold	33	Male	"
do	John S. Barnhisel	"	21	"	Unknown	21	"	"
do	Harriet Hoffman	Idiotic	53	"	"	53	Fem'le	"
Brookfield	Sarah Jewell	Blind			Inflam. in head	50	"	"
do	Nancy Artheholt	Deaf and dumb	54	"	....	54	"	"
do	Isaac Carnes	"	60	"	Unknown	60	Male	"
do	Margaretta A. Deforest	Insane	20	"	Fits	30	Fem'le	"
do	Nancy Burton	Idiotic	17	"	Unknown	17	"	"
Bloomfield	William Smith	Blind	31	"	Accident	43	Male	"
do	Thomas Sealey	"	5	"	Chronic Inflam.	56	"	"
do	Frances A. Northrop	"	15	"	Inflammation	27	Fem'le	"
Hubbard	Lucretia Butler	Deaf and dumb	7	"	Sickness	11	"	"
do	John F. Dilley	Insane	22	"	Unknown	30	Male	"
do	Jane Jewell	Idiotic	16	"	"	16	Fem'le	"
do	Margaret Patterson	Blind	34	"	....	40	"	"
Hartford	Eliza Jones	Idiotic	15	"	Fits	15	"	"
do	Joseph Rider	"	40	"	Unknown	40	Male	"
do	Lester H. Johnson	"	33	"	App. of forceps	33	"	"
Farmington	Jas. O. Strickland	Deaf and dumb	14	"	Unknown	14	Male	"
do	Cyrus P. Wildman	Idiotic	3	"	Rickets	9	"	"
do	Elizabeth Barnard	Deaf and dumb	13	"	Scarlet fever	15	Fem'le	"
Braceville	William Gurdon	Insane	5	"	Unknown		Male	"
Johnston	Isabella Donnald	Idiotic	15	"	"	15	Fem'le	"
do	Sherman Skinner	....			"	40	Male	"
do	Catharine L. Skinner	....			Scarlet fever	29	Fem'le	"
Newton	James A. Hofsteater	Idiotic	5	"	Fits	6	Male	"
do	William Angels Cole	Partially idiotic	29	"	"	34	"	"
do	Netty Ann Hutson	Idiotic	27	"	Unknown	27	Fem'le	"
do	Mary Patterson	"	36	"	Fits	40	"	"
Vienna	Andrew Clark	Deaf and dumb	74	"	Unknown	74	Male	"
do	Stephen Anderson	Partially insane	15	"	"	63	"	"
do	Johnson Runnion	Idiotic	30	"	Fits	30	"	"
do	David Hager	"	20	"	"	20	"	"
do	Sarah Scovill	Insane	15	"	Unknown	63	Fem'le	"
do	Celista Fuller	Idiotic	13	"	"	13	"	"
Bristol	Lydia Ayres	Insane	31	"	....	56	"	"
We'thersf'd	James McCombs	Blind	5	"	....	5	Male	"
Gustavus	Melinda H. Chaffee	Insane	5	months	....	20	Fem'le	"
do	Maria Lyman	Idiotic	18	years	....	18	"	"
do	James Noble Gilmore	Deaf and dumb	19	"	....	19	Male	"
do	James H. Wright	"	21	"	....	21	"	"
Kingman	Anna Splitstone	Blind	15	"	Inflammation	45	Fem'le	"
do	Thomas Lewis	"	4	"	....	27	Male	"
do	Homer Hurlburt	Insane	2	months	Unknown	19	"	"
Lordstown	Moses Stittle	Idiotic	26	years	"	26	"	"
do	Mary Ann Gordon	Dumb	12	"	"	12	Fem'le	"
do	John Landis	Deaf and dumb	43	"	"	43	Male	"
do	Laura Haskell	Simple	23	"	"	23	Fem'le	"

in the county of Trumbull, State of Ohio, on the second Monday of May, 1856.

Occupation.	Birth-place.	Educated or not.	Names of Parents.	Occupation.	Birth-place.	No. children	No. children thus afflicted.	Relationship of Parents before marriage.
....	Ohio	Educated	Harvy and A. Trunkey	Farmer ..	Ct. and Pa.	9	1	None....
Farmer ..	Conn.	do	D. and O. Chapman	"	Conn	9	1	"
....	Ohio	Not	John P. and S. Sackett	"	Ind. & Ct	5	2	"
None	do	do	} Amasa and C. Burns	Hatter ...	Maryland.	12	2	Uncle&} Niece .}
"	do	do						
"	do	do	George and M. Herring	Farmer ..	Penn......	11	1	None....
Farmer ..	Ireland ...	Educated	John and Mary Booth	"	Ireland ...	5	1	"
None	Ohio	do	Henry and S. Barnhisel	"	Pennsylva.	6	1	"
"	Pennsylv'a	Not	Isaac and S. Hoffman	"	do	6	1	"
....	do	do	Robert and S. Jewell	"	do	5	1	....
....	do	do	D. and N. Artheholt	Oil Mill..	do	3	1	....
Farmer ..	do	do	....					....
Knitting .	New Jersey	Educated	G. and Ellen Deforest	Farmer ..	New Jersey	9	1	....
....	Ohio	Not	Warren and M. Burton	"	C nn	4	1	....
Farmer ..	Penn	do	Wm. and Agnes Smith	"	Pa. & N J	4	1	None....
Stonecut'r	England ..	Educated	John and Virtue Sealey	Shoemak'r	England ..	12	1	"
....	New York	do	O. and E. H. Wilcox	Farmer ..	New York	7	1	"
....	Ohio	Not	John and C. Butler..	....	Ohio	3	1	"
....	do	do	Thompson Dilley	....	....			"
....	do	do	J. and Eliz'h Jewell	....	Ohio	3	1	"
....	do	Educated	Isaac Patterson	....	....			"
....	do	Not	John B. and E. Jones	Farmer ..	Ct and Pa	18	1	"
....	New Jersey	do	Benj. and Mary Reider	"	New Jersey	10	1	"
....	Ohio	do	Ransom and C.Johnson	None	Conn.....	6	1	"
....	New York	Educated	J. and M. Strickland	Farmer ..	N. Y. & O.	5	1	....
....	Ohio.....	Not	Silas and L. Wildman	"	do	3	1	....
....	New York	do	Benj. and G. Barnard	"	Vt. & N.H.	11	1	....
Farmer ..	Conn	Educated	....	....	....	3	1	....
....	Scotland ..	Not	Thos. and M. Donald	Farmer ..	Scotland ..	1	1	None....
Farmer ..	Ohio	Educated	James Skincer	Joiner ...	Conn	5	1	"
Tailoress.	Vermont ..	do	Jedediah Calkins ...	Farmer ..	Vermont	10	1	"
....	Ohio	Not	J. and Sarah Hofstaeter	Tailor ...	Ohio	2	1	"
....	do	do	Peter and Caroline Cole	Farmer ..	New York	12	1	"
....	New York	do	Samuel and M. Hutson	"	Penn	1	1	Cousins.
....	Penn.	do	Susan Shafer	"	do	15	1	None....
Carpenter	Conn	do	John and Eliz. Clark	"	Conn	11	2	Cousins.
Farmer ..	Ireland ...	Educated	James and J. Anderson	"	Ireland ...	6	2	None....
....	Ohio	Not	Sons of same mother..	....	....			....
....	do	do						....
....	Conn	Educated	Unknown	....	....			....
....	Ohio	Not	Lor. and H. Fuller..	Bl'cksmth	....	3	1	None....
Farmer ..	New York	Educated	....	....	....			....
....	Wales	Not	E. and Mary Davis..	Boiler....	Wales	4	1	None....
....	Ohio	Educated	Erastus and S. Merry.	Farmer ..	New York	6	1	"
....	do	Not	R and Harriet Lyman	"	O. and N.Y	5	1	"
Farmer ..	do	Educated	John and Eliz. Gilmore	"	Ireland ...	7	1	"
Car'ge m'r	Pennsylva.	do	D. and B. M. Wright	"	O. and N.Y	3	1	"
....	Ohio	Not	S. and Eliz. Splitstone	"	Maryland .	9	1	....
None	do	Educated	Luther and P. Lewis	"	Ct. & Mass	5	4	....
Farmer ..	Penn	do	A. and Eliza Hurlburt	"	New York			....
....	Ohio	Not	Jacob and E'iz. Stittle	"	Penn	5	1	Cousins.
....	do	do	J. P. and Sarah Gordon	"	do	5	1	2d cousins
None	Penn	Educated	Jacob and N. Landis	"	....	6	4	....
"	Ohio.	Not	Moses Haskell	"	New York	6	1	None....

RETURN of the number of Deaf and Dumb, Blind, Insane and Idiotic persons

Townships.	Names of Persons.	Nature of affliction	Duration of affliction.	Cause, where known	Age.	Sex	Color
Sugar Creek.	Solomon Harris....	Deaf.........	34 years..	Fell on knife...	42	Male .	White.
Goshen	Amy Jane McCollum	Deaf and dumb	8 do	Measles	9	Fem'le	do
"	Richard H. Pepper.	do do	15 do	Bad cold......	17	Male .	do
"	Samuel Lytle......	Blind......	4 do	Exposure to cold	70	do	do
"	Henry Meese.....	Insane........	32 do	Unknown.....	32	do	do
"	John Meese........	do	25 do	do	25	do	do
"	Mary Morse.......	do	35 do	do	35	Fem'le	do
"	Anna Morse.......	do	21 do	do	21	do	do
Auburn....	Simon Kutcher...	Dumb........	17 do	....	17	Male ..	do
"	Fred'ck Zimmerman	Deaf and Dumb	21 do	....	21	do	do
"	John Zimmerman..	do	18 do	....	18	do	do
"	Jacob Zimmerman..	do	14 do	....	14	do	do
"	Samuel Snyder....	do	43 do	....	43	do	do
"	Hezikiah Hixon....	Insane........	29 do	By a fall.. ...	41	do	do
Bucks	Philip Jacob Boltz..	blind	8 do	Sickness	31	do	do
Mill.......	Franklin F. Laizure,	Insane........	8 do	Fever	11	do	do
"	Alexander Cahill...	Deaf	7 do	Erysypilas	24	do	do
"	Joseph O. Furguson	Idiotic........	25 do	Unknown.....	5	do	do
"	James Kane.......	do	35 do	do	35	do	do
"	Anna More........	do	44 do	do	44	Fem'le	do
"	——Lewis..	do	12 do	do	12	do	do
"	William Kesner....	do	21 do	do	21	do	do
Warwick ..	Fred'k Hawnekrath.	Deaf and Dumb	23 do	do	23	Male	do
Dover.....	Findley Wetty	Idiotic........	From birth.	Fright of mother	23	do	do
"	Christian Sping....	do	do	Unknown......	33	do	do
"	Matty Myers.......	do	do	do	23	Fem'le	do
"	Hannah Putt......	do	do	do	45	do	do
"	Henry Crite......	do	64 years...	Spasms	66	Male ..	do
"	Elizabeth Fisher...	do	From birth	Hereditary	17	Feml'e	do
"	Catharine S. Hoover	Insane........	do	....	27	do	do
"	Apelonia Hoover...	do	do	....	66	do	do
"	Daniel Beck	do	do	....	45	Male .	do
"	L. Oswalt	Blind........	8 years ..	....	36	do	do
Sandy.....	Daniel Maninger...	Blind and deaf.	30 do	Unknown......	45	do	do
Warren....	Abraham Croft....	Idiotic........	Since birth	....	24	do	do
"	Mary Heycock.....	Insane........	10 years ..	Unknown.....	35	Fem'le	do
Jefferson ...	Caroline Cara.....	Idiotic........	35 do	do	35	do	do
"	Jacob Stroub......	do	12 do	do	30	do	do
Rush......	John Harmon......	Blind........	44 do	Fits	48	Male ..	do
Washington.	Solomon Lee......	Idiotic........	....	....	8	do	do
York.......	John Shull........	do	From birth	....	60	do	do
"	George Shull......	do	do	....	46	do	do
"	Abraham Shull....	do	do	....	40	do	do
"	Hannah Putt......	do	do	....	40	Fem'le	do
"	Margaret Beufer....	do	do	....	16	do	do
Wayne.....	Reudolph Reef.....	Deaf	15 years ..	Over heated...	47	Male .	do
"	John Armstrong...	Idiotic........	58 do	....	58	do	do
"	Cristiana Reed....	Insane.	2 do	Measles	41	Fem'le	do
Clay	Elizabeth Gilmore.	Blind	4 do	Erisypilas.....	77	do	do
"	Thomas Huston....	Idiotic........	4 do	............,...	4	Male .	do
"	Catharine Swigert	Deaf	20 do	Unknown	57	Fem'le	do
"	Jacob F. Rebstock.	Deaf and dumb	56 do	do	57	Male .	do
Salem	Thos. S. Lacey. ..	Insane........	3 do	Fits	24	do	do
"	Andrew Sands....	Deaf and dumb	7 do	....	27	do	do
"	Thos. Everhart, jr.,	Insane........	27 do	Unknown	27	do	do
"	Henry M. Wyant...	do	11 do	do	11	do	do

in the County of Tuscarawas, State of Ohio, on the second Monday of May, 1856.

Occupation.	Birthp'ace.	Educat'd or not.	Names of parents.	Occupation.	Birth-place.	No. children	No. of child'n thus afflicted	Relationship of Parents before Marriage.
Farmer	Penn	Not	Not known			1		
None	Tus.co.,O	"	J. & Susan McCollum	Carpenter	Ohio	4	1	None
Farming	Penn	"	Samuel Pepper	Brick layer	"		1	"
do	Unknown	"	Margaret Candon		Penn	9	1	"
do	Penn	"	George Lytle	Not known	"		1	"
do	"	"	D Meese & N Thomas	Farmer	"		1	"
do	"	"	Catha ine Fodle		"	8	2	
do	"	"						
do	Germany	"	J. and E Kutcher	Farmer	Germany		1	
None	Switz'l'd	"	C. & E. Zimmerman	Laborer	Switz'rl'nd			
do	"	"	"	"	"			
do	"	"	"	"	"		3	
Shoemakr	"	"	Sam. & C. Snyder	Shoemaker	"		1	
None	Penn	"	Amos and Polly Hixan	None	Penn		1	
do	Bavaria	"	Dan. & Cath. Boltz	"	Mullhassen	4	1	None.
do	Ohio	"	Wm. B. & Ann Laizu'e	Carpenter	Penn	5	1	"
Farmer	"	Educated	Wm. and R Cahill	Farmer	Virginia	8	1	"
do	"	Not	Richard & R. Furguson	"	Va & Pa	12	1	"
do	Virginia	"	Illegitimate	"			1	
None	Penn	"	John & Nancy More	"	Penn	8	1	
do	Ohio	"	Zedekiah & J. Lewis	"	Va. & Ohio		1	None.
do	"	"	Adam & R. Kesson	"	Virginia	5	1	"
Farmer	Switz'l'd	"	N. & S. Hawnekrath	Farmer	Switz'rl'nd	8	1	"
None	Dover, O.	"	Jacob & Eliz. Wetty	"	Penn	11	1	"
	Sw'tz'l'd	Educated	E. & Nicholas Spring	Mason	Switz'rl'nd	4	1	"
	St'rkeo,O		A. and Anna Myers	Farmer	Penn	8	1	"
	Penn	Not	Geo. H. & D. Putt	"	Germany	14	1	"
Farmer	"	"	Jacob & E. Crites	"	"	12	1	"
None	Dover, O	"	Henry & E. Fisher	'	Penn	10	1	"
do	Germany	"	Martin & A. Hoover	"	Germany	4	1	"
do	"	"	"	"	"		1	"
Farmer	Penn	"	Peter Beck	"	Penn	6	1	
None	Germany	"	Geo. & Mary Oswalt	"	Germany	9	1	
Laborer	Carrol co.	"	Geo & Eliz. Maninger	"	Penn	9	1	Cousins
None	Ohio	"	Matthew Craft	Blacksmith	England	7	1	None
H'sework	"	Educated	Sherod	Farmer	Ireland	12	1	"
None	"	Not	Jacob Karn	"	Ohio	3	1	"
Farmer	"	"	Parens dead	"	Germany		1	"
Laborer	Penn	"					1	
	Ohio	"	J. and Mary Lee	Farmer	Ohio	8	1	None
	Penn	"	John Shull, deceased	"	Penn	10	3	Unknown
	"	"	"	'	"			
	"	"	"	"	"			
	Prussia	"	Geo. H. Putt		Prussia	11	1	None
	Ohio	"	Iohn M. Benfer	'	"	4	1	"
Farmer	Switz'l'd	Educated	Henry and M. Reefe	'	Switz'rl'nd	4	1	"
None	Penn	Not	A. and B. Armstrong	None	Penn	5	1	"
do	Ohio	Not	Abram & C. Reed	"	Ohio	7	1	"
Weaving	Ireland	Educated	John & Nancy Kelly	Farmer	Ireland	9	1	
	Tus.co.,O	Not	C. and R. A. Huston	St'n.mason	Ohio	1	1	"
Weaving	Penn	Educated	Henry and M. Aim s	Farmer	Penn	14	1	
Farming	Germany	Not	J. and E. Rebstook	"	Germany	9	1	Unknown
do	Carrol co.	Educated	Elijan and C. Lacy	"	Penn	7	1	None
do	Penn	Educated	Wm. Jane Sands	"	Ireland	4	1	Cousins
Saddler	Har'son co	Educated	Thos. and M. Everhart	"	Penn	19	1	None
	Ohio	Not	Adam and J. Wiant	"	"	6	1	"

RETURN of the number of Deaf and Dumb, Blind, Insane and Idiotic

Township.	Names of persons.	Nature of Affliction.	Duration of Affliction.	Cause where known.	Age.	Sex.	Color.
Salem	Jacob Gro-ar h	Insane	13 years	Fits	13	Male	White
Lawrence	Sarah Grove	Insane	8 "	Sickness	10	Fem'le	do
do	John Bauer	Deaf	4 "	"	46	Male	do
do	Martin Ranchenberzer	Deaf and dumb	From birth		30	"	do
do	Aagatha Angele	Blind	"		14	Fem'le	do
do	Emeline G iffith	Insane	21 years	Sickness	22	"	do

persons in the County of Tuscarawas, State of Ohio—Continued.

Birth-place.	Educated or not.	Names of Parents.	Occupation.	Birth-place.	Age.	No. Children thus afflicted.	Relationship of parents before marriage.
Germany..	Not......	C. and Katharine Grosarth....	Farmer...	Germany..	6	1	None...
Ohio	"	George and Sarah Grove......	"	Penna....	8	1	"
Germany..	Educated.	John and Mary Bauer.........	"	Germany..	4	1	"
do	"	M. and Mary Ranchenberzer..	Carpenter.	do	10	1	"
do	....	Jacob and Catharine Angele...	Farmer...	do	3	1	"
....	Not......	Caleb and Eliza Griffith.......	"	Penna....	9	1	"

RETURN of the number of Deaf and Dumb, Blind, Insane and Idiotic persons

Names of Persons.	Nature of affliction.	Duration of affliction.	Cause where known.	Age.	Sex.	Color.	Occupation.
Anna Richardson	Blind	14 years	Fever & inflam.	57	Fem'le	White.	Farming
Nancy Bowen	do	8 do	do	66	do	do	Husbnd Dr
Robt. Reed	Idiotic	11 do	Masturbation	33	Male	do	Farmer
Maria Thackay	Blind	8 do	Cataract	52	Fem'le	do	do
Albert Bam	Insane	1 do		20	Male	do	Farmer
Mary Ann Roach	Deaf and dumb	From birth	Unknown	8	Fem'le	do	
Wm. H. Roach	do	do	do	5	Male	do	
John Oberfield	do	40 years	Fever	44	do	do	Farmer
Ann E. Cooksey	do	6 months	Caused by cold	5	Fem'le	do	
Wm. Meeker	do	36 years	Blow on head	40	Male	do	
Charlotte Wells	Idiotic	12 do	From birth	12	Fem'le	do	
Martha Sparks	do	21 do	Unknown	21	do	do	
Hulah Carter	do	24 do	do	28	do	do	
Sally Green	Blind	40 do	Ague in the face	86	do	do	
Martha Morse	Insane	4 do	Child-bearing	26	do	do	
Austin Clark	Idiotic	34 do	Fits	35	Male	do	Farmer
Miss —— Reed	Deaf and dumb	18 do	Scarlet fever	20	Fem'le	do	
Amor Miller	Insane	13 do	Unknown	52	do	do	

in the county of Union, State of Ohio, on the second Monday of May, 1856.

Birth-place.	Educated or not.	Names of Parents.	Occupation	Birth-place.	No. Children.	No. children thus afflicted.	Relationship of parents before marriage.
Virginia	Partially	Richard and Mary Hall	Farming	Unknown.	10	..	None
Vermont	Educated	Obediah and Hannah Rice	...	Mass	8	..	do
....	....	....	....	....	..	..	....
England	Educated	....	....	....	..	..	....
Ohio	do	Jacob Brown	Farming	....	..	..	....
....	Not	John and Rosey Roach	do	....	2	2	None
....	do	do do	do	....	2	2	do
Virginia	do	Samuel and Nancy Oberfield	do	....	13	1	do
do	....	Simpson and Sarah Cookacy	Hard labor	Virginia	6	1	do
Ohio	Educated	....	....	....	2	1	do
do	Not	John and Caroline Wells	Shoemaker	Va. & Ohio	5	1	do
do	do	Isaac and Martha Sparks	Farming	N. Jersey	10	1	do
do	do	Israel and Agnes Carter	do	Virginia	12	2	do
R Island	do	Henry and Hannah Briggs	Cooper	R. Island	..	..	do
Ohio	Educated	James and Catharine Morse	Farming	Kentucky	6	..	do
do	Not	James and Elizabeth Clark	do	Virginia	6	1	do
Penn	do	James Reed	do	Penn	..	1	do
N. York	Educated	Thomas and K. Warson	do	New York	10	1	Unkno'n

13 —SEC. OF STATE.

RETURN of the number of Deaf and Dumb, Blind, Insane and Idiotic persons in

Townsips.	Names of persons.	Nature of Affliction.	Duration of Affliction.	Cause where known.	Age.	Sex.	Color.
Ridge	Eliza Jane Priddy...	Deaf and dumb	12 years..	Not known....	12	Fem'le	White.
Tully	Emanuel Baker......	Idiotic........	9 do	do	9	Male	do
Pleasant ..	Nancy Roach	Deaf..........	24 do	do	24	Fem'le	do
Pleasant ..	Daniel Wright.......	Deaf..........	33 do	do	33	Male	do
Jennings..	Joseph Berry........	Deaf and dumb	26 do	do	26	Male	do
do ..	Elizabeth Berry......	Deaf and dumb	21 do	do	21	Fem'le	do
Liberty ..	Elias Benton Fox....	Deaf and dumb	6 do	Gather'g in head	7	Male	do
Liberty ..	Mary A. Bottels....	Deaf and dumb	2 do	....	86	Fem'le	do

the county of Van Wert, State of Ohio, on the second Monday of May, 1856.

Occupation.	Birth-place.	Educated or Not.	Names of Parents.	Occupation.	Birth-place.	No. Children.	No. Children thus afflicted.	Relationship of parents before marriage.
....	Ohio	Not	A. and Sarah Priddy .	Farmer ...	Ohio	6	1	None. "
None	Ohio	Not	John & Catharine Baker	Farmer ...	Penn	12	1	....
Dress mkr	Ohio	Educat'd	J. T. & M. A. Roach	Shi'gle mkr	Maryland .	3	1	....
Farmer ..	Ohio	Educat'd	Joseph & Eunice Clark	None	....	3	1	....
Farmer ..	Ohio	Educat'd	Malachia & Polly Berry	....	....	2	2	2d cous.
Seamstre'.	Ohio	Educat'd	" "	....	....	2	2	do
....	Ohio	Not	Collin and Mary Fox.	Farmer ...	Irela'd & O	5	1	None.
....	Penn	Educat'd	Jacob and Mrs. Hipner	Farmer ...	....	.	.	....

RETURN of the Number of Deaf and Dumb, Blind, Insane and Idiotic persons in

Township.	Names of Persons	Nature of Affliction.	Duration of Affliction.	Cause where known.	Age.	Sex.	Color.
Eagle	Rachel Wilkinson	Blind	1 year	Cataract	58	Fem'le	Wh te.
Swan	Lewis Robinett	Idiotic	Life	Congenital	67	Male	"
Knox	Priscilla Dixen	"	11 years	Fits	21	Fem'le	"
"	Harriet McKibben	"	8 "	Unknown	8	"	"
"	Margaret Eason	Deaf	16 "	Cold	41	"	"
Wilkesville	John Samples	Blind	3 "	Accident	19	Male	"
Jackson	Nancy Crambles	"	1 "	Inflammation	72	Fem'le	"
"	George Mosher	"	9 "	Sickness	36	Male	"
Elk	Nancy Winters	Insane	14 "	Unknown	40	Fem'le	"
"	Eleanor Moore	Insane or idiotic	12 "	"	15	"	"
"	David Ogan	Idiotic	12 "	Congenital	12	Male	"
"	Robinson L. Burns	Insane	.. "	Epilepsy	40	"	"
Vinton	Sarah K. Laughlin	Idiotic	60 "	"	60	Fem'le	"
Brown	McHamilton Fee	Insane	12 "	Loss of property	35	Male	"
Clinton	Jonas Robbins	Insane	28 "	Bathing	40	"	"
"	Daniel S. Bard	Deaf and dumb	12 "	Congenital	12	"	"
"	Cath. A. Salmon	Deaf and dumb	5 "	Unknown	5	Fem'le	"
"	Amanda Dill	Insane	3 "	"	34	Fem'le	"

the county of Vinton, State of Ohio, on the second Monday of May, 1856.

Occupation.	Birthplace.	Educated or not.	Names of Parents.	Occupation.	Birthplace.	No children.	No. children thus afflicted.	Relationship of Parents before Marriage.
H'se k'per	Virginia..	Educated	Lewis & Jane Demos..	Farmer ..	Virginia...	7	3	Cousins.
None	Maryland	Not	Ezekiel Robinett	Farmer ..	Maryland,	4	2	2d cous.
"	Ohio	Not	Henry & M. Dixon....	Farmer ..	Ohio	6	1	None.
"	Ohio	Not	Richard & L. McKibben	Farmer ॒	Ohio	8	1	"
Farmer ..	Kentucky	Educated	Daniel & Mary Beach..	Farmer ..	Maryland .	9	1	"
None	Carrol co.	Not.....	Wm. & Mary Samples.	Laborer ..	Unknown .	..	1	....
Farmer ..	Maryland	Not......	Ed. J. & E. Thompson..	Farmer ..	England .	8	1	None.
None	Ohio	Educated	Thomas & E Mosher...	Farmer ..	Mass	11	1	"
....	"	Not	James & Martha Barnes.	....	....	10	1	"
....	"	Not	Jesse & Nancy Moore..	....	....	5	1	1st cous.
....	"	Not	L. & Hannah Ogan....	....	....	10	3	None.
Farmer ..	"	Not	Wm. & Susan Burns...	....	....	..	2	....
None ..	Virginia .	Not	J. & Sarah McLaughlin.	Farmer ..	....	..	1	....
Farmer ..	Ohio	Educated	Ab. & Sarah Fee.	Farmer ..	Va. & N. C.	9	3	None.
Farmer ..	Ohio	Educated	O. & Sarah Robbins...	Farmer ..	Pa. & N. Y.	5	1	"
None	Ohio	Not	E. & M. A. Bard......	Boarding	....	3	1	"
None	Ohio	Not	L. R. & C. A. Salmons.	Farmer ..	Ohio	12	1	"
H'se k'per	Ohio	Educated	Eli & Sarah Cailin	Cooper.	New York.	12	2	"

RETURN of the number of Deaf and Dumb, Blind, Insane and Idiotic persons

Townships	Names of Persons.	Nature of affliction.	Duration of affliction.		Cause where known.	Age.	Sex.	Color.
Massie...	Letitia Burgess........	Insane........	65	years..	Not known....	83	Fem'le	White.
Franklin.	Rose Beancamp.......	Deaf and dumb	33	"	....	33	"	"
"	Barnabas Montgomery.	" "	39	"	....	39	Male.	"
"	Mary Dell...........	Blind	6	"	..Accidental....	20	Fem'le	"
"	Wm. T. Schenck.....	"	30	"	..By Quackery..	40	Male.	"
"	David Crowell........	Idiotic........	56	"	....	56	"	"
"	Catharine Brandon....	"	20	"	....	20	Fem'le	"
Turtle c'rk	Catharine Jarvis......	"	52	"	....	52	"	"
"	Stephen Evans........	Epileptic Fits.	15	"	..Unknown....	29	Male.	"
"	Christian Hatfield....	Deaf and dumb	7	"	..Infla. of brain.	10	"	"
"	John Hollingsworth...	Idiotic........	36	"	....	48	"	"
"	Wm. Hollingsworth...	"	21	"	..Congenital....	21	"	"
"	Harriet Williams......	Epileptic Fits.	30	"	..Unknown....	35	Fem'le	"
"	Benjamin Harkrader...	Blind	3	"	....	70	Male.	"
"	Aaron Monroe........	Epileptic Fits.	27	years..	Unknown....	31	"	"
"	Randolph Ross.......	Idiotic........	35	years..	"	35	"	"
Salem...	Amos M. Meeker.....	Deaf and dumb	20	"	..Ulcer in head..	20	"	"
"	Laura E. Starkey.....	Insane........	6	"	..Deran. of systm	7	Fem'le	"
Warren..	Melissa Langdon......	Deaf and dumb	14	"	....	14	"	"
"	John H. Null.........	Insane........	6	"	....	29	Male.	"
"	David Null..........	"	3	"	....	21	"	"
"	Samuel Brodaway....	"	8	"	..Unknown....	21	"	"
Clear c'rk	Nicholas Fye........	"	1	"	.. "	80	"	"
"	Josehp Graham......	"	16	"	..Cut on big toe.	40	"	"

in the County of Warren, State of Ohio, on the second Monday of May, 1856.

Occupation	Birth-place	Educated or not	Names of Parents	Occupation	Birth-place	No. of child'n	No. of child'n thus afflicted	Relationship of parents before marriage
....	Pennsylva.	Not	J. & Deborah Burgess ...	Farmer .	Penn.. .	12	1	None...
Seamst's	Kentucky .	Educa'ed	S. and Sarah Beancamp .	Laborer .	Virginia	10	2	Cousins.
....	Maryland .	Not	Unknown	....	Delaware	..	..	....
....	Ohio	....	John and Sarah Dell ...	....	Delaware	6	1	Unkn'wn
....	"	Not	J. and Sarah Schenck ...	Merchant	N. Jersey	10	1	do
None ...	N. Jersey .	"	D. and Charlotte Crowell .	Farmer .	Virginia	8	1	None ...
"	Ohio......	"	Wm. and Mary Brandon.	"	"	8	1	do
"	N. Jersey.	"	Jacob Jarvis............	"	"	..	..	....
Farmer .	Ohio	"	N. and Rachael Evans ..	"	Ten & Pa.	9	1	None ...
"	"	"	T. and Hannah Hatfield .	"	Ohio	7	1	do*
"	"	Educa'ed	A. and E. Hollingsworth	"	"	7	1	do
None ...	"	Not	J. and S. Hollingsworth	"	"	9	1	....
....	"	"	L. & Eunice Williams....	S. Teacher	N. Jersey	10	1	None ...
Farming	Virginia ..	Educa'ed	J. & Barbara Harkrader .	Farmer ..	Penn.. .	9	1	do
. . ....	Ohio	Not	Nathan Monroe.........	"	"	6	1	do
....	"	"	T. and Harriet Ross	Lawyer ..	N. Jersey	6	1	do
Farming.	"	Educa'ed	W. & Patience Mecker....	Farmer .	Ohio & NJ	9	1	....
"	"	Not	I. and Phebe Starkey	"	O. & Va.	4	1	....
None ...	Indiana...	Educa'ed	W. and Rebecca Langdon	"	Ohio	3	1	Cousins.
None ...	Ohio	"	Henry and Mary Null ...	"	Virginia	5	2	....
None ...	"	"	Same.....................	"	"	5	2	....
Farming	"	....	W. & Elizabeth Brodaway	"	Ohio	3	1	None ...
Farming	Pennsylva.	Educa'ed	Abraham and Mrs. Fye .	"	Penn ...	8	1	do
Farming	....	"	W. and Phebe Graham ..	"	Ire. & Pa.	11	1	do

*Joseph's grandmother and Sallie's mother were half sisters.

RETURN of the number of Deaf and Dumb, Blind, Insane and Idiotic persons

Townships.	Names of Persons.	Nature of Affliction.	Duration of Affliction.	Cause Where Known.	Age.	Sex.	Color.
Adams	Ezra Sprague	Deaf and dumb	From birth	Unknown	9	Male	White.
"	Rhoda H. Devol	Palsy and fits	20 years	Blue pill	25	Fem'le	"
"	Judith Mason	Blind	5 "	Unknown	71	"	"
Aurelius	Joseph Grant	Idiotic	From birth	"	14	Male	"
Dunham	Benj. Ellenwood	Dumb	35 years	Canker scrofula	36	"	"
Tearing	Harris Foster	Idiotic	30 "	Unknown	30	"	"
"	Phebe Bartell	"	22 "		22	Fem'le	"
Lawrence	Patty Peggs	"	From birth		21	"	"
"	Jacob Miller	"	24 years	Fits	27	Male	"
Ludlow	James Wheeler	Deaf and dumb	From birth	Natural	9	"	"
"	Frances Scott	Insane	41 years	Fits	41	Fem'le	"
"	Mary Wever	"	15 "	Sudden cold	70	"	"
Liberty	James Coon	Deaf and dumb	From birth		18	Male	"
"	Lydia Coon	"	"		16	Fem'le	"
"	Lavina Coon	"			10	"	"
Newport	Rebecca Day	Blind	22 years	Inflammation	30	"	"
Palmer	Polly Molsler	Insane	4 "	Unknown	80	"	"
"	Betsy Palmer	Blind	3 "	Erysipelas	45	"	"
"	Hester Holdron	Idiotic	From birth		26	"	"
Wesley	William Marris	Deaf and dumb	6 years	Convulsions	7	Male	"
"	Elmira Barnes	Blind	6 "		7	Fem'le	"
Watertown	Jacob Woodruff	Insane	5 "	Sun stroke	39	Male	"
Marietta	Rachael Fanbrother	Idiotic	37 "	Born so	37	Fem'le	"
"	Winchester Hall	"	36 "	"	36	Male	"
"	Jane Gilpin	Blind	17 "	Unknown	53	Fem'le	"
"	Susan Johnston	Idiotic	28 "	"	28	"	"
"	George Cherry	"	36 "	Father drunk	36	Male	"
"	William Graham	Insane	13 "	Unknown	63	"	"
"	Anna Klinwort	"	16 "	"	38	Fem'le	"
"	Joel Smith	Blind	13 "	Gouged out	74	Male	"
In Infirm'y	Haman Brackaway	Insane	14 "	Unknown	36	"	"
"	Betsy Anderson	"	13 "	Hereditary	75	Fem'le	"
"	Alvira Cook	"	16 "	Affliction	48	"	"
"	Charlotte Bardsley	"	16 "	Unknown	42	"	"
"	Mary A. Boring	Idiotic	24 "	"	24	"	"
"	Richard Fisher	Blind	10 "	"	92	Male	color'd
"	Louisa Quinby	Insane	10 "	Turn of life	24	Fem'le	White.
"	Esther Vanroy	"	8 "	Unknown	48	"	"
"	Cord. Berenby	"	9 "	"	42	Male	"
"	Julia Phineberger	"	9 "	"	39	Fem'le	"
"	Jefferson Pierce	"	9 "	Masturbation	37	Male	"
"	Ezekiel Haskon	"	10 "	Unknown	77	"	"
"	William Swain	Dumb	24 "	Natural	24	"	"
"	Joseph H. Buell	Insane	6 "	Masturbation	29	"	"
"	Ambrose Harris	Idiotic	68 "	Natural	68	"	"
"	Nancy Hill	Insane	6 "	Unknown	36	Fem'le	"
"	Jane Delany	Blind	3 "	Disorderly con	29	"	"
"	Catharine Manahan	Insane	4 "	Unknown	36	"	"
"	Nicholas Talemus	"	4 "	"	24	Male	"
"	Mary Jane Mull	"	4 "	"	34	Fem'le	"
"	Susan Stear	"	3 "	"	31	"	"
"	Rebecca Miller	Blind	4 "	"	36	"	"

in the county of Washington, State of Ohio, on the second Monday of May, 1856.

Occupation.	Birth-place.	Educated or not.	Names of Parents.	Occupation.	Birth-place.	No. children	No. children thus afflicted	Relationship of parents before marriage.
....	Iowa	Not	John G. & Ellen Sprague	Everyth'g	Ohio	6	1	None ..
....	Ohio	do	S. M. and Ruby Devol..	Farmer ..	do	7	1	do
Housewife.	Penn	do	Jno. Sprague	....	....	6	1	do
None	Ohio	do	Saml and Sarah Grant..	....	Maine ...	6	1	do
Farming	do	do	S. & Pamelia Ellenwood	Farmer ..	Me. & Mas	10	1	do
....	do	....	Leonard and Ruth Foster	....	....	..	..	do
....	Germany .	....	Adam Bartell	Farmer ..	Germany	..	..	....
None	Ohio	do	Sam. and Betty Peggs..	Unknown	Unknown	..	1	Unkno'n
Farming ..	Germany .	do	Jacob Miller	Farmer ..	Germany	11	1	do
None	Ohio	do	Jesse and Sarah Wheeler	do	Ohio ...	4	1	None ..
do	do	do	Jno Precious Scott	do	Va. & Md.	13	1	do
do	Penn	Common .	Geo. and Mary Cook	....	Unknown	5	1	do
Farming ..	Ohio	Not	Sam. and Eliz Cook	Farmer ..	Ohio	6	3	do
....	do	do	do do	....	....	..	..	do
....	....	do	do do	....	....	..	..	do
None	Penn	do	Jacob & Gatharine Day .	Farmer ..	Penn	9	1	do
....	do	....	....	....	....	..	..	....
....	Ohio	....	William Holdron	....	....	..	..	....
....	do	do	B. and Phebe Marris	Farmer ..	Ohio	6	1	None ..
....	do	do	H. and Eliza Barnes	do	Pa. & Md.	8	1	do
Farming ..	do	Common ..	E. and E. Woodruff	do	N. Jersey.	7	1	do
None	England .	Not	Unknown	do	England .	..	1	Unkno'n
Farmer ...	Ve mont .	do	do	do	Vermont	..	1	do
Spinster ..	Virginia .	do	do	do	Virginia .	..	1	do
do	do	do	do	Laborer ..	do	..	1	do
None	New York	do	Dan. and Kezia Cherry .	do	New York	2	1	do
Shepherd .	Ireland ..	Educated	Unknown	....	Ireland ..	..	1	do
Housework	Germany .	do	do	Farmer ..	Germany	..	1	do
Joiner	New York	Not	do	Unknown	New York	..	1	do
Laborer ...	Germany .	do	do	Farmer ..	Germany.	..	1	do
de	Virginia .	do	do	Laborer ..	Virginia	..	2	do
Teacher ..	Vermont .	Educated	Salmon and Mary Cook	Farmer ..	Vermont	..	1	do
Laborer ..	do	Not	Phineas & Eliza Bardsly	do	do	..	1	do
do	Virginia .	do	Unknown	do	Virginia	..	1	do
Miller	Maryland	do	do	do	Maryland	..	1	do
Laborer ..	New York	do	do	do	New York	..	1	do
do	Maryland	do	do	do	Maryland	..	1	do
Stone cutter	Germany .	do	do	do	Germany	..	1	do
Laborer ..	Penn	do	do	do	Penn	..	1	do
do	New York	do	Salmon and Jane Pierce	do	New York	5	1	do
do	Mass	Partially .	Unknown	Unknown	Mass	..	1	do
None	Ohio	Not	do	do	N. Jersey	..	1	do
Shoemaker	do	Educated	D H. and Eliza Buell ...	Lawyer ..	Ohio	6	1	do
Laborer ..	Conn	Not	Unknown	Farmer ..	Conn	..	1	do
do	Ohio ...	Partially .	do	do	Penn	..	1	do
do	Ireland ..	Not	do	Laborer ..	Ireland ..	..	1	do
do	do	Educated	do	Farmer ..	do	..	1	do
do	Germany .	Partially .	do	do	Germany	..	1	do
do	Ohio	do	do	do	Ohio	..	1	do
do	New York	Not	do	do	New York	..	1	do
do	Germany .	Partially .	do	do	Germany	..	1	do

RETURN of the number of Deaf and Dumb, Blind, Insane and Idiotic Persons

Township	Names of Persons.	Nature of affliction	Duration of Affliction.	Cause where known	Age.	Sex.	Color
Elemon	Mary Ann Ford	Insane	22 years	Medicine	44	Female	Wht.
do	Christian Bowman	do	9 months		45	Male	do
do	Samuel Hensburger	Dumb	From birth		12	do	do
do	Simon Burgess	do	7 do	Sickness	8	do	do
Franklin	Elizabeth Busher	Blind	2 do	Not known	80	Female	do
Congress	Eleanor Shaver	Deaf and dumb	7 do	Open'g in head	11	do	do
do	Joseph Cover	Insane	6 do	Not known	23	Male	do
do	Tamer Carlan	Deaf and dumb	12 do	do	12	do	do
Green	Joseph Haines	Idiotic	From birth		7	do	do
do	Samuel Lantz	Insane	30 years		58	do	do
do	Daniel Baker	Deaf and dumb	From birth		61	do	do
do	Benjamin Shaw	Blind			28	do	do
Chippewa	Susan Galehouse	Insane	15 years	Fits	30	Female	do
do	John Dies	Blind	9 do	Not known	9	Male	do
do	William Manning	do	30 do	Blasting rock	55	do	do
Salt Creek	Elizabeth Merriman	Insane	5 do		37	Female	do
do	Hiram Riter	do	17 do		17	Male	do
do	Manilla Mackey	do	20 do	Measles	30	Female	do
do	Christopher P. Clay	Blind	5 do	Cataract	24	Male	do
do	John Freed	Idiotic	7 do	Not known	7	do	do
do	James Armstrong	do	30 do	do	30	do	do
do	Alexander Armstrong	do	21 do	do	21	do	do
do	Matilda Armstrong	do	18 do	do	18	do	do
do	David Barnhill	do	32 do	Whoop'g cough	34	do	do
Wayne	John Byler	Dumb	51 do	Fits	51	do	do
do	Joseph Wernet	Blind	12 do	Splinter	22	do	do
do	Henry Dark	Deaf and dumb	44 do	Fits	45	do	do
Chester	Samantha Garver	Dumb & idiotic	11 do	Not known	11	Female	do
do	J. Crawford		12 do		37	Male	do
Paint	Samuel Kemerly	Idiotic	45 do		45	do	do
do	Christopher Kemerly	do	42 do		42	do	do
do	Susannah Kemerly	do	39 do		39	Female	do
do	Sarah Buckmealter	do	26 do		26	do	do
Canaan	Levi Bartol	Insane	13 do	Fits	17	Male	do
Wooster	Maria Weirick	Idiotic	19 do	Hereditary	19	Female	do
do	Samuel Weirick	do	14 do	do	14	Male	do
do	Daniel Albright	Deaf and dumb	37 do	do	37	do	do
do	Polly Patterson	Insane	Unknown	Not known	60	Female	do
do	Maria Colt	do	do	Sickness	40	do	do
do	Sally Grass	do	8 years	Not known	35	do	do
do	Mary Pollard	do	4 do	Sickness	43	do	do
do	Linny Wells	do	Unknown	Not known	60	do	do
do	Barbara Stratton	Insane	14 do	do	39	do	do
do	Selinola Startton	Deaf, dumb, ins	10 do	Hereditary	10	do	do
do	Simon Burges	Idiotic	8 do	do	8	Male	do
Plain	Elizabeth Goodfellow	do	61 do		61	Female	do
do	John Anderson		44 do		44	Male	do
do	John Neal	Insane	20 do	Fever	30	do	do
do	Polly D. Neal	do	15 do	do	26	Female	do

in the County of Wayne, State of Ohio, on the second Monday of May, 1856.

Occupation.	Birthplace.	Educated or not.	Names of Parents.	Occupation.	Birthplace.	No. children	No. children thus afflicted.	Relationship of Parents before Marriage.
Housework	Penn.....	Educated	William Ford........	Farmer....	N Jersey	5	1	....
Farmer...	do	Not	Christian Bowman ...	Carpenter..	Penn'a..	14	2	....
....	do	do	Joseph Hunsburger ..	Farmer....	do	6	1	....
....	Ohio.....	do	William Burges......	Carpenter.	Germ'ny	5	1	None....
Farmer...	Penn......	Educated	John and Anna Hare	Farmer...	Penn'a..	14	1	do
....	Ohio.....	Not	Robert and M. Shaver	do	do	7	1	do
....	Penn'a....	do	John & Hannah Cover	do	do	7	3	do
None.....	Ohio......	do	Jas. and Sarah Carlan	do	Ohio....	10	1	....
....	do	....	Cyrus and S. Haines	Tailor....	Penn'a..	8	1	....
....	Penn'a....	Educated	....	....	....	..	..	....
Farmer...	do	do	....	....	....	6	1	....
Music tcher	Canada...	do	....	....	....	..	..	....
None.....	Chippewa.	Not	F. and E. Galehouse	Farmer...	Penn'a..	7	1	None....
do	do	do	Peter and Sus. Dies..	Shoemaker	Germ'ny	8	1	....
Farmer...	Ohio.....	do	....	....	....	1	1	....
....	do	Educated	E. and P. Merriman..	Farmer ...	Penn'a..	6	2	....
....	do	Not	Daniel and S. Riter ..	do	Ohio....	1	1	....
....	do	do	Wm. and Mary Mackey	do	Ireland..	11	1	....
....	Penn'a....	do	Chris. and Anna Clay	do	Penn'a..	10	1	....
....	Ohio.....	do	David and J. Freed ..	do	Ohio....	7	1	....
....	do	do	} T. & N. Armstrong.	Farmer...	Ireland .	14	3	....
....	do	do						
....	do	do						
....	do	do	G. and N. Barnhill...	Farmer...	Penn'a..	8	1	....
None.....	Penn'a....	do	Henry and S. Byler ..	do	do	7	1	None....
do	do	do	Chas. and C. Wernet	do	Germ'ny	8	1	do
Farmer,..	do	Educated	J. and Catharine Dark	do	Penn'a..	8	1	do
None.....	Ohio.....	Not.....	Jacob and M. Garver	....	....	..	..	....
do	Penn'a....	....	....	....	....	..	..	....
do	do	Not	} J. and S. Kemerly..	Miller....	Unkn'wn	3	3	....
do	do	do						
do	do	do	M. and N. Buckmealter	Farmer...	Ireland .	5	1	....
do	Ohio......	do	S. and Susan Bartol..	do	Penn'a..	..	1	None....
do	do	do	} H. and S. Weirick..	Farmer...	Penn'a..	12	2	None....
do	do	do						
Gunsmith.	Penn'a....	Educated	Fred. and C. Albright	Gunsmith.	Penn'a..	14	1	....
....	Unknown.	do	Unknown..........	In Infirm'y	....	..	..	....
....	New York	do	do	do	....	..	..	....
....	Penn'a....	do	do	do	....	..	..	....
....	do	do	do	do	....	..	..	....
....	Unknown.	do	do	do	....	..	..	....
....	Penn'a....	do	} Wm. and B. Stratton	None......	Penn'a..	2	2	Unknown
....	Ohio......	Not						
....	do	do	Unknown........	....	....	..	1	None....
None.....	Penn'a....	....	....	....	....	..	1	do
do	do	....	....	....	....	..	1	do
do	do	Educated	....	....	....	..	..	....
do	Ohio......	do	....	....	....	..	..	....

RETURN of the number of Deaf and Dumb, Blind, Insane and Idiotic persons

Townships.	Names of Persons.	Nature of Affliction.	Duration of Affliction.	Cause where known.	Age.	Sex.	Color.
Flounce...	Elizabeth Bostler.	Deaf and dumb	14 years	.. Scarlet fever......	16	Fem'le	White
Madison ..	David Shelheart .	Deaf and dumb	29 "	.. Fits............	30	Male .	do
"	W. James Lawson	Deaf and dumb	6 "	.. Joy of mother	6	Male .	do
"	Mary Rupley....	Blind.........	6 "	.. Disease of eyes ...	6	Fem'le	do
Springfield	Marcilea Fox	Insane........	3 "	.. Unknown.......	45	Fem'le	do
"	Eliza Witt.......	Blind.........	25 "	.. Unknown........	30	Fem'le	do
Pulaski...	Nancy Heater....	Deaf and dumb	45 "	.. Scarlet fever... ..	47	Fem'le	do
"	Elizabeth J. Starr	Dumb	15 "	.. Paralysis	15	Fem'le	do
"	Rhoda Cole..... .	Deaf and dumb	27 "	.. Inflammation head.	32	Fem'le	do
Brady	Lavina Bohner...	Blind.........	42 "	.. Inflamm'n of eyes.	..	......	do
"	J. H. Richardson.	Blind.........	10 "	. Over exertion.....	34	......	do
North West	Isadora Putnam..	Blind.........	13 "	....	.	Fem'le	
"	Jeremiah Baker..	Idiotic........	19 "	....	19	Male .	do
Center	Elizabeth Miser..	Insane........	17 "	.. Cold...........	65	Fem'le	do
"	John Fritch.....	Deaf and dumb	21 "	.. Sickness	21	Male .	do
"	Frederick Weaver	Deaf and dumb	31 "	....	31	Male .	do
Jefferson ..	James Dustin....	Idiotic........	2½"	....	2½	Male .	do
"	William Miller ..	Idiotic.......	13 "	....	13	Male .	do
"	Phillip Miller....	Idiotic..... .	11 "	....	11	Male .	do
"	———— Flegel....	Blind.........	4 "	....	76	Male .	do
"	Wm. Staany.....	Deaf..........	20 "	.. Scarlet fever	50	Male .	do
St. Joseph.	John N. Bowersox	Insane........	8 "	....	8	Male .	do
"	Martha Bowersox	Insane........	2 "	.. Religious excitem't	37	Fem'le	do
"	Joseph Kearns...	Insane & dumb	32 "	.. Unknown........	32	Male .	do

in the county of Williams, State of Ohio, on the second Monday of May, 1856.

Occupation.	Birth-place.	Educated or not.	Names of parents.	Occupation.	Birthplace.	No. of child'n	No. Children thus Afflicted	Relationship of parents before marriage.
Housework	Ohio	Not	Jacob and Cath's Bostler	Carpenter.	Penn	1	1	None.
Farmer	Penn	"	C. and Elizabeth Shelheart	Farmer	Penn	9	1	None.
....	Ohio	....	George & Elizabeth Lawson	"	Penn	9	1	....
....	....	....	....	....	....	..	..	....
....	Ireland	Not	Peter and Ellen West	Farmer	Ireland	6	1	....
....	N. York	"	Thomas and Mary Barber	....	N. York	2	1	....
Housework	Ohio	"	John and Phebe Heater	Farmer	Va. & Md.	9	1	None.
....	Ohio	"	George and Lucinda Starr	"	Md. & Pa.	5	1	None.
Housework	N. York	Educat'd	Solomon & Hester Cole	Cooper	....	6	1	None.
....	Ohio	Not	Jacob and Susanna Bohner	Farmer	Penn	10	1	....
Farming	Ohio	....	Richard & Ann Richardson	"	Va. & Pa.	5	1	....
None	Ohio	Not	Miles and Mary Putnam	"	N. Hamp.	7	1	None.
"	Ohio	"	David and Maria Baker	"	Penn	3	1	None.
Farmer	Penn	Educat'd	....	....	....	..	..	....
"	Ohio	Not	Jacob and Marg. Mifer	Farmer	Germany	7	1	....
"	Germany	Educat'd	Chas. & Elizabeth Weaver	"	Germany	3	1	....
....	....	....	S. and Mrs. Dustin	....	Germany	..	..	....
....	....	....	Wm. and Mrs. Miller	....	Germany	..	..	....
....	....	....	" "	....	Germany	..	..	....
Farmer	....	Educat'd	....	....	....	..	..	....
....	Ohio	Not	D. and Martha Bowersox	Farmer	Maryland	6	1	None.
....	Marylnd	Educat'd	....	....	....	..	..	....
....	Ohio	Not	Thomas & Mary Kearns	Farmer	Maryland	9	1	None.

RETURN of the number of Deaf and Dumb, Blind, Insane and Idiotic persons

Names of Persons.	Nature of Affliction.	Duration of Affliction.	Cause where known.	Age.	Sex.	Color.	Occupation.
Matthew Taylor	Insane	18 years	Convulsions	26	Male	White	
Orison Cross	do	Unkown	Not given	26	Male	do	
Mary Ann Butler	do	14 years	From Infancy	14	Fem'le	do	
Ida Freeman	do	8 months	Convulsions	7	Fem'le	do	
Eleanor Reed	Deaf and dumb	16 years	Inflama. in head	25	Fem'le	do	
Henry Bell	do do	7 "	Unknown	9	Male	do	
David Stoner	do do	Born so	do	34	Male	do	Carpenter.
Clementina Stoner	do do	"	do	25	Fem'le	do	H'usewife
Ann Fair	do do	"	do	30	Fem'le	do	"
Hiram Fair	do do	"	do	32	Male	do	Farmer
Philander Fair	do do	"	do	26	Male	do	"
Jeffrey Shiner	do do	"	do	14	Male	do	
David Heath	Deaf	44 years	Firing cannon	68	Male	do	Farmer
Johnson B. Holcomb	Dumb	7 "	Unknown	9	Male	do	
Jane Johnson	Idiot	F'm birth	do	44	Fem'le	do	
Henry Campbell	Blind	24 years	Scarlet Fever	26	Male	do	Br'mmakr
Vinton J. Younker	do	Unknown	Not given	16	Male	do	

in the county of Wood, State of Ohio, on the second Monday of May, 1856.

Birth-place	Educated or not.	Names of Parents.	Occupation.	Birth-place	No. Children	No. Children thus Afflicted	Relationship of parents before marriage.
England	Not	John and Frances Taylor	Farmer	England	6	1	None
New York	Educated	Abraham and Clarissa Cross	do	Connectic't	7	1	"
Ohio	Not	J. P. and Lucinda Butler	Carpenter	New York	4	1	"
	Not	Robt. and —— Freeman	Farmer	do	8	1	"
Scotland	Not	Robt. and Isabella Reed	Baker	Scotland	10	1	"
Ohio	Not	Wm. and Elizabeth Bell	Farmer	Unknown	4	1	"
New York	Educated	Jeremiah and Mary Stoner	do	New York	11	2	Cousins.
New York	Not	Same	do	do	11	2	"
Ohio	Not	Elisha and Susan Fair	do	Unknown	12	6	None
do	Not	Same	do	do	12	6	"
do	Not	Same	do	do	12	6	"
do	Not	Jacob Shiner and Anna Fair			2	1	"
Vermont	Educated						
Ohio	Not	Wilson and Theresa Holcomb	Farmer	Maryland	12	1	None
do	Not	John and Elizabeth Johnson	do	New York	4	1	"
Pennsylva	Educated	Wm. and Elizabeth Campbell	do	Pennsylva	6	1	"
Ohio	Educated	David and Abigal Yunker	do	do	1	1	"

208

RETURN of the number of Deaf and Dumb, Blind, Insane and Idiotic persons

Townships.	Names of persons.	Nature of Affliction	Duration of Affliction.	Cause where known	Age.	Sex.	Color.
Antrum...	Harriet Woolsey.....	Fits	5 years ..	Pressure on br'n	5	Fem'le	White.
do ...	——— Becktell.....	Lunatic	18 do	Not known....	30	Male .	do
Sycamore .	Charles Kirk James..	Blind	14 do	Torn out by hog	18	Male .	do
do	Peter Bretty	Deaf & dumb	46 do	....	46	Male .	do
do	Isabell Hitchew	*	5 do	....	5	Fem'le	....
do	Clary Yates.........	Idiot	45 do	Not known....	45	Fem'le	do
Pitt	Harriet McClean.....	Idiot	From birth	....	16	Fem'le	do
Pitt	John McClean	Idiot	do	....	14	Male .	do
Crawford .	John Stewart........	Idiot	do	....	56	Male .	do
do	Harriet Turner	Insane	5 months	....	28	Fem'le	do
do	Mary M. Purd	Insane......	5 years ..	Bad disposition	65	Fem'le	do
Jackson ..	....	Idiots	2 & 7 do	....	2 & 7	Fem'ls	do
Marsailes .	Iry Renick..........	Insane......	16 years ..	Disappointment	43	......	do
do	Mary M Pencer.....	Idiot	9 years ..	Dropsy	10	Fem'le	do
do	George W. Holden...	Idiot	6 years ..	Fits	6	Male .	do
Salem	N. Nichelfetter	Idiot	20 do	....	2'	Male .	do
Ridge	Wm. M. Montage....	Blind	3 years ..	Burnt with pow.	17	Male .	do

* Likeness and color of a monkey ; also similar actions, said to be caused by the Mother being at an animal show, previous to birth.

in the County of Wyandot, State of Ohio, on the second Monday of May, 1856.

Occupation.	Birthplace.	Educated or not.	Names of Parents.	Occupation.	Birth-place.	No. Children.	No. children thus afflicted.	Relationship of parents before marriage.
None....	Ohio....	Not....	Walter and H. Woolsey.	Farmer..	New York.	7	1	None.
None....	Penn....	Not....	Jacob Becktell.........	Farmer..	Penn	5	1	do
Br'm mkr.	Ohio....	....	Jas. Gaines............	Shoemakr	New York	4	1	do
None....	Ohio....	....	Coonrad Bretty........	Farmer..	Penn.....	7	1	do
....	Ohio....	....	L. and A. Hitchew.....	Bl'ksmith	Maryland.	4	1	do
....	Virginia.	....	Abner and A. Yates....	Farmer..	Virginia..	4	1	do
....	Ohio....	....	David & R. McClean..	Farmer..	Penn.....	6	...	1st cous.
....	Ohio....	....	do do	Farmer..	Penn	..	2	do
....	Maryland	....	....	Farmer..	Scotland..	...	....	do
....	Ohio....	....	——— Turner.........	Farmer..	Mass.....	...	....	do
....	Germany.	....	....	....	Ohio.....	..	....	....
....	....	....	Henry Beer...........	Farmer..	Ohio.....	..	....	....
....	Ohio....	Educat'd	A. & O. Renick........	Sto'k raisr	Virginia..	3	1	None.
....	Ohio....	....	H. & D. Pencer	Farmer..	....	7	1	None.
....	Ohio....	....	M. & E. Holden.......	Gunsmith	O. & N. Y.	3	1	None.
....	Germany.	....	John Nichelfetter	Laborer..	Germany..	8	1	None.
....	....	....	....	....	....	5	1	None.

14—SEC. OF STATE.

INDEX

This index lists all surnames. Variations in names are common and each name has been listed here as it is recorded in the text. Some names appear more than once on a page.

ABBOTT, 64 65
ABERCROMBIE, 78 79
ACKLEY, 44
ADAMS, 112 113 134 135
ADDISON, 36 37
AFFALTER, 180 181
AIMES, 189
AIRHEART, 46
AKINS, 26 27
ALBRIGHT, 202 203
ALDRICH, 146
ALEXANDER, 75
ALFELD, 88
ALGIRE, 168 169
ALICESSOR, 114 115
ALINGTON, 78
ALLBAUGH, 116 117
ALLEN, 148 149 184
ALLINGHAM, 88
ALLINGTON, 79 146 147
ALLISON, 26 27 100 101
ALSWORTH, 131
AMES, 22
ANDERSON, 22 23 40 41 130 131 150 186 187 200 202
ANDREW, 172 173
ANDREWS, 76 142 143
ANGELE, 190 191
ANGLE, 98 99
ANNIS, 56 57
ANSHUTZ, 140 141
ANTONI, 62 63
APPLEGATE, 32 33
APRIL, 88 89
ARCHER, 123
ARMITAGE, 134 135

ARMSTRONG, 88 89 152 153 188 189 202 203
ARNOLD, 66 67 78 79 94 97
ARROWSMITH, 36 37
ARTHEHOLT, 186 187
ARTZ, 68 69
ASHENFETTER, 96
ASHWELL, 147
ATEN, 104 105
ATHERTON, 110 111
ATKIN, 29
ATWELL, 22 23
AUGHRY, 142
AULTMAN, 52
AUNNON, 142 143
AUSTIN, 102 103 177
AUTH, 124
AWMILLER, 134 135
AYERS, 150
AYRES, 186
BABCOCK, 102 103 122
BACHMAN, 140 141
BACON, 122 123 152
BAINBRIDGE, 122
BAIRD, 22 23 48 49 66
BAKER, 36 37 62 63 66 82 83 96 168 169 194 195 202 204 205
BALDWIN, 66
BALEY, 66 67
BAM, 192
BANCROFT, 28 162 163
BANGHAM, 44
BANKS, 122 123
BARANDT, 88 89
BARBEE, 156 157
BARBER, 205

BARD, 196 197
BARDSLEY, 200
BARDSLY, 201
BARKER, 86
BARKEY, 101
BARKLEY, 40 41
BARNARD, 28 29 186 187
BARNES, 24 25 110 111 197 200 201
BARNET, 108
BARNHART, 58 170
BARNHILL, 202 203
BARNHISEL, 186 187
BARNHOUSE, 34
BARR, 30 31 38
BARRET, 97 100
BARRETT, 96 106
BARSHARE, 150
BARST, 92
BARTHOLOMEW, 28
BARTIN, 81
BARTOL, 202 203
BARTON, 28 80
BASH, 148 149
BASHON, 44
BATEMAN, 142 143
BATES, 106 107 114 115 140 141
BATTHIAS, 116 117
BATTLE, 56 57
BAUER, 178 179 190 191
BAUHOFF, 180 181
BEACH, 197
BEALL, 66 100 101
BEAN, 57
BEANCAMP, 198 199
BEANS, 48
BEAR, 72 73
BEARD, 129
BEARDSLEY, 154
BEASON, 168 169
BEATTY, 72 73
BEAUCHAMP, 173
BEAUMONT, 50
BEAVER, 68 69
BECHTOL, 52
BECK, 82 83 142 143 188 189
BECKET, 97
BECKMAN, 82
BECKTELL, 208 209
BECKWITH, 62 156 157
BEEBE, 126 127
BEER, 209
BEESON, 178 179
BEHER, 76 77
BELBEY, 166 167
BELL, 108 148 149 206 207
BELLOWS, 134 135
BEMINGER, 86 87
BEMSBURGH, 172
BEMUS, 28
BEND, 88
BENEDICT, 146 147
BENFER, 189
BENGAMAN, 32 33
BENHAM, 102 176 177
BENNAGE, 184 185
BENNET, 66
BENNETT, 102 103 106 107
BENSONHAVER, 98 99
BERENBY, 200
BERGMAN, 136 137
BERRY, 194 195
BETZER, 171
BEUFER, 188
BEVERICK, 102
BIBER, 86 87
BIERMAN, 84
BIERS, 26 27
BIGELOW, 117
BIKEL, 132 133
BILLMAN, 172 173
BILLS, 102 103
BINGHAM, 96
BINGMAN, 97
BISH, 66 67
BISHOP, 110 111 185
BISSELL, 132 133
BLACK, 40 41 44 66-69 82
BLACKWELL, 94 95
BLAIR, 112 113 120
BLAKELEY, 179
BLAKELY, 48 49 178
BLAKESLEE, 29
BLALOCK, 36
BLANK, 169
BLAUSER, 66
BLAZER, 66 67
BLAZIER, 152 153
BLISS, 56 57
BLOCH, 180 181
BLOOM, 58
BLUE, 178 179
BLUEBAUGH, 110
BODEN, 184 185

BOGGS, 170
BOHNER, 204 205
BOLAND, 84
BOLINGER, 84
BOLTZ, 188 189
BONNER, 70 71
BOOTH, 186 187
BOPE, 176
BORDER, 144 145
BORER, 38
BORING, 200
BOSLER, 34 35
BOSTLER, 204 205
BOSTON, 62 63 118 119
BOTTELS, 194
BOUZER, 143
BOWEN, 192
BOWER, 66 86
BOWERS, 148 149
BOWERSOCK, 138 139 178 179
BOWERSOX, 204 205
BOWMAN, 118 148 149 176 177 202 203
BOWMIN, 70 71
BOWSER, 156 157
BOYD, 52 108
BOYLAND, 82
BRACKAWAY, 200
BRADEN, 106 107 137
BRADLEY, 73 122
BRAG, 44 138 139
BRAKAW, 54 55
BRAND, 158 159 176 177
BRANDENBURG, 38 39
BRANDON, 198 199
BRANEN, 30 31
BRANKER, 162
BRANT, 174 175
BRATON, 154
BRATTON, 96 97
BRENMAN, 100 101
BRETTENHAM, 126 127
BRETTY, 208 209
BRIAN, 36
BRICE, 58 59
BRIGGS, 193
BRINDLEY, 94 95
BRISTLEIB, 180 181
BROCKERT, 30 31
BROCKMAN, 82
BROCKSMITH, 89
BRODAWAY, 198 199

BROHNER, 82
BROKSMITH, 88
BROOKOVER, 150
BROOKS, 76 77 135
BROTHERS, 34 35
BROTTON, 152
BROUGHN, 122 123
BROWER, 42 164 165
BROWN, 23-25 34 35 46 56 80 81 114 115 120 121 146 147 150 156 157 165 170 171 193
BROWNSON, 181
BRUBAKER, 36 37
BRUCE, 38 39
BRUKETT, 142 143
BRUMBAUGH, 142 143
BRYANT, 120
BUCK, 128 129
BUCKLEY, 104 105
BUCKMAN, 162 163
BUCKMEALTER, 202 203
BUELL, 200 201
BUGBEE, 28 29
BUHEE, 168
BUHLMAN, 86
BULHAND, 132 133
BULTMAN, 82 83
BUNDY, 102 103
BUNIS, 113
BURGAN, 26 27
BURGER, 100 101
BURGES, 202 203
BURGESS, 198 199 202
BURK, 28 29
BURKEY, 150
BURNS, 86 112 113 186 187 196 197
BURTON, 44 45 54-57 186 187
BUSH, 70 71 172 173
BUSHER, 202
BUTCHER, 93
BUTLER, 186 187 206 207
BUTTERS, 96 97
BUTTON, 48
BUZARD, 70 71
BUZZARD, 67
BYLER, 202 203
BYRNS, 48 49
CABLE, 116
CADIE, 22
CADWALLADER, 23
CAHILL, 188 189

CAHOL, 32 33
CAILIN, 197
CAIN, 176 177
CALAHAN, 85
CALDWELL, 148 158 159 165
CALHOUN, 128 129
CALKINS, 187
CALLADER, 22
CALLAHAN, 84
CALVIN, 84 148
CAMERON, 106 107
CAMES, 170
CAMPBELL, 62 63 106 107 142 206 207
CANAHAN, 100 101
CANAN, 73
CANDLE, 111
CANDON, 189
CAREY, 146 147
CARIGAN, 86 87
CARLAN, 202 203
CARLE, 113
CARMAN, 106 107
CARMINE, 174
CARMON, 105
CARN, 188
CARNAGEY, 26 27
CARNAHAN, 134 135
CARNES, 186
CARNS, 150
CARPENTER, 106 107 132 133 152 153 184 185
CARR, 74
CARRICK, 94 95
CARRIGAN, 150
CARTER, 102 103 108 110 111 130 131 192 193
CASE, 72 73 88 89 184 185
CASIP, 54 55
CASSELL, 26 27
CASTOR, 174 175
CATLEY, 88
CATTAN, 96
CESSNEE, 128
CHADWICK, 62 63
CHAFFEE, 186
CHANDLER, 26 27 72 73 148 149
CHANEY, 66 67
CHAPIN, 112
CHAPMAN, 32 33 116 135 181 186 187
CHASE, 134 135

CHENOWOTH, 126 127
CHERRY, 200 201
CHESNUT, 160 161
CHIDDESTER, 128
CHILSON, 76 77
CHRIST, 143
CHRISTIAN, 116 117
CHRISTOPHER, 86
CHRISTY, 146 147
CHUBB, 136
CLARK, 40 41 49 62 63 88-90 96 97 106 107 128 132 133 186 187 192 193 195
CLAWSON, 30 31
CLAY, 202 203
CLEMENTINE, 150
CLEVELAND, 28
CLICE, 34 35
CLIFTON, 142 143
CLINCATTO, 114 115
CLOSE, 106 107
CLOSSON, 124 125
CLUSE, 40 41
CLUTZ, 34 35
COATE, 138 139
COATS, 130
COE, 110 111
COFENBERY, 168
COFFEE, 86 87
COFFEY, 36 37 142
COFFMAN, 32
COFFY, 143
COGAN, 66 67
COIL, 30 31 70 71
COLE, 106 107 112 113 186 187 204 205
COLEGATE, 86
COLEMAN, 114
COLGROVE, 28 29
COLLINGS, 22 23
COLLINS, 80-82 164 165
COLT, 202
COLVIN, 149
COMEFORD, 36 37
CONAWAY, 95
CONGER, 164 165
CONGROW, 134 135
CONKEY, 132 133
CONNOR, 134 135
CONOWAY, 94
CONRAD, 100 101 119
CONROY, 84

CONWAY, 110 111
COOK, 26 27 62 63 66 84 114 115 122 200 201
COOKACY, 193
COOKSEY, 192
COOL, 128 129
COOLEY, 72 73
COOLY, 56 57
COON, 129 168 169 200
COONEY, 48 49
COOPER, 171
COOSARD, 162
COPAS, 96 97 160 161
CORDELL, 26 27
CORDERY, 150
CORNELL, 52 53
CORRY, 88
COSSIBONE, 150
COTLEY, 89
COUNTRYMAN, 28
COUNTS, 126 127
COUP, 176 177
COURTNEY, 128 129
COVAULT, 138 139
COVER, 128 129 202 203
COVINGTON, 37
COWAN, 72
COWDRY, 176
COWDY, 177
COWEN, 82
COWGILL, 44 153
COX, 40 41 106 107 126 128 174 175 184
COZENS, 114 115
CRABB, 141
CRABTREE, 104 105
CRAFT, 189
CRAIG, 104 105 136 137 140 141
CRAIL, 106 107
CRAMBLES, 196
CRAMEA, 54 55
CRAMER, 42 43
CRANE, 40 41
CRAWFORD, 152 202
CREMAN, 24 25
CRESIP, 52 53
CRESWELL, 22 23
CREW, 96 97 144 145
CRIST, 184
CRISTI, 150
CRITE, 188
CRITES, 189

CROFT, 188
CRONE, 26 27
CRONIN, 140 141
CROSS, 206 207
CROTY, 82
CROUT, 52 53
CROW, 88 89
CROWELL, 198 199
CRULL, 174 175
CRUM, 96 97
CRUMBAKER, 164 165
CULLEN, 134
CULP, 128
CUMPTON, 64
CURL, 156 157
CURREN, 92
CURRY, 48 49
CURTIS, 162
CURWIN, 84
DAILEY, 140 141
DAILY, 82
DAIN, 84 85
DAIR, 40 41
DAKIN, 44 45
DALE, 44
DANES, 88 89
DANIELS, 112
DARBY, 44
DARK, 202 203
DARROUGH, 74 75
DART, 28 29
DAUGHERTY, 66
DAVIDSON, 82 142 143 152 153
DAVIS, 36 37 48 52-55 66 67 95 102-105 112 116-119 128 134 135 150 154 155 187
DAVISON, 82 156 157
DAVY, 86 87
DAWSON, 86 87 156
DAY, 62 63 84 85 88 89 162 172 173 178 179 200 201
DAYMUDE, 110 111
DEAL, 26 27 180 181
DEALAND, 123
DEBEWISE, 116 117
DEEVER, 156 157
DEFOREST, 186 187
DELANEY, 70
DELANY, 200
DELEMETER, 150
DELL, 198 199
DEMENY, 37

DEMING, 32 33
DEMOS, 197
DENLIN, 44
DENNISON, 72 73
DENNON, 56 57
DEVAULT, 70 71
DEVOL, 200 201
DEVORSE, 53
DICKENSON, 150
DICKERSON, 94 95
DICKSON, 118 148
DIES, 202 203
DILL, 89 196
DILLEY, 186 187
DILLON, 23 114 115
DILTZ, 156 157
DIMELING, 132 133
DINGY, 128
DINSMORE, 82
DIPLE, 142
DISSINGER, 184
DITTERICK, 130 131
DIXEN, 196
DIXON, 38 39 72 73 197
DOAN, 158 159
DODD, 156 157
DOLAN, 82 83
DONAHOO, 36 80
DONALD, 187
DONALDSON, 144 145
DONALLY, 110
DONE, 112
DONNALD, 186
DONNARD, 134 135
DONNELLY, 111
DONNILY, 32
DONOVAN, 72 73
DOOLAN, 82
DORNAN, 116 117
DORSEY, 62
DOUGHERTY, 74 75
DOUGHTY, 41
DOUGLASS, 106 107 134 135 184
DOWLAND, 54 55
DOWNER, 150 151
DOWNING, 24 25 158 159
DRACE, 96
DRAKE, 38 39 156 157
DRAN, 128
DRENNEN, 84
DRUMMOND, 114
DRYCHANS, 82

DUBOIS, 102 103
DUCHER, 81
DUEHER, 80
DUFFIELD, 89
DUMMER, 128
DUNCAN, 134 135
DUNDERMAN, 132 133
DUNHAM, 96 97
DUNLAP, 94 95 110 111
DURBIN, 110 111
DUSTIN, 204 205
DUTERER, 128
DYE, 138-141
DYEN, 88 89
DYER, 78 79
EARLE, 96
EARNEST, 165
EASON, 196
EASTER, 102 103
EATON, 38 148 149
EBERZ, 142 143
EDGAR, 23
EDMINSTER, 62 63
EDMUNDSON, 48
EDWARDS, 40
EESON, 148
EICHHOLTZ, 36 37
EKEY, 106 107
ELDER, 52 53
ELDRIDGE, 48 49
ELESON, 149
ELINE, 136 137
ELLENWOOD, 200 201
ELLER, 164
ELLIOTT, 110 176 177
ELLIS, 44 45 70 71 103 156 157
ELLISON, 28
EMECK, 48
EMELON, 146 147
EMERSON, 40 41
EMMONS, 91 164 165
ENGLAND, 106 107
ENGLISH, 30 31
ENITH, 49
EPMYER, 84
ERLINE, 136 137
ERNST, 176
ESHELBY, 84
ESTEL, 84
ETTENSON, 84 85
ETTINGER, 146 147
EVANS, 32 33 54 55 104 105 138

EVANS (continued)
    139 146 198 199
EVERETT, 28
EVERGREEN, 150
EVERHART, 82 83 188 189
EVERITT, 68 69
EVERNHAM, 36 37
EVERTON, 134
EVERTS, 158 159
EVINS, 72
EWING, 128
EXTINE, 48
FAGLEY, 88 89
FAIR, 206 207
FAIRCHILD, 167
FAIRCHILDS, 166
FALLANCE, 134
FALLS, 152
FALMON, 64 65
FANBROTHER, 200
FANHOUSER, 140 141
FARAW, 168
FARRIS, 96
FEAGANS, 116 117
FEBLE, 176 177
FEE, 196 197
FELTON, 154 155
FENDER, 96 97
FENNER, 84 172
FENSEBECK, 88 89
FERGURSON, 84
FERGUSON, 73 80 81 162 163
FERRECE, 40
FERRIE, 178 179
FICKENSON, 152 153
FICOX, 154
FIELD, 72 73
FIELDER, 120
FIELDING, 108 109
FIELDS, 22 23 28 29 162 163
FIGHT, 184
FIGLEY, 26 27 107
FINCH, 117
FINDLEY, 80
FINNEY, 149
FINSTEWALD, 82
FIREBAUGH, 24 25
FISHER, 44 49 72 73 96 97 141
    188 189 200
FISK, 28 64 65
FITE, 32 33
FITZGERALD, 156 157

FITZPATRICK, 30 31 72 73
FLANEGAN, 72 73
FLEGEL, 204
FLEMMING, 44
FLINN, 86 87 96
FLOOD, 48
FODLE, 189
FOERST, 32 33
FOLDEN, 134 135
FONSER, 184 185
FONTZ, 142 143
FORD, 48 94 95 104 105 110 111
    202 203
FOREST, 140 141
FORREST, 120 121
FORTUNE, 100 101
FOSTER, 22 23 77 156 157 200
    201
FOURMAN, 59
FOURMEN, 58
FOUTS, 48 144 145
FOX, 148 149 156 157 194 195
    204
FRAME, 80
FRANCE, 148 149
FRANCIS, 72 73 84 113 116 117
FRANKLIN, 24 25 96
FRANKS, 118 119
FRAZEE, 88 89
FRAZER, 48 49
FRECH, 86-89
FREDENHOUR, 156
FREED, 49 202 203
FREEMAN, 206 207
FREET, 48
FRENCH, 146-149
FREYMAN, 128 129
FRICKER, 66 67 98 99
FRILER, 102
FRINK, 28 29
FRITCH, 204
FRYER, 32 33
FULLER, 80 186 187
FULLERTON, 24 25
FULMER, 180 181
FULTON, 120 150
FULTZ, 62 63
FUNKIN, 84
FURBY, 150
FURGUSON, 188 189
FURMP, 96
FURNACE, 150 180 181

FURNEY, 94 95
FURRY, 162 163
FYE, 198 199
GAGE, 28 29
GAINES, 209
GAKING, 166 167
GALAHER, 81
GALBREATH, 49
GALEHOUSE, 202 203
GALIAM, 142
GALL, 156 157
GALLAHER, 80
GALLREATH, 48
GARBRICH, 55
GARDNER, 52 53 84 156 157
GARLOCH, 156 157
GARRET, 98 99
GARRETT, 129 184 185
GARRISON, 40 41 44
GARVER, 164 202 203
GARVEY, 84
GARWOOD, 22
GASSER, 88 89
GAVER, 116 117
GEISLER, 86
GEISTEVITE, 162
GELLASKIE, 40 41
GELLER, 70 71
GEORGE, 152
GERE, 59
GERMAN, 148 149
GERRARD, 126 127
GERTARL, 154
GERVES, 60
GETZ, 180 181
GHRIST, 114 115
GIBSON, 80 81 128 168-170
GILBERT, 28 29 66
GILDERSLEVE, 132 133
GILL, 40 41
GILLISON, 94 95
GILMORE, 134 135 186-188
GILPIN, 23 200
GILVERY, 48
GLANNER, 66 67
GLASPIE, 60 61
GLASS, 88 89
GLEASON, 82 83
GLOID, 162
GLOVER, 116
GOBLE, 156 157
GOFF, 150

GOODFELLOW, 202
GOODWIN, 30
GORDON, 186 187
GOUCHER, 124
GOUDY, 27
GOULBOURN, 48 49
GOULD, 132 133
GOWDY, 56 57 78 79
GRADY, 70
GRAHAM, 122 185 198 199 200
GRANDSTAFF, 118 119
GRANT, 200 201
GRASS, 202
GRATEFENK, 84
GRAVER, 152
GRAY, 63
GREEK, 68 69
GREEN, 38 76 84 120 192
GREENE, 44
GREGORY, 102
GREW, 48
GRICE, 23
GRIDLEY, 132 133
GRIFFIS, 164 165
GRIFFITH, 190 191
GRIGSBY, 130 131
GRILL, 154 155 184 185
GRISWOLD, 103 147
GRONGER, 162
GROOMS, 22 23
GROSARTH, 190 191
GROUNTIZOR, 52
GROVE, 25 36 128 190 191
GROVES, 40 41
GRUBER, 34 35
GTRATEFENK, 85
GUARD, 88 89
GUILGURT, 134 135
GULICK, 158 159
GUNN, 74 75
GURDON, 186
GUTSHALL, 94
GUYER, 102 103
HAAFORD, 184
HADDLER, 86
HADGRON, 44
HADLEY, 138 139
HAGER, 186
HAGERMAN, 92 93
HAGERTY, 22 23 86 87
HAINES, 116 117 202 203
HALE, 104 105

HALL, 28 32 33 80 81 96 97 162
  193 200
HALLIDAY, 134 135
HAMAN, 96
HAMILTON, 106 107 122
HAMMAKER, 54 55
HAMMEL, 110 111 158 159
HAMMON, 164 165
HAMPTON, 74
HAN, 84
HAND, 27 72 73 142 143
HANES, 44
HANEY, 87 154 155 184
HANN, 126 127
HANNERS, 162 163
HANSUCKER, 158 159
HANY, 86
HARBAUGH, 156 157
HARDESTY, 66
HARDING, 104
HARDMAN, 48 49
HARDYSHELL, 96
HARE, 152 153 203
HARKRADER, 198 199
HARLAN, 148 149
HARMAN, 52 53
HARMON, 188
HARNESS, 78 79
HAROFF, 30
HARPER, 153
HARRICUT, 150
HARRIS, 40 41 62 63 132 133 152
  153 158 160 161 188 200
HARRISON, 116 117
HARSHBERGER, 30 31
HART, 58 59 74 75 96 97 150
HARTELL, 200 201
HARTMAN, 26 27 110 111
HARTZELL, 162 163
HARVEY, 30 31
HASKELL, 152 186 187
HASKON, 200
HASLAN, 96
HASLEN, 97
HASTINGS, 132 133
HATCHER, 48
HATFIELD, 198 199
HATT, 86 87
HATTEN, 54 55
HAUN, 26 27
HAUSBROOK, 58 59
HAWARTH, 148 149
HAWK, 104
HAWKINS, 177
HAWNEKRATH, 188 189
HAYDEN, 122 123
HAYHURST, 128 129
HAYMAN, 134 135
HAYMARN, 134
HAYNS, 160 161
HEACHT, 86
HEADLEY, 46
HEATER, 204 205
HEATH, 206
HEATHERINGT'N, 96
HEATON, 78
HEAVIN, 84
HEDGES, 66 67 72
HEDRICK, 136 137
HEFT, 98
HEGE, 66 67
HEIN, 30 31
HEITE, 83
HELMAN, 26 27
HENDERSON, 34 35 38 39 41 156
  157
HENGST, 54 55
HENGSTER, 30
HENN, 86
HENRY, 48 72 73 174 175
HENSBURGER, 202
HENSKEY, 30
HENTZELL, 180 181
HERCULES, 58 59
HERRICK, 28
HERRIN, 66 67
HERRING, 186 187
HERSH, 148 149
HERSHBERGER, 100 101
HERWIG, 82
HESS, 34 35 38 118
HETHERINGTON, 97
HEYCOCK, 188
HICKEY, 158 159
HILBERT, 174
HILL, 26 27 40 41 60 61 84 140
  141 200
HILLERY, 156 157
HILLIARD, 138 139
HILLMAN, 82 84
HINELINE, 92 93
HINES, 94 95
HINKS, 86
HINMAN, 44

HIPNER, 195
HIPSLEY, 152
HITCHCOCK, 112 113
HITCHEW, 208 209
HITE, 156 157
HITZELBERG, 132 133
HIVELEY, 48
HIVELY, 49
HIXAN, 188 189
HOADLEY, 128 129
HOAK, 38 39
HOBSON, 44
HOBY, 82
HODGMAN, 132 133
HOFFER, 176 177
HOFFMAN, 88 89 176 186 187
HOFFNER, 176 177
HOFSTAETER, 187
HOFSTEATER, 186
HOLBRADE, 142
HOLCOMB, 184 185 206 207
HOLDEN, 132 133 208 209
HOLDRON, 200 201
HOLLADAY, 40 41
HOLLEN, 119
HOLLFORD, 84
HOLLINGSWORTH, 30 31 198 199
HOLLISTER, 124 125
HOLLOWELL, 94 95
HOLMES, 106 107
HOLSTEIN, 82
HOLT, 148 149
HOMAN, 40 41
HOMER, 142
HONNING, 142
HOOD, 24 25
HOOVER, 142 143 188 189
HOPFER, 56 57
HOPKINS, 28 29
HOPMAN, 86 87
HOPPER, 148
HORNER, 178 179
HORTON, 104 105
HOSBROOK, 88
HOSKINSON, 166 167
HOTT, 134 135
HOUCK, 116 117
HOUNING, 143
HOUSE, 28
HOUSEHOLD, 84
HOUSER, 66 67

HOUTS, 132 133
HOVEY, 76
HOWE, 48
HOWELL, 148 149
HOWENSTINE, 181
HOWLEN, 32 33
HOWNESTINE, 180
HOYT, 116 117 150
HOZELBAKER, 23
HOZELLAKER, 22
HUBBARD, 88 89
HUFF, 88
HUFFMAN, 39
HUGGINS, 96
HUGH, 40 41 87
HUGHES, 32 38
HUGHS, 82 86 128 150
HULBEN, 181
HULDA, 129
HUMMEF, 82
HUNSBURGER, 203
HUNT, 28 46 146 147 162 163
HUNTER, 40 41 96 97 102 103 136 137 148 149
HURLBURT, 162 163 186 187
HUSTON, 28 120 188 189
HUTCHES, 156 157
HUTCHINSON, 100 101
HUTCHISON, 54 55
HUTER, 176 177
HUTSON, 186 187
HYNES, 158 159
ICKES, 48 49
IDLE, 36 37
IREMAN, 48 49
IRWIN, 48
ISENBARG, 72
JACK, 102 103
JACKANAW, 58 59
JACKSON, 126 127 178 179
JACOBS, 28 29 88 112
JACOBY, 168 169
JAMES, 208
JAMISON, 117 148 149
JARVIS, 198 199
JEFFRIES, 66 67
JENKINS, 36 37 146 162
JEWELL, 186 187
JINKS, 56 57
JOHN, 116
JOHNSON, 26 36 37 44 74 75 110 149 164 165 186 187 206 207

JOHNSTON, 86 87 200
JONEES, 87
JONES, 32 33 38 39 44 86 94 95
    100-103 106 107 120 121 148
    149 156 157 170 171 186 187
JORDAN, 28 29 152 170 171
JOSEPH, 114 115 150
JUDGE, 140
JUDY, 120
JUMP, 103
JUSTICE, 102 103
KAFF, 134 135
KALAR, 100 101
KALPHOFF, 136
KANE, 188
KARN, 180 181 189
KARNES, 44 45
KATE, 164
KAUFFMAN, 136 137
KAUFMAN, 88 89
KEARNS, 204 205
KEEFER, 172 173
KEIM, 110
KEITH, 24 25 136
KELLER, 88
KELLEY, 48
KELLOG, 102 103
KELLY, 106 107 189
KELSEY, 152 153
KELSO, 86 87
KELTS, 150
KEMALA, 128
KEMERLY, 202 203
KEMPER, 84
KENDAL, 134 135
KENEDY, 32 33
KENNEDY, 82 85
KERR, 48 49
KESNER, 188
KESSLER, 174
KESSON, 189
KEYES, 148 149
KEYSECKER, 128
KID, 80
KILGORE, 180 181
KIMBLE, 80
KINDLE, 97
KINER, 72 73
KING, 54-57
KINSEL, 54 55
KIRBY, 44
KIRCHNER, 86 87

KIRK, 144 145
KIRKLAN, 48
KIRKPATRICK, 106 107
KIRTLAND, 49
KISER, 178 179
KISLING, 160 161
KIST, 36 37
KLECKNER, 128
KLINE, 100 101
KLINWORT, 200
KLOFFIER, 138
KNAPP, 102 103
KNEPPER, 66
KNIGHT, 111 146 147
KNOUFF, 129
KOCHLER, 156 157
KOLEY, 100
KONIG, 30
KOONTZ, 162 163
KOPFER, 56
KRESKADDEN, 85
KRUS, 66
KUHN, 176 177
KUNREEL, 84
KUPLEY, 74
KUTCHER, 188 189
LACEY, 188
LACY, 116 117 189
LADDEE, 180 181
LAGOR, 142 143
LAGRANGE, 28 29
LAIRD, 106
LAIZURE, 188 189
LAKE, 52 53 100
LAKLEAR, 180 181
LAMBERT, 54 55 114 115
LANCE, 24 25 96 98 99
LANDIS, 186 187
LANE, 56 57 122 148 150
LANEAR, 164 165
LANEY, 120
LANG, 122
LANGDON, 198 199
LANGHORN, 182 183
LANTZ, 202
LANY, 121
LAPSLAY, 168
LARIMER, 156 157
LATTLE, 86
LAUGHLIN, 48 106 107 196
LAWSON, 204 205
LEACHLEY, 180 181

LEAK, 27
LEAR, 66 67
LEASER, 24
LEASERS, 25
LEE, 72 73 188 189
LEFEVER, 178 179
LEFEVIN, 82
LEGSTON, 111
LEHEW, 144 145
LEIB, 72
LEIZURE, 94 95
LEKINS, 106
LEMING, 88 89
LEMON, 78
LEONARD, 66 67 163
LEVENGOOD, 100 101
LEVERING, 66 67
LEWIS, 26-29 40 41 46 52 53 56
    102 103 106 107 114 115 126
    158 159 186-189
LICKENS, 107
LIEB, 73
LIGMAN, 80
LIKENS, 162 163
LIMPACH, 176
LINCH, 46
LINN, 48 49
LINUS, 48
LISHEE, 140
LISLER, 44
LISPER, 93
LITTLE, 52 53 144 145
LOCK, 123
LOCKHARD, 120 121
LOEH, 82
LOGAN, 48 49
LOMISON, 175
LONG, 36 82 110 111 138 139 166
    167 176 177
LONGADORF, 120
LONGWELL, 140 141
LOOKER, 67
LOOMIS, 28 29
LORTON, 178 179
LOUCK, 66
LOUPER, 158 159
LOVELAND, 162 163
LOW, 67
LOWINGRUTH, 179
LOWINGUTH, 178
LOWMILLER, 94 95
LOWRY, 26 27

LUCAS, 96
LUDWIG, 24-27
LUPTON, 106 107
LYLE, 120
LYMAN, 186 187
LYNCH, 134 135 176
LYON, 146
LYONS, 116 117
LYTLE, 188 189
M'CLANE, 149
M'CONN, 42 43
M'DILL, 164
M'GINNIS, 149
M'GREW, 164 165
M'VEIGH, 164 165
M'WHINNEY, 164 165
MACK, 150
MACKEY, 202 203
MADDOCK, 164 165
MAHAFFEY, 22 23
MAHONEY, 128
MAIN, 62 63
MAINE, 146 147
MALCOLM, 26 27
MANAHAN, 102 200
MANCHESTER, 34
MANINGER, 188 189
MANN, 90 91
MANNING, 40 41 202
MANOR, 26 27 78 79
MARCKS, 152 153
MARCY, 123
MARIOT, 180 181
MARKLE, 106 107 126 127
MARKS, 26 27
MARR, 170 171
MARRIS, 200 201
MARSH, 38
MARSHALL, 164 165
MARTIN, 48 84 88 89 104 116 142
    143 170 171
MARTZ, 36 37
MARVIN, 84
MASON, 116 117 152 153 184 200
MASSEY, 79
MASSIE, 114 115
MASTERS, 152
MATHERS, 108
MATSON, 122 123
MATTON, 84
MAXWELL, 32 33 128 129
MAY, 88

MAYHER, 84
MAYS, 120 121
MAZE, 62 63
MCADAMS, 106 107
MCALLISTER, 22 23
MCBRIDE, 160 161
MCCANN, 82 83
MCCELLAND, 88
MCCLAIN, 106 142
MCCLANE, 148
MCCLARY, 176 177
MCCLAVE, 102 103
MCCLEAN, 208 209
MCCLELLAND, 89
MCCLEUGHEN, 22
MCCLOUD, 62
MCCOLLUM, 22 38 39 188 189
MCCOLUM, 23
MCCOMBS, 186
MCCONNELL, 106
MCCONNOUGHLY, 184
MCCORD, 142 143
MCCORMACK, 22 23 106 107
MCCORMICK, 100 101
MCCOY, 36 72 73 80 81 158 159
MCCULLOUGH, 52 53 94
MCCULLUM, 40 41
MCCUTCHEN, 74 75
MCDONALD, 82 146 147
MCELROY, 24 25
MCEWEN, 26 27
MCFARLAND, 128 129
MCFARLIN, 37
MCFETRIDGE, 52
MCGACHE, 86 87
MCGEARY, 152 153
MCGIFFIN, 38
MCGILVERY, 49
MCGINNIS, 148
MCGOHON, 156 157
MCGOWAN, 92
MCGUNEGAL, 144 145
MCINTIRE, 26 27 86
MCINTOSH, 28 29
MCJUNKIN, 168 169
MCKAY, 70 71
MCKEE, 26 27 152
MCKENDEL, 132 133
MCKIBBEN, 196 197
MCKINNEY, 138 139
MCLAIN, 107

MCLAUGHLIN, 49 86 87 134 135 197
MCMILLAN, 44 45
MCMILLEN, 86 87 96
MCMILLER, 172
MCMURRY, 126 127
MCNEIL, 22 23
MCPHEREN, 24 25
MCVEY, 140 141
MCZANE, 157
MECKER, 199
MECORD, 72
MEEKER, 192 198
MEESE, 188
MELDEN, 55
MELDER, 54
MELL, 56 162 163
MELLROSS, 79
MELOTT, 140 141
MELROSS, 78
MENAKLY, 128
MEPHORD, 86
MERCER, 78 79
MEREDITH, 150
MERITTE, 38 39
MERRILL, 106
MERRIMAN, 202 203
MERRY, 187
MERVINE, 166 167
MESKIMINS, 80
MESSERLEY, 66
MESSERLY, 67
MESSIAST, 84
METCALF, 26
MEYER, 25 85
MICHAEL, 86
MIDDAGH, 156 157
MIDDLETON, 128 129
MIFER, 205
MILLER, 22-25 30-32 34 35 56 66 67 72 73 88 100 101 120 140 141 164 180 192 200 201 204 205
MILLIKAN, 70 71
MILLS, 46 97 106 126 127 148 149
MINERE, 180 181
MINES, 104 105
MINICUM, 120
MINNEAR, 138 139
MINSTER, 122

MINTER, 62 63
MINUS, 122
MIRKUL, 122
MISER, 204
MITCHEL, 36
MITCHELL, 30 31 37
MOBLEY, 52
MOCK, 110 111
MOCKS, 176 177
MOLDEN, 80 81
MOLSLER, 200
MONG, 138 139
MONGER, 28
MONNIER, 180 181
MONROE, 120 121 148 178 179 198 199
MONTAGE, 208
MONTANEY, 146
MONTGOMERY, 134 135 158 159 198
MONTZ, 121
MOOMAW, 170 171
MOON, 60
MOORE, 32-35 38 49 66 67 72 73 98 99 112 116 117 121 140 141 148 149 152 153 164 165 181 196 197
MOOTH, 46
MOOTS, 170 171
MORE, 188 189
MOREHEAD, 52 53 86 168
MORIO, 176 177
MORRIS, 84 124 125
MORRISON, 36 37 116
MORROW, 148 156 157
MORSE, 113 188 192 193
MORTON, 120
MOSHER, 196 197
MOSS, 170-173
MOSSER, 128
MOTT, 138 139
MOTTS, 141
MOWRY, 114
MOZIER, 146 147
MULALLY, 84
MULIGAN, 82
MULL, 200
MULLEN, 117
MULLER, 84
MUNDELL, 88 89
MUNGER, 133
MUNK, 143

MUNYER, 132
MURPHEY, 84
MURPHY, 76 77
MURRAY, 87 144 145 153
MURRY, 86 87
MUSSERE, 152 153
MUSTED, 176 177
MYER, 24 82
MYERS, 78 79 106 184 185 188 189
NAHIR, 166 167
NAIL, 48
NANCE, 114 115
NASH, 40 41
NAUMAN, 170 171
NEAL, 202
NEEB, 64 65
NEELY, 144 145
NELSON, 97
NEWBURN, 48
NEWELL, 76 77
NEWMAN, 144 145 176
NEWSON, 39
NEWTON, 38 122 123 144 145
NICEWARNER, 167
NICHELFETTER, 208 209
NICHLES, 122 123
NICHOLAS, 142 143
NICKELL, 104 105
NIHART, 152 153
NISBET, 185
NISWANGER, 178 179
NOBLE, 40 41 48 49 170 171
NOLAND, 178 179
NOLENBURG, 133
NOLINBURG, 132
NORRIS, 66 67 148 149 168 169
NORTHROP, 186
NORTHWAY, 28 29
NORTON, 106 107
NOTTS, 140
NUCKELS, 70 71
NUGENT, 82 83
NULL, 198 199
NYMAN, 162
O'CONNER, 86 87
O'NEIL, 124
O'NEILL, 125
OAKS, 143
OBERFIELD, 192 193
OBLINGER, 164 165
ODELL, 174 175

OGAN, 196 197
OLINGER, 100 101
OLIVER, 46
ORTON, 172 173
ORVILER, 54 55
OSBORN, 42 43
OSWALT, 188 189
OTT, 26 27
OTTIS, 82
OVIATT, 185
OWEN, 76 77
PACKER, 38 39
PADOVAIN, 82
PAGE, 132 133
PAINE, 177
PAISLEY, 106 107
PALMER, 134 135 140 141 168 200
PANGBORN, 122 123
PANGBURN, 32 33
PARIS, 140 141
PARK, 72 73
PARKER, 84 96 97 164
PARKESON, 117
PARKISON, 116
PARR, 116 117
PARRAT, 26
PARRELL, 40
PARRY, 152 153
PATERSON, 28 29 116
PATTEN, 130
PATTERSON, 42 43 48 49 117 156 157 186 187 202
PATTON, 95 131
PAUL, 32 33 84 174
PAXTON, 144 145
PEALER, 110 111
PEARCE, 30
PEARCH, 31 34 35
PEARSON, 138 139
PEASE, 184 185
PEASLEE, 116
PECK, 72 73 102 103
PECKMAN, 96
PEGGS, 200 201
PENCE, 22 23
PENCER, 208 209
PENNOCK, 48 49
PENROSE, 130 131
PEPPER, 188 189
PERCIVAL, 122 123
PERINE, 142 143 149

PERKINS, 86 87 126
PERRINE, 148
PERRY, 32 33 65 84 86 87 134 135
PESSINGER, 58
PETER, 88
PETERS, 84-86 127 164 165
PETERSON, 126
PFITZMYER, 128
PFLEIDERA, 54 55
PHEBE, 33
PHELPS, 56 113
PHILIPS, 158 159
PHILLBROOK, 116 117
PHILLIP, 111
PHILLIPS, 110 123 164 165
PHILLIS, 144 145
PHINEBERGER, 200
PIDD, 76 77
PIER, 116 117
PIERCE, 64 82 83 200 201
PIERSON, 136
PIFER, 32
PILE, 174 175
PINKSTOCK, 67
PITTENGER, 22
PITTMAN, 140
PLANKARD, 49
PLUMMER, 22 23 40 41
PLYMPTON, 28
POLEFF, 84
POLING, 156 157
POLLARD, 202
POOL, 40 41
POORMAN, 163
PORDUE, 52
PORTER, 72 73 154 155
PORTS, 110
POST, 34 35 103 156 157
POWELL, 37 176 177
POWERS, 40 41 96 97 102 103
PRENTICE, 28
PRENTISS, 162
PRESBEE, 54 55
PRICE, 32 33 104 105-107 176
PRICER, 170 171
PRIDDY, 194 195
PRIEST, 116 117
PRIFFING, 56
PRIOR, 148 149
PROMITZ, 84
PRUDEN, 43

PURD, 208
PURDY, 52 53
PURGIT, 170 171
PURSEL, 72 73
PURSHALL, 128
PUTNAM, 204 205
PUTT, 188 189
QUINBY, 200
QUINLAN, 40 41
QUINTON, 83
RABE, 136 137
RADER, 22
RAFFERTY, 126 127
RAKESTRAW, 116 117
RAMBO, 52
RAMSAY, 148
RANCHENBERZER, 190 191
RANDALL, 40
RANDOLPH, 128 178
RANKIN, 72 73 115
RANSHART, 84
RANSOM, 152 153
RAPP, 82 83
RATER, 22 23
RATLIFF, 80 81
RAULL, 176
RAY, 152 153
RAYMOND, 64 65
REACHARD, 74 75
READ, 110 111
REBSTOCK, 188 189
REDDINGTON, 122 123
REED, 72 120 123 128 154 155 180 181 188 189 192 193 206 207
REEF, 188
REEFE, 189
REEL, 98 99
REID, 68
REIDER, 187
REINEGER, 174
RENICK, 208 209
REYNOLDS, 150 176 177
RHADABAUGH, 104 105
RHINEHART, 84 85
RHODES, 148
RIAN, 86
RIBLE, 116 117
RIBLEY, 54 55
RICE, 28 29 40 66 88 89 102 103 164 165 193
RICHARDS, 46 117 162

RICHARDSON, 116 148 192 204 205
RICKET, 149
RIDDLE, 80 134
RIDENHOUR, 156 157
RIDENOUR, 24 25
RIDENOW, 116 117
RIDER, 180 181 186
RIDGEWAY, 116
RIDGWAY, 62 63 117
RIFE, 180 181
RINCHART, 170
RINEBOLD, 176 177
RINEGER, 175
RINEHART, 171 176 177
RITER, 202 203
RIX, 150
ROACH, 180 181 192-195
ROADS, 22
ROBB, 40 41
ROBBINS, 32 33 196 197
ROBE, 32 33
ROBERTS, 128
ROBERTSON, 180 181
ROBINET, 150
ROBINETT, 156 157 196 197
ROBINSON, 48 49 76 77 102 103 120-122 148 149 158
ROCHAFELLOW, 113
ROCK, 158 159
ROCKAFELLOW, 112
RODGERS, 116 117
ROE, 22
ROGERS, 28 32 33
ROLAND, 138
ROLL, 38
ROMINE, 135
RONGHER, 140
ROOD, 162 172
ROOF, 67
ROSE, 128 142 143
ROSS, 26 27 106 149 198 199
ROUSTBERER, 32
ROUTT, 170 171
ROWE, 113
RUBY, 94 95
RUCKER, 114 115
RUDOLPH, 66 67
RUDY, 180 181
RUMMEL, 24 25
RUMMELL, 24
RUNK, 142 143

RUNNION, 186
RUNNIONS, 164 165
RUNSER, 180 181
RUPLEY, 204
RUSHAW, 136
RUSSEL, 32 33
RUSSELL, 60 61 86 87 128
RUTLEDGE, 34 106
RYAN, 84
RYTS, 162 163
SACKETT, 186 187
SAGRE, 134 135
SALLANCE, 135
SALLSBURY, 78
SALMON, 106 107 196
SALMONS, 197
SAMPLES, 196 197
SAMPSON, 102
SANDERSON, 28
SANDS, 188 189
SANDY, 72 73
SANFORD, 152 153
SANSOM, 100
SANTZINGER, 84 85
SAP, 87
SARGEANT, 110 111
SATIR, 84 85
SAUNDERS, 56 57 123 134 135
SAVILL, 78 79
SAWHILL, 72 73
SAYRE, 138 139
SCHANAVER, 82 83
SCHENCK, 142 143 198 199
SCHENK, 168
SCHEYING, 164 165
SCHILTZ, 180 181
SCHLICHTER, 180 181
SCHNECK, 169
SCHOENLAUB, 88 89
SCHOTT, 84
SCHRADER, 24
SCHUDERMAN, 86
SCHULTZ, 82 162 163
SCHWARTZ, 84
SCHWAVERLY, 176
SCISCO, 99
SCOFIELD, 150
SCOTLAND, 114
SCOTT, 34 35 44 48 76 77 104
    106-109 114-117 152 153 200
    201
SCOVAL, 56

SCOVEL, 56 57
SCOVILL, 186
SCRIBER, 56 57
SEAL, 44
SEALEY, 186 187
SEARL, 112
SEARLS, 102 103
SEATON, 34 35
SEBRIL, 162 163
SEERY, 54 55
SEIDMER, 128
SEIDNER, 129
SEITZ, 176 177
SELLERS, 158 159
SELLS, 136
SELOVER, 150
SERANTON, 132
SERENER, 54 55
SETTLES, 148 149
SEWELL, 44 45
SHACKLEFORD, 66
SHADO, 142 143
SHAFER, 70 71 128 129 187
SHAFFER, 120 178 179
SHANHOLZER, 66 67
SHANK, 169
SHANNICH, 98
SHAUL, 38 39
SHAVER, 202 203
SHAW, 76 77 106 107 158 159
    176-178 202
SHEARER, 138 139
SHEETS, 24 25
SHELBY, 86
SHELHEART, 204 205
SHELLENBEGER, 28
SHELY, 86
SHEPHERD, 152 153
SHEPNER, 89
SHERER, 52 53
SHEROD, 65 189
SHERWICK, 24 25
SHILLING, 180 181
SHINER, 206
SHIPLEY, 81
SHIPLY, 80
SHOCK, 24 25
SHOCNESEE, 106
SHOCNESEESS, 107
SHOEMAKER, 92
SHOTTS, 170
SHOULTS, 170 171

SHOUP, 146 147
SHOW, 164 165
SHOWMAN, 116 117
SHRADNEY, 40 41
SHRIGLEY, 150
SHROLL, 54 55
SHUGA, 54
SHULL, 188 189
SHULTZ, 168 169
SHUMWAY, 56 57
SHUNK, 180 181
SHUTT, 180
SIBERT, 30 31
SILBER, 98 99
SILVER, 178 179
SIMMONS, 32 108 117 158 159
    182 183
SIMPKINS, 116
SIMPSON, 128 129
SIMS, 56 57
SINCLAIR, 96 97
SINGLETARY, 184
SIRRELL, 44
SISCO, 98
SKEEN, 96
SKINNER, 186 187
SLACK, 174 175
SLATER, 102 103
SLOAN, 26 27 134 176
SLYMDTZ, 40 41
SMALLEY, 150
SMELTS, 34 35
SMITH, 26-29 40 44 52 53 56 57
    66 72 73 76 77 82 83 94-96 98
    99 102 103 114-120 123 129
    140 141 148 149 164 172-174
    184 186 187 200
SMOOT, 48
SMUTZ, 156 157
SMYTH, 56
SNEIDER, 122
SNELBAKER, 82
SNELL, 146 147
SNIDER, 84 85 123 152
SNOOK, 48 49
SNOW, 130
SNOWDEN, 78
SNOWDON, 79
SNYDER, 114 115 138 139 164
    165 170 171 180 181 188 189
SOLOMON, 88
SOLOR, 84

SOUDER, 72 73
SOUTH, 41
SOWERS, 178 179
SPADE, 184 185
SPANGLER, 180 181
SPARHAWK, 184 185
SPARKS, 192 193
SPAULDING, 148 149
SPENCE, 82
SPENCER, 48 49 120
SPEVNLY, 86 87
SPICHER, 100 101
SPIKERMYER, 24 25
SPING, 188
SPISMESSER, 78
SPLITSTONE, 186 187
SPOONER, 62 63 84
SPOTTS, 184 185
SPRADLING, 114 115
SPRAGUE, 200 201
SPRING, 189
SPRINGER, 146 147
STAANY, 204
STAFFORD, 44
STALEY, 142
STALL, 128 129
STANBURY, 84
STANCART, 134 135
STANDISH, 74
STARKEY, 156 157 198 199
STARR, 116 204 205
STARRETT, 148 150
STARTTON, 202
STCHOB, 163
STEAR, 200
STEBBINS, 76
STEDGER, 35
STEEL, 120 121
STEELE, 104 105 142 143
STEFFLER, 104 105
STEGLE, 30
STEIGLER, 86
STEINLE, 83
STEMEN, 66
STEPHENS, 40 41
STEPHENSON, 104 105
STERICK, 168
STERRITS, 88
STEVENS, 144
STEVENSON, 144 145
STEWART, 52 53 56 57 78 79 134
    135 208

STIDGER, 34
STILES, 82
STILLEY, 146 147
STILLWELL, 88 89 154 155 171
STILTZ, 86
STINEBAUGH, 176 177
STINER, 156 157 180 181
STITTLE, 186 187
STIVER, 142 143
STOCKBARGER, 116 117
STOLL, 162 163
STONE, 28 29
STONEBRAKER, 116 117
STOVER, 148 149 206 207
STONG, 102
STORER, 104
STORY, 80
STOTT, 146 147
STOTTS, 148-150
STOUFFER, 168
STOUT, 78 79
STRAHL, 144 145
STRAIGHT, 56
STRATTON, 202 203
STRAW, 54 55
STRAYER, 66 67
STREATOR, 162 163
STRICKLAND, 186 187
STROUB, 188
STRUBLE, 74
STUART, 40 41 152 153 178 179
STUCKEY, 140 141
STULL, 110 111
STUMP, 40 41 56 57 148 149 180 181
STURGEON, 30
STURTEVANT, 122 123
STUTLER, 132 133
SULLIVAN, 36 37 44 131
SULTZ, 146
SUMMERLOT, 146
SUNDAY, 26
SUPP, 124 125
SURBER, 32 33
SURLINE, 28 29
SUTER, 141
SUTHERFIELD, 22
SUTTAN, 54
SUTTER, 140
SUTTON, 22 23 52 53 88 89
SWAIN, 164 165 200
SWALLEY, 98 99

SWANEY, 38
SWARENGER, 49
SWARTZ, 130 131 177 180 181
SWARTZEL, 142 143
SWIGERT, 188
SWIM, 40 41
SWISHER, 54
SWITZER, 26 27 52
TAGGART, 48 49
TAGUE, 82
TALEMUS, 200
TANI, 141
TANNER, 82 83
TAP, 86
TAVENER, 156 157
TAYLOR, 26 27 36 37 58 59 106 107 118 119 148 158 159 162 163 206 207
TEFLER, 172 173
TEMPLAR, 78 79
TENNEMANN, 88 89
TERRACE, 40 41
TERRY, 22-25
TEST, 48 49
TEW, 172 173
THACKAY, 192
THACKER, 116 117
THEUS, 86
THOMAS, 60 61 78 79 156 157 170 171 189
THOMPSON, 56 57 70 71 82 83 86 90 91 102 103 117 120 150 164 174 175 184 185 197
THORN, 78 79 104
THORNTON, 120 123 174 175
THORP, 88
THRALL, 62 63
TIFFANY, 184
TILLROW, 102 103
TINKER, 28 29
TITTLE, 176 177
TITUS, 56
TOBIAS, 83
TODD, 176 177
TODHUNTER, 70 71
TOMAS, 88
TOMB, 140
TOMPKINS, 102 103
TOOKER, 168 169
TORRENCE, 54 55 134 135
TOTTEN, 89
TOTTON, 88

TOUSLEY, 184 185
TOUTTS, 49
TOWER, 155
TOWERS, 158 159
TOWNSEND, 44
TRANLEY, 88 89
TREHAPPAT, 140
TRENTMAN, 30
TRESSET, 82
TROTO, 180 181
TROTTER, 22 23
TROWBRIDGE, 58 59
TRUMP, 180 181
TRUNKEY, 186 187
TRUXELL, 102 103
TSCHAPPAT, 141
TUBBLE, 106
TUBS, 135
TUCKER, 40 41 168 174 175
TUMEY, 120
TUNISON, 116 117
TURNER, 66-69 78 138 208 209
TURNIPSED, 70
TURRILL, 90 91
TUSSEL, 142 143
TUSSET, 83
TUSTISON, 54 55
TUTHILL, 96
TUTON, 84
TWADDLE, 106 107
TYLER, 122 123
ULLERY, 138 139
ULRY, 82
ULTHOFF, 154 155
UNDERWOOD, 138 139
UNGER, 142
UPSON, 28
UTZIE, 100 101
VAIL, 143
VANATOR, 102 103
VANATTA, 116 117
VANCE, 100 101 150
VANDIVORT, 148
VANDIWORT, 149
VANDUZOR, 146
VANHORN, 144 145
VANKIRK, 88 89
VANLIEW, 102
VANNERT, 141
VANROY, 200
VANSYOC, 49
VANVICKEL, 158

VANWENKEL, 27
VARIANN, 104
VAUGHAN, 120
VAUGHN, 168 169
VERNER, 86
VESEY, 105
VIAN, 110 111
VICKROY, 156 157
VINCENT, 170 171
VIRGARD, 54 55
VOLLY, 146
VOLMAR, 56 57
VONSCHRITTZ, 134 135
WABER, 88
WACHTEL, 101
WADE, 100 101
WAGGONER, 176 177
WAGNER, 30 31
WAGONER, 34 35 138 139 171
WAKDEN, 123
WALCUTT, 72 73
WALKER, 32 33 84 94 95 112
   128-130 140 141 158
WALLACE, 22 80 81 150 180 181
WALPOLDT, 100
WALSH, 82
WALSTON, 158 159
WALTER, 128 129
WALTERS, 168 169
WARD, 36 37 48 90 91
WARE, 72 73
WARNE, 148 149
WARNER, 116 117
WARSON, 193
WATCHTEL, 100
WATERLAKE, 96 97
WATERMAN, 32 33
WATERS, 122 123 170 171
WATKINS, 106 107
WATSON, 72-75 84 176 177
WATTNER, 166 167
WATTS, 96
WAY, 50
WEAVER, 204 205
WEBB, 110 111 118 119
WEBER, 89 146 147
WEBSTER, 26 27 76 77 134 135
WECKEL, 142 143
WEDDEL, 82
WEDDELL, 73
WEEKLY, 148 149
WEIHART, 24

WEIKER, 176 177
WEIOFF, 26 27
WEIRICK, 202 203
WELBER, 132 133
WELCH, 38 62 63 83 150 176 180 181
WELKER, 110 111
WELLS, 30 31 52 53 192 193 202
WELSH, 39 80-82 86
WENKLE, 87
WENMOTH, 140 141
WERNET, 202 203
WERNKLE, 86
WESLING, 83
WEST, 36 37 120 121 205
WETTY, 188 189
WEVER, 200
WEYER, 97
WHEELER, 106 107 116 117 200 201
WHELPLEY, 122 123
WHIPPLE, 112
WHISLER, 110 111
WHITE, 44 52 53 78 80 81 144 146-149 180 181
WHITEHEAD, 114-117
WHITEMAN, 164 165
WHITING, 76
WHITNEY, 28
WHITTEN, 74 75
WHITTLE, 162 163
WHYDE, 148 149
WIANT, 188 189
WIEHART, 25
WILBER, 76 77
WILCOX, 72 130 131 187
WILDER, 88
WILDMAN, 186 187
WILES, 61 156 157
WILEY, 48 156
WILKIN, 116
WILKINS, 30 117
WILKINSON, 196
WILLIAMS, 30 31 38 44 45 48-51 104 105 118 122 123 128 198 199
WILLIAMSON, 50 66 67 88 89
WILSON, 32 33 44 45 64 65 80 81 126 127 129 132 133 176 177
WINDER, 150
WINE, 150
WINKLER, 82

WINNEMAKER, 124
WINTEROW, 58
WINTERROW, 59
WINTERS, 112 113 196
WINTZ, 56 57
WISE, 140 141 162 176-178 184 185
WISHON, 104
WITNER, 172 173
WITT, 204
WITTCHE, 140 141
WOLF, 116 117
WOLFSPERGER, 182 183
WOLONMAN, 82
WOLPOLDT, 101
WOLTZ, 98 99
WONDERLING, 128 129
WOOD, 85 112 113 144 145
WOODLING, 54
WOODRUFF, 150 200 201
WOODS, 97
WOODSON, 86 87
WOOLCUT, 162
WOOLMAN, 164
WOOLSEY, 208 209
WORDEN, 164 165
WORTHINGTON, 150
WRIGHT, 28 48 49 164 165 174 175 184 186 187 194
WYKLE, 164 165
WYLE, 32
WYLER, 33
WYNANT, 36 37
YATES, 72 73 208 209
YESLEY, 168 169
YOCKEY, 182 183
YOHO, 140 141
YOUMANS, 88 89
YOUNG, 22 23 112 113 171 178
YOUNKER, 206
YOUNKIN, 114 115
YUNKER, 207
ZANGLINE, 30 31
ZIGLER, 138 139
ZIMERMAN, 170
ZIMMERMAN, 26 27 188 189
ZINNERMAN, 170 171
ZINNERMON, 171
ZOOK, 138 139
ZUNKLE, 150

www.ingramcontent.com/pod-product-compliance
Lightning Source LLC
Chambersburg PA
CBHW050146170426
43197CB00011B/1984